WOMEN OF THE NATION

Women of the Nation

Between Black Protest and Sunni Islam

Dawn-Marie Gibson and Jamillah Karim

NEW YORK UNIVERSITY PRESS

New York and London

NEW YORK UNIVERSITY PRESS
New York and London
www.nyupress.org
© 2014 by New York University

References to Internet websites (URLs) were accurate at the time of writing. Neither the author nor New York University Press is responsible for URLs that may have expired or changed since the manuscript was prepared.

Library of Congress Cataloging-in-Publication Data
Gibson, Dawn-Marie.
Women of the nation : between black protest and Sunni Islam / Dawn-Marie Gibson, Jamillah Karim.
pages cm Includes bibliographical references and index.
ISBN 978-0-8147-6995-9 (hbk.) — ISBN 978-0-8147-3786-6 (pbk.) —
1. Muslim women—United States—History. 2. Women and religion—United States—History. 3. Nation of Islam (Chicago, Ill.)—History. I. Karim, Jamillah Ashira, 1976-II. Title.
HQ1170.G53 2014
305.48'6970973--dc23   2014004205

New York University Press books are printed on acid-free paper, and their binding materials are chosen for strength and durability. We strive to use environmentally responsible suppliers and materials to the greatest extent possible in publishing our books.

Manufactured in the United States of America

10 9 8 7 6 5 4 3 2 1

Also available as an ebook

This book is dedicated to Khayriyyah Faiz and Lauryn McCullough.

CONTENTS

ACKNOWLEDGMENTS

JAMILLAH KARIM. I thank Dawn-Marie for the idea to write a book on women in the Nation of Islam and inviting me to co-write it. Dawn learned of my interest in women and the NOI from my article "Through Sunni Women's Eyes." I thank my mother, Marjorie Karim, and one of my "community mothers," Lynda Najlah Abdul-Salaam, for the hours of interviewing that led to the article, which led to collaboration with Dawn. I thank my mother for modeling excellence and keeping the company of other pious, loving women who positively influenced me. I dedicated my first book to her, and I dedicate this book to one of her dearest friends, Khayriyyah Faiz, a constant servant of God and His creation. I thank my father, Ahmad Abdul-Karim, for planting the seeds for me to write this book, with his unwavering faith in me and his love and gratitude for the Honorable Elijah Muhammad, Imam W. D. Mohammed, and Minister Louis Farrakhan. I thank all of the women who gave generously of their time to participate in interviews for the book. I share with many of them ideals about family and work. When I took a break from teaching to work at home with my two sons, Yahya and Lut, it was my husband, Hud Williams, who convinced me that I could write the book while keeping commitments to my growing family. Furthermore, he ensured that I had time to devote to research and writing. I thank him for "making my goals his goals" and surpassing my expectations as a great father and spouse. I love you, Hud. I thank Hadiya Staine for her devoted sisterhood and generous spirit as she assisted with taking care of my sons while I wrote. I thank my aunt Jonetta Tilghman Winters for her steady acts of kindness and for always being there when I needed help with the boys. In this regard, I also thank Zakiyyah Waheed and all of my family. I thank Ayesha K. Mustafa and Zubaydah Madyun for loaning me issues of the *Bilalian*

News, and Amatullah Um'rani and Ana Karim for providing other rare documents and materials. I thank Rosetta Ross, Nami Kim, Khalil Abdullah, and Zakiyyah Muhammad for their professional support and conversations. I thank Cecilia Cabanatan and Virginia Nakitari for transcribing interviews. Finally, I thank God for perfect timing, allowing me to complete the manuscript a week before the birth of my third son, Zayn Mohammed.

DAWN-MARIE GIBSON. I thank Jamillah for taking on this project and for all she has brought to the book. I thank the women in the Nation of Islam and the Imam W. D. Mohammed community for being so generous with their time. This project could not have been completed without their assistance and willingness to take part in interviews. I thank my colleagues in the Department of History at Royal Holloway, University of London, for their encouragement. My family has supported the completion of this work, and for that I am grateful. My parents, Marie and Thomas, have been a constant support. I thank Lindsay, Gemma, Lauryn, and Christie for distracting me from work when at home. I thank Lauryn for her beautiful spirit and for the joy she brings to our lives. I dedicate my portion of this work to her as a token of my appreciation for her faith, kindness, and love. No one has supported my efforts on this project more than my husband. He has been a constant source of wisdom, unconditional love, and true friendship. I thank him for his many sacrifices on my behalf and for being my rock and best friend. I love you, Zuruvi.

Introduction

When you went into the Nation, the first thing they taught you was, your brothers and sisters are in the temple and no one else matters. You can't have any other friends; you turn your back on everyone. Everything they want you to do, they got a place for you to do it.
—Sonji Clay, first wife of Muhammad Ali

The Nation gave me a place to develop the confidence that I needed. It was a womb that got me ready to come out into the world.
—Lynda, Sunni Muslim woman

Both popular media and scholarly accounts of the Nation of Islam (NOI) tend to focus on dominant male figures such as Malcolm X, Muhammad Ali, and Louis Farrakhan. In the rarer cases in which literature on the Nation features women's experiences, Nation women are often presented in relation to these dominant men, as in the case of Sonji Clay, whose comments at the start of this Introduction were included in a biography of Muhammad Ali.[1] Or they tend to be accounts of ex-Nation women who describe the NOI as controlling and repressive, as also mentioned in Clay's comments. Missing have been the accounts of everyday NOI women, many of whom, unlike Clay, consciously chose the Nation independent of their husbands or fathers. Also absent have been the voices of ex-Nation women who, like Lynda, also quoted at the start of this Introduction, have left the NOI for Sunni Islam but describe the Nation as an organization that bettered their lives.[2] This book brings such voices to the center of analysis. It portrays women of the Nation of Islam from various perspectives, recognizing the group's patriarchal dimensions and revealing how women have experienced and shaped the Nation.

This book explores how women have understood, experienced, and contributed to the Nation of Islam throughout its eighty-year history. It illuminates how women have interpreted and navigated the NOI's gender ideologies and practices in light of their multilayered identities as women of ethnic minorities in America. It portrays the diverse experiences of mostly African American and also Latinas and Native American women within the NOI and their changing roles in the group. Women of the Nation of Islam include those who joined the organization under Elijah Muhammad, its second leader; those who followed Elijah's son W. D. Mohammed when he inherited leadership of the Nation of Islam and enacted a shift toward Sunni Islam; and those who have followed Louis Farrakhan after he resurrected the Nation of Islam for those dissatisfied with W. D. Mohammed's transition to Sunni Islam.

Women's accounts of the Nation of Islam vary, but generally they are far more positive than indicated by feminist critiques of the NOI and other scholarly and popular histories of the Nation. Misperceptions of the Nation of Islam can be attributed to two factors: (1) that women's experiences have been presented and understood outside of historical context and (2) that a broad spectrum of women in the Nation of Islam have not been represented in their own voices. This book corrects this tendency, providing historical and ethnographic detail of women's participation in and perspectives on the Nation of Islam from the 1930s to the present.

This book argues that the racial climate of the United States has made the Nation of Islam particularly appealing to African American women. In its early years, these women were primarily interested in its race-uplift and community-building messages, but they also embraced the Nation's traditional gender roles given Black women's generally lower socioeconomic status and American notions of respectability and economic advancement. As the Nation of Islam moved into its post–civil rights formations and toward Sunni Islam, women's experiences generally became even more favorable. We attribute this in part to the ways in which the two leaders following Elijah Muhammad—W. D. Mohammed and Louis Farrakhan—incorporated ideals regarding women's public leadership and racial diversity based in both American culture and Islam, albeit in varying degrees and from different directions. Moreover, women's positive experiences relate also to how women themselves have interpreted and navigated expressions of their faith, including those of their leaders, in light of their social and personal concerns as African American women, and in a few cases, Latinas and Native American women. In sum, we argue that the Nation of Islam experience for women has been characterized by an expression of Islam sensitive to American cultural messages about race and gender but also by gender and race ideals in the Islamic tradition. While this expression of Islam, which includes an honoring of traditional gender roles and prescribed female dress and decorum, is not always in harmony with popular notions of women's advancement in American society, it certainly speaks and appeals to the continuing concerns about race, family, and community among many African American women.

The NOI's Beginnings

The NOI finds its origins in 1930s Detroit. Wallace D. Fard Muhammad, its founder, remains something of an enigma in the history of African American Islam. For decades, scholars have contested Fard's origins, ethnicity, and the extent of his affiliations with Black nationalist and Islamic organizations in the United States. Fard was neither native to the United States nor of African descent. Recent research by journalist Karl Evanzz and historian Fatimah Fanusie suggests that he was of Pakistani origin.[3] According to FBI surveillance, Fard entered the United States illegally in 1913. Fard's light-skinned complexion set him apart from the plethora of small-scale peddlers and African American preachers in Detroit. According to sociologist Erdmann Beynon, Fard introduced himself to Detroit's African American migrant community as a peddler. Soon after gaining the confidence of his customers, he began to censure Christianity and the Black church. Beynon notes that Fard taught his customers that Islam was their "true" and "natural" religion, that the "Asiatic Black man" was "the God of the universe," and that Caucasians were "blue-eyed devils" created by an evil scientist, Yakub, on the island of Patmos. Fard's audiences grew rapidly in size. Two factors in particular are important when considering Fard's success. First, his exclusive African American following comprised predominantly working-class migrants from the American South who found their dreams of economic opportunity unfulfilled as a result of the economic depression of the 1930s. Thus, when they first encountered Fard, they were receptive to his message. Second, Fard's followers proved unhappy with the existing religious landscape of Detroit as evidenced by the growth of storefront churches in the city. Indeed, it is estimated that by 1930 storefronts accounted for 45 percent of African American churches in Detroit.[4] Migrants were enthralled by Fard's critique of the U.S. racial hierarchy and his rhetorical attacks on Caucasians, whom he described as the "natural enemy" of Blacks. Beynon comments that Fard's customers collectively financed the hiring of small halls and basements in order to accommodate all of the migrants who proved eager to hear the peddler "teach" them about their "natural" religion. It was at this point that the NOI was born.

Fard's theology and racial politics were the product of multiple competing influences. Fard was a contemporary of both Marcus Garvey and Noble Drew Ali. The Garvey movement, the Universal Negro Improvement Association (UNIA), was an early-twentieth-century Black nationalist and separatist organization. Garvey's organization proved hugely popular with the urban Black proletariat, but the UNIA collapsed following Garvey's deportation on charges of mail fraud in 1927. Early historians and sociologists who studied the NOI noted that it also had commonalities with another group, the Moorish Science Temple of America (MSTA). The MSTA was founded and led by Noble Drew Ali in Newark, New Jersey, in 1913. The MSTA's members were a discernible group within their larger communities. They were close-knit and entrepreneurial, and they identified themselves not as Negroes but as Moors—"a nation that emerged out of a more general group of Asiatic peoples."[5] The MSTA was afflicted by power struggles, the most volatile of which was launched by MSTA member Sheik Claude Green. The struggle resulted in Green's sudden death. Police arrested Ali on suspicion of murder but released him soon after. In the weeks that followed his release from police custody, Ali died under mysterious circumstances. The confusion surrounding Ali's death allowed several individuals to launch succession bids that included controversial claims of reincarnation. It is thought by some historians that Fard Muhammad was one of these individuals.[6]

Fard Muhammad's theology was inspired primarily by UNIA and MSTA dogma. However, it also borrowed from the Bible and the writings of Joseph F. Rutherford, leader of the Jehovah Witnesses. Fard taught his followers that the Bible had been contaminated and distorted by the "blue-eyed devils" and that heaven and hell were nothing more than realities to be faced while on earth. Fard referred to his followers as Asiatics and as members of the original Lost-Found Tribe of Shabazz. Fard's following is estimated to have included thousands of members. Fard marketed his message to migrants as being rooted in their ancestral religion, Islam. However, Beynon's observations, accounts by early members, and police surveillance illustrate that Fard's knowledge of Islam was rudimentary. Moreover, his claim that Islam had been the ancestral religion of his African American followers was fallacious. African American studies scholar Alan D. Austin notes that approximately 10 percent of African slaves taken from the west coast of Africa by European slave traders were Muslim.[7] Muslim slaves made "genuine and persistent" efforts to observe and fulfill the requirements of their faith in the United States.[8] Yet such efforts proved tenuous and insufficient given the pressure on Muslim slaves to abandon their faith for Christianity. Islam did not begin to thrive among African Americans until the twentieth century, when Muslims increasingly migrated to the United States from Asia and Africa. African Americans were introduced to Islam in the 1920s by Muslim missionaries in the form of the Islamic Mission of America, the Universal Islamic Society, and the Ahmadiyya movement. The Ahmadiyya, an Islamic sect from the Indian subcontinent, had the greatest impact. Islamic studies scholar Aminah B. McCloud notes that the Ahmadiyya's most important contribution to the spread of Islam among African Americans was their circulation of Islamic literature and English translations of the Qur'an.[9] Although they gained African American adherents, all three missionary groups failed to address and provide a panacea for the unique socioeconomic problems afflicting African Americans. It appears that Fard Muhammad learned from their collective error, as his eclectic theology addressed both the spiritual isolation and socioeconomic realities of his followers.

Beynon's research tells us little about why women may have been attracted to the NOI. The emphasis Fard appears to have placed on morality and asceticism, however, is likely to have been a characteristic that women embraced in the hope that it would regulate their spouses' behavior. Nation members formed their own close-knit community. Yet they were a sizable group in Detroit and known for their work ethic and refusal to be called by their anglicized surnames, which they replaced with an X. The "X" was adopted by Nation members for two reasons. First, it represented their unknown ancestral names and, second, it implied "that the Muslim is no longer what he was."[10] A new member took a numbered X, as in Carla 3X, when others with her first name had already joined the group. Fard developed a number of internal organizations for his followers, including an independent school for Nation children, the Muhammad University of Islam (MUI). Fard's female followers were educated in domestic science in what became known as Muslim Girls Training and General Civilization Class (MGT & GCC), which was generally shortened to Muslim Girls Training, or MGT. Male members of the organization likewise attended gender-segregated classes known as the Fruit of Islam (FOI), which operated as a para-military division of the organization. Members of both the MGT and the FOI were responsible for providing security during NOI meetings, which included searching individuals before they entered NOI temples.

Fard's Early Followers, Clara and Elijah

Clara Poole was one of Fard's earliest followers in Detroit. Her unexpected journey to the NOI began in 1923, when she and her husband, Elijah, left their native Georgia for Detroit with their two infant children, Emmanuel and Ethel. Elijah relocated to Detroit ahead of his wife and children to secure work in industry. The family shared the optimism, turmoil, and despair of the migrant experience. Their decision to relocate to the North was inspired by the promise of economic opportunity and the desire to raise their children in a more racially tolerant society.[11] Elijah found work in numerous industries, including the Detroit Copper Company and later the Chevrolet Axle Company, while his young wife assumed the role of homemaker. In 1925 Clara gave birth to another daughter, Lottie, and a year later to another son, Nathaniel. Her fifth child, Herbert, was born in 1929. The family survived on Elijah's stints of temporary employment until the late 1920s, when the city's economy began to suffer the effects of a national economic downturn. Clara's fears about the economic well-being of her family intensified when she discovered that she was pregnant with their sixth child, Elijah Jr., in 1931. Elijah's inability to provide for his family quickly drove him from the family home and into the nearest gutter, where he was often found drunk.[12] Unable to secure full-time employment, Clara began to venture out of the home in search of day-to-day employment in domestic work. She later described this tumultuous time as the family's "lowest ebb":

> Once my family and I were at our lowest ebb–in a bad condition. With five children, there were times we didn't have a piece of bread in the house, nor heat, water or even sufficient wearing apparel. My husband would walk the streets looking for a job daily, but would come home with no job. I would go out and try to help him, but with five children I could not work steadily. However, I was successful when I went door to door, asking for work.[13]

Keeping her family together required nothing short of a herculean effort, but Clara's plight was not unique. The proliferation of female-headed households among urban Black communities was a direct consequence of wider employment practices that favored the employment of Black women as cheap, noncontractual domestic servants. Black men, on the other hand, encountered a job market that was anything but a level playing field. Jobs that had been traditionally considered the preserve of the African American proletariat were increasingly pursued by whites as competition for work intensified. Indeed, the 1930 census report revealed that in the North unemployment rates were 80 percent higher for African Americans than whites.[14]

Clara's work kept the family afloat, but nonetheless Elijah detested domestic service—an industry known to carry the very real potential for physical and sexual abuse.[15] The plight of the Poole family improved in the spring of 1931, when Elijah's drinking eased after he confessed to his mother that he felt there was something "warning" him to be a "better man" and to "teach religion or preach."[16] The Poole family was steeped in the traditions of the southern Black church. Elijah's family was active in the surrounding Baptist churches in Cordele and Sandersville, Georgia, where his father preached. Clara was born into the Bethel Christian Methodist Episcopal Church in Cordele, where her father was heavily involved in the ministry.[17] Clara appears to have cherished deeply her faith and her close-knit church family. Historian Claude Clegg observes that Clara's "piety" was an attribute Elijah found particularly attractive.[18] The migration north disconnected the Poole family from the refuge the church had provided them. Elijah and his young wife struggled to find a spiritual home in Detroit, as did thousands of migrant families.

Clara was particularly unprepared for the realities of the urban North. Racial violence, discrimination, and disregard for the lives of Black Americans were evidenced in race riots and discriminatory employment practices. Her host city tested Clara's faith. Religious studies scholar Debra Majeed comments, "Without the closeness of her immediate or church families, Clara found herself searching for a tangible anchor in an environment where many disillusioned Blacks hunger[ed] for a religion that spoke to their 'material reality.'"[19]

Womanist scholars Rosetta Ross and Debra Majeed contend that it was Clara who introduced her husband to the NOI's founder, Fard Muhammad.[20] Their contention, while disputed, is not without merit. Fard's door-to-door activity as a peddler in Detroit's African American neighborhoods lends credence to the revisionist theory offered by Majeed and Ross. Elijah's frequent absences would likely have meant that when Fard did approach the home of the Poole family, it was Clara whom he encountered.

Clara cherished the Nation's ideals of respectability and patriarchy. Elijah became devoted to Fard, which ensured a renewal of commitment to Clara and their children. More important, however, his new devotion liberated Clara from the need to rescue her husband from the vices to which circumstances had driven him. Clara became pregnant with her seventh child, Wallace, in 1933. Wallace was the only child Clara conceived during Fard's stay in Detroit. NOI literature suggests that Wallace was predicted by and named after Fard.[21]

Elijah's commitment to the Nation was rewarded in a series of promotions, including to that of Supreme Minister. Supreme Ministers were responsible for relaying Fard's instructions to NOI members and for overseeing the daily affairs of the organization. Supreme Ministers took on an increasingly important role in the NOI starting in 1932, when Fard began to withdraw from the organization. Fard's activity in Detroit was monitored by the police department following allegations that Nation members were engaging in acts of sacrificial murder.[22] The arrest of one of Fard's alleged followers on charges of murder in

1932 prompted what became an all-encompassing effort on the part of the police department and later the Federal Bureau of Investigation to destroy the NOI. Fard disappeared mysteriously from Detroit in May 1933, following a threatening encounter with the local police department. His sudden and unannounced exit produced panic among his followers. Several ministers immediately launched succession bids, including Elijah. The intimidation Elijah faced from other Supreme Ministers, including his brother Kallat, forced him out of Detroit in 1934. He was to spend the next few years under a constant "shadow of persecution."[23] Clara remained in Detroit with her young children while Elijah sought refuge in Chicago, Milwaukee, and Washington, D.C., establishing NOI temples and starting the group's newspaper *The Final Call to Islam*. Elijah later relocated with his family to Chicago, where they sought to establish the Nation's central headquarters in 1940. However, their efforts were interrupted in 1942 when the police arrested eighty NOI members, including Elijah, for draft evasion.[24] According to the testimonies of these men, NOI teachings prohibited them from carrying arms. Elijah was found guilty of encouraging draft evasion and sentenced to a five-year prison term to be served at the Milan, Michigan, Federal Correctional Institution. He refused parole in December 1943 and was released on August 24, 1946.

Elijah's incarceration forced the burden of managing the NOI onto Clara, who became the organization's Supreme Secretary during Elijah's absence. Much of Clara's efforts to manage the NOI during Elijah's incarceration is undocumented. However, historian Ajile Rahman notes that Clara became a conduit through which her husband's orders were relayed to ministers.[25] Clara also visited other NOI members who had been incarcerated and covertly passed on correspondence to and from NOI members. It is arguable that without Clara's leadership during this time, the Nation would have ceased to exist. Historian Manning Marable contends that the NOI's membership had dwindled to around 400 members by 1946.[26] The mass exodus of men and women from the NOI should not, however, be construed as evidence of ineffective leadership on the part of Clara. Rather, intimidation from police and the harassment of NOI members played a significant part in the demise of the NOI. Police records contained in Fard Muhammad's and Elijah Muhammad's respective FBI files reveal that dozens of NOI members were routinely harassed and intimidated by local police departments solely because of their association with the NOI.[27] In an article for the *Muhammad Speaks* newspaper in 1964, for example, Beatrice X noted, "We suffered extreme hardships to help the Honorable Elijah Muhammad establish Islam here. I served twenty days in jail. My sons, James and Johnny, were taken away from me and placed in Blue Plains, D.C. . . . . [F]or the slightest provocation—or for no reason at all—Muslims were arrested and thrown in jail."[28]

Elijah Muhammad worked diligently to establish the NOI in Chicago following his release from prison in 1946. According to his son Wallace, who took on the name Warith Deen Mohammed,[29] Elijah Muhammad was eager to set an example for his followers by establishing his own businesses and enacting an economic policy that would ensure the Nation's financial security:

> The Honorable Elijah Muhammad said, "We have to show the people something—we cannot progress by talk." So, he changed from preaching this mysterious doctrine to doing something practical. He said, "We have to have businesses." So he began to promote the opening of businesses. He said, "You have to produce jobs for yourself." Soon the Honorable Elijah Muhammad had a restaurant on 31st Street and Wentworth in Chicago. He had a grocery store and he, himself, was the butcher. . . . He showed them how to butcher meat and how to sell groceries. He, himself, with his own apron, had his children in the business with him.[30]

Elijah Muhammad also made important alterations to the NOI's theology following his release from prison. Historians generally agree that Fard elevated himself to the position of a prophet in the NOI. However, it was Elijah Muhammad who propagated the idea among NOI members that Fard was a deity. Elijah Muhammad's own writings on the issue illustrate that although Fard never claimed to be a deity, he did not correct Muhammad when he suggested it. In interviews with sociologist Hatim Sahib, for example, Elijah commented:

> I said that we should call him the "Almighty God" himself in person because according to what he has taught us, that must be the work of God and not of a human being. Then I took it with him, but, although

he did not tell me exactly, but he did mention that I will find out who he was. He was referring to himself as the one coming to save us and that he was the Messiah that we were looking for.[31]

Elijah's efforts to rebuild the Nation paid dividends. In 1954 he purchased a headquarters for the NOI on Chicago's South Side. The NOI established at least a dozen temples throughout the United States between 1945 and 1955.[32] NOI temples were opened in Harlem, Roxbury, San Diego, Atlanta, and Philadelphia prior to the Nation's mass exposure to the American public in 1959. Temples were assigned a number by Elijah Muhammad in the order that they were established.[33] For example, Chicago's temple was designated as Temple No. 2. Muhammad recruited a significant number of young ministers, including Malcolm X and Louis X. In these ministers, Muhammad found the dynamism, eloquence, and charisma that he lacked. Muhammad targeted the NOI's recruiting efforts at those individuals most affected by the psychology of white supremacy or those he referred to as "blind, deaf and dumb" to the truth of their history and greatness.[34] Muhammad described and promoted his message as "a practical religious teaching based on sound reasoning and common sense and void of the stupid emotionalism and imaginations that have influenced the religious thinking of our people in the past."[35] Muhammad's "practical" teachings appealed to thousands of African Americans who had grown disillusioned with the slow pace at which legislation chipping away at segregation affected their realities as disenfranchised citizens.

Elijah Muhammad's Gender Ideology

While most women and men were attracted to the Nation by its racial message, they also found its gender ideology agreeable as it was based upon notions of race building. Elijah Muhammad held deeply conservative and contradictory beliefs about the nature of the roles and positions that women should occupy in society. His gender ideology was undoubtedly influenced by and symptomatic of a postwar mass culture that tied women to the domestic sphere. Religious studies scholar Herbert Berg notes that Muhammad's most "oft-repeated directive for women was the practice of modesty."[36] This was apparent in the conservative dress codes for women—for example, covering the hair and wearing long skirts—which eventually led to a strict uniform. Qur'an-based teachings had little role in shaping Muhammad's ideas about gender spheres. Muhammad provided the rationale for his gender ideology in his 1965 publication *Message to the Blackman in America*, in which he wrote:

> Our women have been and are still being used by the devil white race, ever since we were first brought here to these States as slaves. They cannot go without being winked at, whistled at, yelled at, slapped, patted, kicked and driven around in the street by your devil enemies right under your nose. Yet you do nothing about it, nor do you protest [or] stop our women from trying to look like them.[37]

It is important to note that, in this quotation, Muhammad is addressing men and not women. Indeed, Muhammad rarely addressed women directly in any of his public addresses or writings.[38] His comments reveal a protectionary ethos, but more sinisterly they can also be read as sanctioning male control of women. African American women were often stereotyped as sexually loose and void of the qualities associated with the Victorian concept of "true womanhood." Elijah Muhammad's gender ideology resisted this stereotype by promoting the belief that Black women were "naturally beautiful."[39] At the same time, the NOI adhered to Victorian ideals of respectability and chastity. These ideals were taught and implemented within the Nation via MGT classes.

Malcolm X

According to Manning Marable, the NOI grew exponentially between 1953 and 1961. Scholars including C. Eric Lincoln and Marable have noted that the demographics of the NOI's membership altered considerably during this period. During its formative years, Nation members were characterized as predominantly middle-aged and recent migrants. In the late 1950s and early 1960s, however, the most discernible characteristic of the Nation's members was their youth. Indeed, Lincoln observed that up to 80 percent of NOI members during this period were between the ages of seventeen and thirty-five.[40] The Nation's popularity with young African Americans led to a tenfold increase in membership between 1956 and 1961.[41] Nation ministers played a leading role in popularizing the organization among young African Americans. No minister was more influential during this period than Minister Malcolm X.

Malcolm Little joined the NOI while incarcerated for larceny at the Norfolk County (Massachusetts) Prison. Malcolm was born in Omaha, Nebraska, in 1925. His parents, Earl and Louise Little, were dedicated organizers for the Marcus Garvey movement. Indeed, in reflecting upon his father, Malcolm noted that "still the image of him that made me proudest was his crusading and militantly campaigning with the words of Marcus Garvey."[42] Malcolm's family was torn apart as a result of his father's death and the subsequent deterioration of his mother's mental health. Earl Little was killed when Malcolm was just six years old. Throughout his life, Malcolm believed that the Ku Klux Klan had been responsible for his death. Earl Little's death forced the burden of care for the family onto Louise, who struggled to secure the family's economic survival. According to Malcolm, his mother's mental health deteriorated further when the state social agency began to visit the family home in Lansing, Michigan, to assess how Louise was coping with the children. Louise eventually suffered a breakdown and was institutionalized at the State Mental Hospital at Kalamazoo. Her children were separated and placed with foster parents. Malcolm excelled at school despite staunch racism from his white teachers. Indeed, he had aspirations to become a lawyer. Malcolm's formal education came to an abrupt end after a candid discussion with his teacher Mr. Ostrowski, who forever ended Malcolm's dream of pursuing a career in law:

> He [Mr. Ostrowski] kind of half-smiled and said, "Malcolm, one of life's first needs is for us to be realistic. Don't misunderstand me, now. We all here like you, you know that. But you've got to be realistic about being a nigger. A lawyer—that's no realistic goal for a nigger. You need to think about something you can be.[43]

Malcolm's exodus from formal education led him eventually to Harlem, where he drifted into a life of crime and self-degradation. In his autobiography Malcolm comments that his efforts to "conk" or straighten his hair marked his "first really big step toward self-degradation."[44] It was during his time in Harlem that he met and began dating a white woman, Sophia, with whom he had an ongoing affair. Malcolm's descent into a life of crime, pimping, and drugs eventually caught up with him. In 1946 Malcolm, aged twenty-one, and his friend Shorty were arrested with two white women for robbery. It was in prison that Malcolm was to find the Nation of Islam. He was introduced to the NOI and the teachings of Elijah Muhammad via his brother Philbert, who had joined the organization. Malcolm's life was transformed while he was in prison. He returned to his love of reading and adopted an ascetic lifestyle. On his release from prison Malcolm went straight to Detroit, where he was employed as an NOI minister in 1953. His dedication was rewarded in 1954 when Muhammad appointed him the minister of Temple No. 7 in Harlem. According to Malcolm's autobiography, Temple No. 7 grew more rapidly than any other.

The Media

The NOI remained relatively unknown in the United States until the 1950s, when Elijah Muhammad established a Public Relations Committee under the direction of his son Herbert Muhammad.[45] Muhammad's early writings exhorting African Americans to "join their own" were featured regularly in numerous African American newspapers, including the *Pittsburgh Courier*, the *Los Angeles Herald Dispatch*, the *Afro-American*, and the *New York Amsterdam News*. In addition to propagating its teachings via the African American press, the NOI also published its own magazines, *The Supreme Wisdom* and *The Messenger Magazine*. The NOI's frequent appearances in the media also received attention from the national press in the form of a 1959 documentary on the NOI, *The Hate That Hate Produced*. The five-part series was designed to shock moderate viewers and present the NOI as "hate mongers."[46] Remarkably, Elijah Muhammad was featured only briefly in the documentary. Muhammad's oration was regarded as "inaudible" and subsequently the news cameras moved swiftly to the NOI's regional minister in Harlem, Malcolm X.[47] With the spotlight on Malcolm X, known for his talent to capture audiences, the documentary had a great impact on popularizing the organization. Following the documentary, Malcolm X encouraged Elijah Muhammad to authorize the creation of the NOI's own official newspaper, *Muhammad Speaks* (*MS*). The newspaper was to become an important source of information on the Nation and often the primary means by which potential members learned about it. The success of the paper, however, also came at a cost for NOI members. Muhammad instructed his male followers to buy a set quota of papers and resell them during their free time.[48] This often placed an intolerable financial burden on Muhammad's followers. Yet the quotas remained in place. Malcolm X rose through the ranks of the NOI more quickly than any other minister. In 1960 Muhammad created a new post for Malcolm: that of National Minister.

Power Struggles

Malcolm enjoyed what could be described as a father–son relationship with Muhammad. Indeed, Muhammad considered Malcolm his "most faithful" minister.[49] Elijah Muhammad suffered from chronic health problems that were largely kept hidden from his followers. Muhammad's increased health issues caused much speculation that Malcolm X would succeed him. Such speculation led to heightened power struggles within the Nation and eventually resulted in Malcolm's exodus from the organization in March 1964. Malcolm was suspended from the NOI in 1963 following his decision to make unauthorized comments about the assassination of President John F. Kennedy. The suspension, however, became indefinite when Muhammad discovered that Malcolm had been informed of Muhammad's affairs with several of his secretaries. In his autobiography Malcolm notes that he heard rumors of Muhammad's affairs as early as 1955 and chose to ignore them. Malcolm's enemies in the Nation, however, persuaded Muhammad that Malcolm had been gossiping about him. Malcolm realized quickly that his prospects of reentering the Nation were slipping away, and he defected from the organization in March 1964. Upon his exit from the Nation, Malcolm established two organizations, Muslim Mosque Inc. and the Organization of Afro-American Unity. Both organizations were created between March and June 1964. Malcolm made the transition to Sunni Islam after performing the *hajj* (pilgrimage to Mecca). Malcolm's exodus from the

Nation did not end his problems with the organization, however. When he informed the press of Muhammad's affairs, Nation members, and the FOI in particular, reacted angrily. Indeed, on November 4, 1964, Louis X, whom Malcolm had recruited into the NOI, wrote in the *MS* paper:

> Only those who wish to be led to hell, or to their doom, will follow Malcolm. The die is set, and Malcolm shall not escape. . . . Such a man as Malcolm is worthy of death, and would have met with death if it had not been for Muhammad's confidence in Allah and victory over his enemies.[50]

Malcolm encountered constant threats on his life and his family's safety. His assassination on February 25, 1965, marked a turning point in the NOI and Elijah Muhammad's relationship with his ministers.[51] Louis Farrakhan replaced Malcolm as the Nation's National Minister and was appointed by Muhammad to oversee Temple No. 7.

Imam W. D. Mohammed and Minister Farrakhan Lead Two Nations

When Elijah Muhammad passed away in 1975, his son Wallace Mohammed (1933–2008) found himself leading the Nation the very next day. Many in the Nation were surprised by Wallace's succession, about which there are at least three competing narratives.[52] The first suggests that Wallace, who had been a minister under Elijah Muhammad, had been predestined to one day lead the Nation. The second contends that Elijah Muhammad had privately appointed Wallace to succeed him. The third narrative suggests that Wallace was unanimously elected to succeed his father by a six-man ruling committee composed of his close family members and world heavyweight boxing champion Muhammad Ali. Wallace's succession sounded the death knell for the Nation's doctrine. Indeed, Wallace had earned a reputation for his proclivity toward Sunni Islam as early as 1958.[53] Wallace's constant questioning of his father's particularistic appropriation of Islam resulted in his suspension from the Nation on more than one occasion.

Wallace's succession was also somewhat of a surprise to many given that Muhammad had repeatedly suspended him from the NOI.

Elijah Muhammad and his future successor endured a tense and often strained relationship. There can be little doubt that Wallace revered his father. However, it is also true that he questioned his father's teachings. Yet at some point in his ministerial career, Wallace did regard himself as the "Second Man" in the Nation. In an interview with political scientist E. U. Essien-Udom in 1960 he remarked:

> I am sent by the Messenger wherever there is a need. I have to be in town when the Messenger is out because the Messenger relies on me. He has confidence that I can carry out the work. The followers have come to look upon me as the second man. Besides, I had four years of Koranic teachings. Many of the ministers are qualified but there are always people who seek information on Islam and if the Messenger is not around I am the next logical man [from] whom they can obtain most reliable information. People seek information continuously.[54]

Wallace was sworn in as his father's successor in February 1975 at the Nation's Saviour's Day convention—an event held annually in honor of Fard Muhammad—where he pledged to "carry on in the tradition" of his father. Wallace's inaugural address, however, also made explicitly clear that race baiting would be a thing of the past: "They named us Black Muslims . . . but I want you to know that we are not a people to harbor racism."[55]

The NOI's new leader quickly restructured the organization, introducing Sunni Islam at a speed that alarmed many. Wallace took on the title Imam W. D. Mohammed, the NOI was renamed the World Community of Al-Islam in the West (WCIW), and its business empire was liquidated in 1976. The changes that swept through the Nation left many disillusioned. High-profile figures defected from the WCIW and formed their own splinter groups, the most notorious of which was to become Louis Farrakhan's "Resurrected NOI."

The ideological split within the Nation ran deep throughout 1975 and 1976. It would be erroneous to suggest that NOI members in 1975 were unaware of the charge that their practices and teachings were far removed from those of their Sunni counterparts. Moreover, this awareness may have heightened after 1965, when the national media published Malcolm X's critiques of Muhammad's teachings. Elijah

Muhammad had surrounded himself with sycophants who vied not only for his approval but also for a share of the Nation's spoils. Such corruption left Wallace deeply embittered. At one point, for example, he described a segment of the Nation's leadership as "wearing pimp's clothes and preaching nation building."[56] Thus, for some NOI members, Wallace's introduction of Sunni Islam and efforts to domesticate Islam in the U.S. context came as a "mercy" to a community already deeply divided along theological lines.[57] For others, however, the departure from NOI dogma had arrived too quickly. The rupture between W. D. Mohammed and Louis Farrakhan separated Sunni women in the WCIW from their former friends who now formed an integral and important part of Farrakhan's newly created Nation in 1977.

Despite his popularity within the NOI prior to 1975, Louis Farrakhan was unable initially to attract a significant number of former Nation members to his Resurrected Nation. Moreover, he departed from the WCIW with neither the financial resources nor manpower necessary to market the group as effectively as he had done in the late 1960s when he replaced Malcolm X as the Nation's National Minister. Farrakhan remained relatively true to his promise not to depart from Elijah Muhammad's apolitical and theological teachings within the Resurrected NOI until 1984, when he announced publicly his support for Jesse Jackson's bid for the U.S. presidency. Farrakhan's anti-Semitic rhetoric during the campaign received national media attention, thus launching him and the Resurrected NOI into the national spotlight almost overnight. Farrakhan's departure from Elijah Muhammad's rule of non-engagement in the political process was censured by Imam Mohammed, who suggested that the relationship between Farrakhan and Jackson was "puzzling."[58]

Farrakhan's NOI flourished in the 1980s for many of the same reasons that Elijah Muhammad's Nation did. Deteriorating race relations, poverty, ghettoization, and government indifference coupled with the emergence of the prison industrial complex combined to create a fertile context in which the NOI and its leader could thrive. Such realities vindicated Farrakhan's critique of the racial hierarchy in the United States and helped propel him to the apex of his career in 1995, when he led the Million Man March (MMM) in Washington, D.C. Farrakhan's path to popularity in pockets of the United States was aided not only by the context of Reaganomics but also by the advent of African American musical genres that voiced both the discontent and aspirations of African American youths. Farrakhan's ascent also owed much to the willingness of clergy and secular groups to work with the NOI.

Like its predecessor, Farrakhan's NOI earned a reputation for promoting and helping to enforce socioeconomic improvement in numerous African American communities. Such work earned Farrakhan a degree of prestige among young African Americans and particularly the hip-hop generation. Hip-hop and rap artists including Nas, The Fugees, and Notorious BIG paid homage to the "Honorable Minister Louis Farrakhan" in their artistic work. Farrakhan's celebrity status in pockets of the United States throughout the early 1990s remained dependent upon his ability to secure a working relationship with the Black church and secular groups. Nowhere was his dependence on both groups more apparent than in the buildup to the Million Man March in 1995. Farrakhan's decision to exclude women from the March led to fervent charges that the NOI advocated "outdated models of male dominated approaches to rebuilding Black families and communities."[59] Such criticism, however, neglected the important leadership and administrative roles that women played in organizing and financing the March.

The flurry of censure that engulfed the NOI and its patriarchal structure in the buildup to and the aftermath of the March overshadowed the harsh socioeconomic realities that had made it a success. Perhaps more important, however, charges of misogyny masked the emergence of NOI women as ministers, managers, and administrators in the group. As early as 1998 Farrakhan appointed Ava Muhammad, a high-profile lawyer, as the Resurrected NOI's first female minister. Ava's appointment was quickly followed by the emergence of Tynetta Muhammad, Elijah Muhammad's former secretary; Claudette-Marie Muhammad; and Farrakhan's daughter Donna Farrakhan Muhammad as high-profile figures in the group.

African American women have steadily climbed the Nation's patriarchal structures. Their achievements have been matched by their Latina and Native American counterparts. Theresa X Torres, for example, serves on the NOI's Prison Reform Ministry and writes regularly for the Nation's paper, *The Final Call.* Similarly, YoNasDa Lonewolf Muhammad serves as the director for the Indigenous Nations Alliance and also

writes regularly for the paper. Farrakhan's promotion of Latinas and
Native American women within the NOI has been strategic and part
of his overarching goal to make the Nation more inclusive. Contrary
to popular belief, the NOI has never been a racially exclusive group.
According to the organization's National Latino Minister, Abel Muhammad, Elijah Muhammad invited Latino families to join the Nation
in the early 1940s. Moreover, in his published work Elijah Muhammad exhorted Latinos and Native Americans to join and support the
Nation. The presence of Latinos in the NOI grew steadily throughout
the late 1980s and early 1990s. Yet fully integrating Latinos into the NOI
remains problematic. In 2009, for example, at the annual Saviours'[60]
Day convention, Latinos hosted a workshop titled "Bridging the Gap"
to discuss prejudice directed toward them within the Nation. During panel discussions, Brian Muhammad noted that some within the
Nation had been "hesitant to embrace members of the Latino family"
despite the fact that they make up more than an estimated 20 percent
of the group's national membership.[61] Native Americans also remain a
minority within the NOI. Farrakhan has made efforts since the early
1980s to market the Nation to this ethnic group. In the early 1980s, for
example, he employed Wauneta Muhammad, a young Native American
woman who had married into the NOI, to help oversee the recruitment
of Native Americans.

The NOI and the MGT have attempted to make the Nation more
appealing to women by relaxing certain rules in recent years, particularly the dress code. That the strict dress code in the NOI has been a
deterrent to women's joining the group is well known. Under the watch-
ful eye of the MGT, the dress code for women in the NOI has been
gradually modernized. The NOI now annually hosts designer competi-
tions and fashion shows to promote modest fashions for women. Project Modesty is one such show. Its focus is on stimulating the creation of
designs from women in the group. The annual design contests are open
to girls and women aged fourteen to twenty-four and carry a lucrative
prize offer: "Project Modesty will clothe our girls with the garments
that will reflect their beauty and culture without being tight, revealing
or skimpy."[62] Alongside this initiative, the NOI no longer forbids the use
of birth control or prevents interracial marriage. Interfaith marriage is
also no longer prohibited.

Farrakhan's travels abroad in the immediate years following the MMM placed him at odds with Sunni Muslims, including followers of Imam Mohammed. After much-publicized meetings with Muammar Gaddafi of Libya and Saddam Hussein of Iraq in 1996 and the censure that followed from the U.S. Senate Foreign Relations Committee, Sunni Muslims in Chicago became increasingly concerned that they would be mistaken for NOI converts and therefore be subject to the negative press coverage that Farrakhan's tours abroad had received in the United States. Sunni Muslims were not alone in fearing association with Farrakhan on his return to the United States. Many who had reluctantly supported the MMM withdrew support for Farrakhan when he returned from Africa and the Middle East. During the first gathering of grassroots organizers of the MMM in February 1996, for example, only 50 of the nearly 350 local organizing committees attended. The absence of 300 local organizers was construed by the national media as evidence of disappointment with Farrakhan's activities.[63] The NOI's relationship with its Sunni counterparts continued to sour until February 2000, when Farrakhan's NOI publicly reconciled with Imam Mohammed's community. The reconciliation saw Farrakhan bring the NOI relatively in line with its Sunni counterpart. Many observers remarked that the event marked a significant change in the NOI's theological and racial trajectory.[64]

No less than a year after the 2000 Saviours' Day address, Farrakhan sought to challenge reports that he was a shadow of his former self. In his 2001 Saviours' Day address at Christ Universal Temple in Chicago, he refuted notions that illness had resulted in his apparent change. Farrakhan's Nation made another push toward Sunni Islam in October 2008 at the re-dedication of its national center at Mosque Maryam in Chicago. The event was attended by representatives of the Muslim, Christian, and Jewish faiths. The re-dedication ceremony saw the NOI's leader ask his followers to take on an "expanded" mission and accept a "New Beginning" for the NOI. The "expanded" mission that Farrakhan envisioned involved his followers' serving all sectors of society, including whites.[65] News coverage of reactions from NOI members to the "New Beginning" and "expanded mission" in *The Final Call* differed notably. Initial optimism over the Nation's "New Beginning" proved fleeting as the NOI quickly retreated to its original doctrine.

The NOI, however, is no longer a replica of its predecessor. The NOI's female demographic is diverse both in its ethnic makeup and in terms of the socioeconomic backgrounds from which its membership is drawn. Indeed, it appears that the only constant is the religious persuasion of women before they arrive at the NOI. According to Nisa Islam Muhammad, an NOI member, 99 percent of the women who end up in the arms of the NOI are nominal Christians.[66] In the Chicago area, where the NOI is strongest, its female converts are drawn from many of the surrounding Christian churches, including President Barack Obama's former church, Trinity United Church of Christ. In an interview, President Obama's former pastor Dr. Jeremiah Wright recalled losing one of his strongest female members to the NOI. According to Wright, this loss was a result of her relationship with an NOI member:

> One of the girls who grew up in the church, a strong womanist theologian, went away to college. She graduated and I didn't see her so I asked her mom two years after she graduated, and she said, "She's waiting on her X; she's at the Nation." I said, "Will she talk to me?" and she said, "Yeah," and so she called and we made an appointment, and she showed up with two women from the Nation. . . . We went into my office and I said, "Explain to me what happened," and she said, "Reverend, when it comes to a man who is only trying to get me into bed, who drinks, who does reefer . . . but who's saying he's sanctified and filled with the Holy Ghost and hopping in bed with all the women as opposed to a man who does not drink, a man who does not do drugs, a man who's working and supporting and respecting me and who's a Muslim, I'll take *as-salamu ʿalaykum* [Muslim greeting] all day long." I said, "But the theology . . . and the women are inferior," and she said, "I don't believe none of that. . . . I've got a good man."[67]

Nation Women's Leadership

African American women made significant contributions to building and sustaining the NOI's educational and economic structures throughout the 1950s and 1960s. Women's roles in the NOI have changed dramatically since its inception in 1930. Yet rarely are these changes noted by scholars and outside observers of the Nation. Women exercised leadership roles in various aspects of Elijah Muhammad's NOI but particularly within the Muslim Girls Training and the NOI's plethora of small business ventures, including its national newspaper, *Muhammad Speaks*. Women now exercise powerful ministerial, management, editorial, and senior administrative roles within Louis Farrakhan's NOI. A manifestation of this progression can be seen in the fact that women currently sit on the NOI's exclusive Executive Board.

Early Nation women were rarely visible in the public sphere. Indeed, concerns about their safety and dictates about gender spheres resulted in their activism's being confined to within the walls and boundaries of the NOI's structures and communities. Early Nation women exercised both formal and informal leadership positions in the Nation. Nation women devoted their collective energies to the task of erecting, overseeing, and strengthening Nation businesses, temples, and schools. Popular discourse relating to gender spheres helped shape the roles and positions that women could occupy in the Nation. Unlike their counterparts in the civil rights movement and the Black church, Nation women exercised agency *within* their religious setting. African American women have historically constituted a majority in Black churches. Yet they often remained in the "background" of the church setting. Evelyn Brooks Higginbotham, for example, notes, "Male biased traditions and rules of decorum sought to mute women's voices and accentuate their subordinate status vis-à-vis men. Thus tainted by the values of the larger American society, the Black church sought to provide men with full manhood rights, while offering women a separate and unequal status."[68] Ministers dominated the upper echelons of the civil rights movement for pragmatic reasons. Their dominance of such positions resulted in women's being excluded from executive positions in several civil rights organizations, including the Montgomery Improvement Association (MIA), the Student Non-Violent Coordinating Committee (SNCC), and the Southern Christian Leadership Conference (SCLC). Women made invaluable contributions to the campaigns of these organizations, but they did so outside of their religious setting. Research by sociologists Belinda Robnett and Teresa Nance illustrates that women in the civil rights movement served as bridge leaders, field secretaries, and activists in local communities. Put simply, women's formal and informal leadership in the civil rights movement occurred largely outside of the realm of the Black church. Nation women had the opposite experience. They found themselves almost daily in the temple, where they led and attended MGT classes and created and worked for business enterprises.

Oral history narratives have captured the resentment that many women who engaged in the civil rights movement felt at being collectively excluded from the decision-making process. Perhaps the most vocal of such women was Ella Baker, who once remarked that her exclusion from executive positions was a result of both ageism and sexism:

> In the first place, the combination of being a woman, and an older woman, presented some problems. Number one, I was old enough to be the mother of the leadership. The combination of this basic attitude of men, and especially ministers, as to what the role of women in the church setup is—that of taking orders, not providing leadership—and the ego that is involved—the ego involved in having to feel that here is someone who had the capacity for a certain amount of leadership and, certainly, had more information about a lot of things than they possessed at that time—this would never had lent itself to my being a leader in the movement there.[69]

Women who protested the patriarchal structures of civil rights groups often found that their grievances fell on deaf ears. Johnnie Carr, a former MIA member, remarked:

> Well, it was not a stated thing but just an understanding thing. . . . Now of course when you spoke out against things like that, a lot of times you were even criticized by other women that felt like . . . this is not what we ought to be doing. I think we just accepted the servant role and done what we could because we felt like togetherness was the point.[70]

Belinda Robnett's research on the gender dynamics of the civil rights movement reveals that many women relished seeing their male counterparts exercise authority in the regional and national leadership structure of the movement. Women's support of their male counterparts' dominance of such positions appears to have stemmed from the fact that they were acutely aware of and sensitive to the fact that Black men had historically been denied such influential positions of power in the larger society.[71]

The NOI's structures did enable women to exercise leadership. Nation women's opportunities for such leadership were found in the MGT, the Nation's schools, and business enterprises. The Muslim Girls Training served three purposes within the overall structure of the NOI. It provided an arena in which NOI women could foster a greater sense of community, it educated women in all things relative to the domestic sphere, and it was a forum in which women could be disciplined for failing to adhere to either the Nation's strict moral codes or the standards imposed by the MGT. The MGT's emphasis on traditional gender roles has often led outside observers to conclude that female members of the group were prisoners of the domestic sphere. This conclusion indicates a poor understanding of the context in which the NOI operated. Elijah Muhammad's NOI encouraged women, first and foremost, to fulfill their obligations to their families. Opportunities for working-class African American women to pursue employment were often restricted to domestic work for whites, as well as other unskilled jobs.[72] In this context, the prospect of not having to pursue menial employment was seen by some women as a welcome and protectionary measure. Moreover, the Nation's dress code would have made certain forms of menial labor more difficult for women to carry out.

The Muhammad University of Islam (MUI) was a space in which women could exercise considerable influence over the direction of the NOI's educational program. The schools accepted both Muslim and non-Muslim children and educated them in the rudiments of NOI dogma and core subjects. The NOI's school curriculum was drastically out of sync with the norms of U.S. public schools, but it nonetheless provided a refuge in which NOI children could enjoy a sense of protection from hostile forces. The NOI's educational curriculum was designed with the aim of encouraging children's individual talents and thus acted as a great leveler. Former MUI pupil Sonsyrea Tate remarks:

> I think self-awareness and self-discipline are a huge part of education and I appreciate getting that in the NOI. Other aspects of our education, however, were questionable. For instance, the American history and

world history we learned in the NOI didn't square with the mainstream American history. The difference left some of us at a disadvantage when it was time to pass standardized tests. What I considered superior was the focus on our individual talents.[73]

Women exercised a greater degree of influence in the NOI's school structure than their male counterparts. Charlene Johnson, for example, served as the director of the MUI in Chicago in 1960, and numerous women were employed as assistant directors, teachers, and secretaries in regional NOI schools.

The NOI provided educators with an opportunity to contribute to the management of the MUI on a number of levels. NOI schools stood as a beacon of stability and discipline in African American communities. Such attributes made the NOI's schools appealing to African American parents, especially in the midst of the chaos and confusion that school desegregation created in the 1950s and 1960s. MUI schools were known for their dedicated and disciplined teaching staff. Former MUI teacher W. Muhsinah Abdullah notes:

I did teach in the school at one point and we did an excellent job. In terms of educating we were really committed; we would get there at 8 am and not leave until 7 pm working on lesson plans or developing extra-curricular activities. . . . For me personally, it offered an opportunity to contribute and to realize my potential as a teacher.[74]

Aside from fulfilling teaching and administrative roles in the MUI, women took advantage of numerous opportunities to support the NOI's host of small businesses and to pursue their own entrepreneurial enterprises. NOI women secured employment in various businesses, including the Temple No. 2 clothing factory in Chicago and the Muslim Thrift Shop. The NOI's emphasis on "Buying Black" and fostering group cohesion provided would-be entrepreneurs with an existing consumer base. Women regularly advertised their businesses in *Muhammad Speaks*. A "Shirt Hospital" that Ida 4X Gidas operated was advertised regularly in the paper, as was "Sister Meda's Sesame Seed Candy." Such businesses may have been rather small, but they nevertheless provided women with an opportunity not only to seek out a livelihood from their membership in the NOI but also to contribute actively to its overarching economic goal of self-sufficiency.

The Original NOI's Gender Ideology in Context: Black Women and Slavery

Black feminist and womanist scholars have argued that Black feminist perspectives develop from the everyday struggles of African American women, represented by the intricate and overlapping power plays of gender, race, class, and sexuality.[75] In other words, grasping what may have or have not been liberating for Black women requires careful consideration of the context of their lives. African Americans were only two generations out of slavery when the Nation's teachings began attracting African Americans in Detroit and Chicago, destination cities of the Great Migration. The Nation spoke directly to the devastating impact of slavery on African Americans. Slavery "made us blind, deaf, and dumb to the knowledge of self or anyone else and it stands true today that the American so-called Negroes don't know themselves or anyone else," Elijah Muhammad asserted.[76] The Nation promised to return to African Americans their true identity and original religion. In reality, it instilled many white American middle-class ideals. The NOI appropriated the mainstream essentialist construction of whites as "civilized" and African Americans as "savage," but reversed it. In doing so, the NOI ascribed cultural conceptions of the white middle-class male to the "Black Muslim," making him the hardworking provider in a suit.

As the Nation was determined to undo the physical and psychological brutality of slavery, it attracted women whose lives were still haunted by its violence on their bodies, their families, and their institutions. The cruelties of slavery left African American women bound to a number of stereotypes that marked them as undeserving of respect and honor. The NOI resisted such notions of Black women, again by borrowing from the dominant ideology's existing constructions of white women. Claiming to protect white women from Black men's "savagery," white men constructed white women as the symbol of the white race's honor and purity. The thought to "sanction a white woman enduring the embrace of a colored man" was an abomination to the "highest race," preventing women from "no holier duty" than to "preserve the purity of the type." Woman as an embodiment of honor provided white men with the rationale to lynch African American men for the "protection" of white women and the white race.[77]

In an anonymous article in *Muhammad Speaks*, the category "woman" was also manipulated as a symbol of honor but for the purpose of exposing white men's savagery: "Today the so-called Negro woman is living a jungle life." The writer held the white man, who is "by nature an adulterer and a fornicator," responsible for her condition. The white man "has seduced our women of Africa and Asia. . . . He was the crook who first put our women out on the streets that they may disgrace our morals and tear down the future of our nation."[78] Although the NOI borrowed from the dominant ideology as it used women as a symbol of honor and an object of protection to assault the white race, we cannot ignore the painful reality lying behind the NOI's critique: the systematic raping of slave women by white slaveholders. This is an example of the NOI's bold exposure of white men's injustices, which has played an integral part in attracting women to the movement.

The construction of white women as preservers of the race's honor was expanded with conceptions of "true womanhood." Based on mid-nineteenth-century American popular literature, the four cardinal virtues that distinguished a "true woman" were "piety, purity, submissiveness, and domesticity."[79] The ideology of "true womanhood" inherently excluded African American women as it was used to rationalize "opposing definitions of womanhood and motherhood" for white and Black women. Constructions of the two groups of women were mutually reinforcing, "each dependent on the other for its existence," with the aim to legitimize the sexual exploitation of slave women. Slave women were vulnerable to sexual abuse because they did not possess "the assets of white womanhood: no masculine protector or home and family, the locus of the flowering of white womanhood."[80] Historian Deborah White argues that such skewed sexual myths were reinforced by various factors, including Europeans' misconception of semi-nudity in parts of Africa as a sign of promiscuity, enslaved women's bodies' being displayed at auctions and whippings, the primary role of enslaved women to produce children, and boasts from masters that they were not required to exert force to secure the sexual compliance of their enslaved women.[81]

At the same time that enslaved women were raped and expected to bear children, they were not exempted from the demands of labor. "The grueling demands of fieldwork constrained slave women's experience of pregnancy and child-rearing." In this way, African American women have always been working mothers. As slave women worked throughout the day, the care of their children was left to slaves who were "too weak, too old, or too young to join them in the fields." Often children were left for hours without their mothers' returning to nurse them. As a result of such conditions, "the infant mortality rate among slaves in 1850 was twice that of whites, with fewer than two out of three Black children surviving to age ten. Death from malnutrition and disease was more likely to snatch a mother's children than sale to a new owner."[82] Directly speaking to African American women's historical experience of having to produce and reproduce against their will, the NOI's focus on honoring and protecting women's roles as wives and mothers continues to attract African American women and other women of color.

Alongside images of African American women as sexually loose, other stereotypes have emerged to simultaneously legitimize and mask the racism and sexism directed toward Black women. Feminist scholar Patricia Collins describes the most prominent of these stereotypes, calling them "controlling images." They have their roots in slavery but have been used to blame African American women for the current ills in their communities caused, in reality, by the injustices of racism and capitalism. These images are mammy, matriarch, welfare recipient, and jezebel.[83]

The mammy is "the faithful, obedient domestic servant," an image created to "justify the economic exploitation" of Black women serving as domestics in white homes during and after slavery. With mammies, the nurturing of African American women is displaced from her children to white children. This image has been falsely portrayed as rewarding for African American women, who were depicted as submissively and merrily serving the white race. While the "mammy represents the 'good' Black mother, the matriarch symbolizes the 'bad' Black mother." The matriarch is blamed for the breakdown of Black families because she defies the traditional domestic role. Taking a job outside the home, she emasculates her man and takes attention away from the proper raising of her children. This image displaces responsibility for economic, educational, and moral decline in African American homes. Instead of faulting the class dimensions of racism, it blames African American women.[84]

The image of Black women as welfare mothers reduces African American women to child breeders. The welfare mother's dependency on assistance enforces the notion that African Americans are lazy "by blaming Black welfare mothers for failing to pass on the work ethic." Also, because welfare mothers are usually portrayed as unwed mothers, they lose any value owing to the "dominant gender ideology positing that a woman's true worth" is claimed only through marriage. The fourth controlling image that Collins discusses is "the Jezebel, whore, or sexually aggressive woman." As discussed above, this image has served as justification for the ongoing sexual assault against African American women.[85]

The NOI's ideology constructed the Black *Muslim* woman to defy these controlling images. By portraying the Muslim woman as the one who provides "proper spiritual guidance," for "our children, the future generation," the NOI rejected the mammy image. By portraying the Muslim woman as provided for and protected by her husband and not speaking "in a demanding voice to her husband," the NOI defied the matriarch image. Because the Muslim woman seeks marriage, and her Muslim husband is not a lazy beggar, the welfare image was challenged. Finally, because the Muslim woman never wears "vulgar, immodest, or indecent attire," the jezebel image was refuted. Ultimately, the NOI reversed the language of the dominant ideology, teaching that "Black women are the Mothers of Civilization, and by nature, they are the most beautiful women on earth."[86] In this way, Nation notions of the ideal woman were based on white middle-class American values, not Sunni Islam, and sought to present Black women as the symbol of the Black race's purity and dignity, who therefore needed the protection of Black men.

Central Issues

This book's focus on women's contributions and experiences in the NOI centers on several core issues. The NOI's gender ideology stipulated separate gender spheres for women and men, emphasizing women's roles as homemaker and mother and men's roles as breadwinner and protector. The ways in which Nation women interpreted and negotiated their role as domestics will emerge across the following chapters. At the same time, complementing the analysis of separate gender spheres is an exploration of how women transcended their "ideal" roles within the home and worked alongside men in the educational and economic structures of the Nation. Here we find the Nation's larger goals of Black protest and self-help providing women with opportunities to contribute to the building of the Nation and, later, to the development of their Sunni *masjid* (mosque) communities. Outlining women's contributions to and work in the NOI is a central goal of the book.

Women's reinterpretation and negotiation of the Nation's gender ideology have developed into a larger tradition of Nation women defining and producing thought, voice, and image for themselves. Certainly their leaders have greatly influenced them, but women have also reinterpreted the guidance of their male teachers, applying it as they see fit. We will see how women have regularly negotiated voice and leadership in their religious communities, including a discussion of the controversial topic of women imams. Moreover, Nation women have assessed and claimed for themselves meanings of gender liberation against the backdrop of notions of gender liberation in the larger society. Like womanist and Black feminist thinkers who have proclaimed that mainstream white feminism does not speak to or for their experiences in the struggle for gender justice, African American Muslim women have proclaimed the same. Diverse conceptions of gender liberation therefore are a central focus of this book.

The NOI's protest against white superiority, particularly the famous pronouncement "The original man is the Asiatic Black man, the maker, the owner, the cream of the planet earth, God of the universe," was also articulated to apply in specific ways to women, most notably in NOI notions of Black women's superior beauty and their worthiness of ultimate respect. Similarly, NOI policies and practices intended to both transform the second-class circumstances of African Americans and to defy inferior images of them were expressed in ways specifically meaningful to women. These practices include dress codes, as Nation women designed and donned various uniforms including ones resembling the attire of nuns, and diet, as women significantly contributed to the NOI legacy with the creation of the bean pie, a product of the

Nation's dietary rules that resisted the historical slave diet. As we consider what made the NOI appealing to women, constructions of beauty, respect due to women, dress, and diet emerge as ongoing topics.

The Nation of Islam is not only a Black nationalist movement but also a religious movement.[87] Its references to and dialogue with Christianity have made it relevant to many who were once committed Christians. At the same time, the NOI introduced practices meant for Black uplift that are unmistakably embedded in the religion of Islam, so much so that some former Nation members believe that the creator of NOI doctrine intended for the movement to eventually lead African Americans to Sunni Islam. The religious nature of the Nation makes Black women's spirituality and religious protest, not unlike the "righteous discontent" of Black Baptist women in the South, an ongoing theme explored in the book.[88]

Featuring women currently in the Nation and those who left the Nation for Sunni Islam—namely, those in Imam Mohammed's community—central topics of this book also include the ongoing relationship between the Nation and Sunni Islam and Nation women's journeys into Sunni Islam. We explore not only changes in the Nation's gender ideology brought by Imam Mohammed and the ways in which women responded but also current Nation women's conviction of the continuing relevance of the teachings of Elijah Muhammad as the best way to present Islam to African Americans today. This consideration of the NOI as "Islam for Black people" complements analysis of the revised Black consciousness in Imam Mohammed's community as articulated in the voice and work of Sunni women. Nation women, former and current, find themselves in the complex and fascinating places between Black protest and Sunni Islam.

Methodology

The research for this book is based primarily on the oral histories of women whose membership in the NOI spans the period 1950s to the present. We refer to women who joined the NOI before 1975 and followed Imam Mohammed into Sunni Islam as former Nation women, Sunni women, or, as below, women in the Warith Deen Mohammed (WDM) community. Preferring the simple label Muslim, these women do not regularly use these terms to describe themselves; however, we appropriate them to distinguish between former and current women in the Nation. The term "Sunni" is likely the most problematic term for these women because it is often used in reference to the Sunni–Shi'ah divide; however, it is still appropriate as it is a term widely used among African Americans, both Muslim and non-Muslim, to distinguish between Sunni Islam and the Nation of Islam. During discussions of the World Community of Al-Islam in the West, female followers are referred to as women in the WCIW. However, that name was abandoned by the 1980s, and because the community went through several name changes over the years but has always been popularly described as the Warith Deen Mohammed community by various groups of Muslims, we have used the terminology "women in the WDM community" in discussing female followers after the transition from the Nation.[89] We refer to women who are currently in the Nation of Islam as Nation women or women in the NOI. Many of these women also prefer the simple title Muslim but also refer to themselves as MGT or members of Muhammad Mosque.

We approach the oral testimonies of informants as authentic accounts of what membership in the Nation has meant to women. While these accounts are diverse, "there are no 'false' oral sources." No matter the extent to which women's views of the Nation differ from one another or from scholarly analysis of NOI gender ideology as documented in NOI literature, women's oral accounts are "psychologically 'true.'" Oral histories tell us how individual life experiences inform how women remember the past. Given their subjective nature, it is expected that women's narratives will differ, providing a more comprehensive and, therefore, more accurate picture of the Nation than any one account.[90]

Our approach also pays attention to the fact that roughly half of our research participants left the Nation almost four decades ago and now practice Sunni Islam. We recognize that Sunni women's changed religious position influences how they interpret and recall their Nation past. Oral histories "tell us not just what people did, but what they wanted to do, what they believed they were doing, what they now think they did." As we portray and analyze the narratives of women in the WDM community, we especially keep in mind how they remember the NOI in terms of "what they now think they did."[91] We do not, however, make any generalizations about how this new consciousness affects their recollection. Former Nation women often describe the NOI as their doorway into Sunni Islam, a recognition that engenders a positive view of the Nation. However, this view does not prevent women from describing what they disliked about the NOI. At the same time, some women favorably recall aspects of the Nation that they once found appealing, although these aspects now contradict their current theological position. In summary, while we recognize that the embrace of Sunni Islam affects women's oral histories, we find among women multiple possibilities for remembering the Nation.

Former Nation women appear generally more open to criticizing certain aspects of Elijah Muhammad's NOI. Contemporary Nation women, however, appear less willing to censure or complain about aspects of Minister Farrakhan's NOI. That is not to say, however, that their narratives are less authentic. Minister Farrakhan's Nation is a very different organization from its predecessor. Women have much more freedom to contribute to and hold positions of authority within Minister Farrakhan's NOI. Moreover, current Nation women are encouraged to pursue their educational and entrepreneurial aspirations in the NOI. Perhaps, unsurprisingly, we find that when women do speak about their involvement with the Nation, they are eager to deconstruct and challenge myths about their treatment and their work in the organization. Together we interviewed current Nation women located in several different cities. We found, however, that current Nation women were more willing to consent to interviews with the non-Muslim author than with the author in the WDM community. The reluctance of current Nation women to speak with the Muslim author we found to be largely a result of concerns about questions relating to NOI theology and Sunni Islam. Current NOI member Yasmin Otway, for example, explains that Nation women may have felt hesitant because "they feel they may be invalidated. . . . Even I have encountered some tension, even among Blacks [non-Muslim], which is crazy: [this attitude of] well who's real and who's not."[92]

Together we interviewed roughly one hundred women currently or formerly in the NOI. Our objective was less to achieve a specific quantitative goal than to acquire an abundance of perspectives. As scholars of ethnography note, more important than the number of research participants is the range of participants' experiences. This view complements our emphasis on the diversity of women's experiences in the Nation. Moreover, we recognize that time and place have a major impact on women's experiences and contributions. Ministers, captains, and lieutenants have varied on the extent to which they have implemented the Nation's gender ideologies or other national NOI practices or mandates. With this in mind, we interviewed women who joined the Nation at different times and have highlighted these differences in this book, indicating the ways that we understand their shaping women's individual experiences.

Place matters significantly in the diversity of Nation women's contributions and experiences. In particular, there is a popular understanding among past and present Nation members that the NOI has differed by region or city based on various factors, including the size of the temple or mosque community and the larger socioeconomic and historical context. Together we interviewed past and present Nation women in several different cities, including Atlanta; Chicago; Philadelphia; New York; Jersey City; Detroit; Washington; San Francisco; Houston; Charlotte and Durham, North Carolina; and Tallahassee and Jacksonville, Florida. In addition to conducting interviews with past and present Nation women in these cities, we also interviewed Nation women who engage with the organization almost exclusively via its online forums.

Our research also employed the use of numerous archival sources, including the Nation's papers, mainstream media coverage, and government surveillance. The primary archives we have surveyed include *Muhammad Speaks*, *Bilalian News*, *Muslim Journal*, and the Resurrected NOI's national newspaper, *The Final Call*. These archives help shed light on not only the portrayal of women within the NOI and the WDM community but also the extent to which women served as regular editors and journalists for the papers. Our research has illustrated that NOI women have contributed significantly to the content and editorial production of *Muhammad Speaks*, *Bilalian News*, *Muslim Journal*, and *The Final Call*. Our use of the newspaper archives has served a number of purposes. They have helped shape our understanding of how women understood the NOI's framework and purpose in the African American communities where it operated. Our survey of NOI women's conversion testimonies in the *Muhammad Speaks* newspaper, known as

"What Islam Has Done for Me," has offered a contrast and complement to the oral history interviews we have conducted. These testimonies are a valuable source for understanding the NOI's attraction to women. Nevertheless, our approach considers the fact that these testimonies were conducted and published as part of the NOI's proselytizing efforts and thus are not entirely accurate accounts of how women's lives had improved as a result of their membership in the Nation.

Our archival research has not been limited to the Nation's papers. We have also consulted a number of African American and mainstream newspapers that have informed our critique of the multifaceted ways the NOI and its female following in particular have historically been presented in the national media. Our engagement with these publications has helped shape our analysis of various responses to the NOI and particularly African American women's responses to the Million Man March.

A third archival source comes from the plethora of declassified governmental records on the NOI. We employed this archival source while keeping in mind the context, tactics, and purpose with which this data was collected. We have employed selective evidence from these files as it relates to the NOI's history and the women within the group. We have found that very little of the FBI's surveillance was devoted to the place of women in the NOI. Indeed, with the exception of references to Elijah Muhammad's domestic quarrels with Clara Muhammad and his sexual exploits with several of his secretaries, it is apparent that investigative officers attached little importance to women in the Nation.

Chapter Summaries

Chapter 1 explores women's encounters with the Black Muslims, women's experiences of life within the NOI, and their collective and individual contributions to building and sustaining the Nation's structures. While this chapter is not focused on the inner power struggles and leadership abuses that engulfed the Chicago and New York branches of the movement, it does consider women's responses to leadership crises within the group. The majority of the women highlighted in this chapter are former members of the Nation, currently in the WDM community, who joined the Nation in the 1960s and '70s.

Chapter 2 focuses on Nation women who followed Imam Moham-med into Sunni Islam when he succeeded his father in 1975. The first part of the chapter describes women's responses to the selection of Imam Mohammed to lead the Nation. It includes historical details of Imam Mohammed's personal journey to Sunni Islam while still in the Nation and the strategy he later used to bring an entire community to Sunni Islam. The second part of the chapter contextualizes and analyzes Imam Mohammed's new gender ideology. The third part focuses on changes in the structure of the Nation that supported his new gender outlook, including the transitioning out of Muslim Girls Training and the appointment of the first female minister of the Nation and the first female editor of *Muhammad Speaks*. It also features the ways in which women responded to some ministers, and later imams, who resisted the new gender philosophy. The final part of the chapter demonstrates the ways in which women adapted to the five pillars of practice in Sunni Islam as well as reading the Qur'an, learning about the Prophet Muhammad, and expectations of modest dress.

Chapter 3 examines the experiences and contributions women have made to Louis Farrakhan's Resurrected NOI from 1977 to the present day. This chapter considers the Nation's appeal to women and how they exercise agency and leadership in the group. The chapter exam-ines the elevation of women to ministerial positions in the Nation and highlights the varied ways in which they are collectively revising the boundaries of the NOI's gender norms. The chapter closes with a dis-cussion of Nation women's efforts to remake their image in the popular imagination.

Chapter 4 focuses on dialogue between Nation women and women in the WDM community. It begins with a rare exchange between Imam Mohammed and Minister Ava Muhammad that sets the stage for the main themes explored in this chapter: the two groups' levels of engagement with mainstream Islam, engagement with concerns in the Black community, and conceptions of gender equality, especially as it relates to women's leadership in mosques. Having found that encoun-ters and conversations between women of the two groups are few and far between, the chapter next proposes what women of the two groups would want the other to know about their practice and understanding of Islam in light of mutual misconceptions. It then highlights women's

voices as they might respond to these misconceptions, providing wom-
en's views on various topics, including the continued relevance of the
Nation of Islam in a context in which Sunni Islam prevails as the version of Islam practiced by most African Americans and the controversial practices of female imams and polygyny.

The Conclusion summarizes the book's main argument and the key
insights we expect readers to take away. Further, it highlights the way in
which the NOI legacy makes Nation and Sunni women more alike than
they might imagine, particularly through their commitment to traditional gender roles. It offers additional stories and insights into how
attitudes toward whites have changed in the two communities. Last,
it discusses the book's contribution to relevant academic fields, particularly the emergence of Muslim women's contributions to womanist
thought.

1

"Our Nation"

Women and the NOI, Pre-1975

I really felt that I was going to die if I had stayed in the streets. I had suicidal tendencies. I really just didn't have much of a motivation for living. I felt like a failure and the Nation of Islam took me as I was, and not having my degree wasn't a big deal. . . . Initially the idea of the white man being the devil was appealing to me. I was very angry. I grew up under the Jim Crow laws. My mother worked in a restaurant where we couldn't go in the front of it. If we wanted to buy something, we had to buy it through the back door. My grandmother worked for $17.00 a week for a family that was nice and kind, but my grandmother was still like a slave to them. My granddad died at the age of 52 as a result of alcoholism—he was a sharecropper, and it was because he felt he had no manhood and he couldn't demonstrate his dignity as a result of the way he was treated by white people.
—Jessica Muhammad

The Nation of Islam was about business. They established businesses, they treated their women well and they educated their children. They were model citizens. I mean, if you did something wrong, you were banned. It was just unacceptable.
—Safiyyah Shahid

Look at this sister here. She came to Chicago about twelve years ago from a town seventy-two miles from Little Rock, Arkansas. She reunited with the Nation seven years ago. She was nothing when she came in. Now she is morally regenerated and materially well-to-do. She lives on the West Side. She owns a gas station and rents out two flats. All praise is due to Allah for His blessings upon us the Lost-Found Nation of Islam.
—Elijah Muhammad

Jessica arrived at the Nation of Islam's Temple No. 15 in Atlanta in 1974 while struggling to overcome low self-esteem, homelessness, drug use, and fractured family relationships. Prior to attending the NOI, Jessica had been a promising student at Spelman, a historically Black college for women. Jessica's experiences of race, gender, and class discrimination made the NOI's critique of the U.S. racial hierarchy and castigation of

Caucasians as "blue-eyed devils" particularly attractive. Elijah Muhammad's NOI provided a framework and structure that enabled women like Jessica to transform their lives, relying almost exclusively on their isolated community via the creation of alternative kinship networks. Indeed, the organization prided itself on its perceived ability to convert disillusioned men and women into what former Nation member and school director Safiyyah Shahid describes as "model citizens." Safiyyah's belief that the NOI converted women like Jessica into "model citizens" is shared by countless observers of the Black Muslim movement. In a speech delivered at Imam Mohammed's inauguration in February 1975, for example, Rev. Jesse Jackson described Elijah Muhammad as having "transformed his followers from shooting dope in their veins to pushing hope in their brains."[1]

Elijah Muhammad's gender ideology was intensely conservative and contradictory yet fully compatible with the national discourse on traditional gender roles and spheres of influence. The NOI placed the development of progressive patriarchal communities, communal regeneration, and independence from white institutions above all other concerns. Nation women were integral to the fulfillment of these ideals. African American women encountered Elijah Muhammad's patriarchal group via several outlets, including the Nation's official newspaper, *Muhammad Speaks* (*MS*), and recruiting efforts by local ministers. Women were attracted to the Nation for many of the same reasons as their male counterparts. They embraced the NOI's critique of race relations and pooled resources to achieve the NOI's nation-building aims. It is important to note that Elijah Muhammad's gender ideology was rarely a significant consideration in women's decisions to join the Nation. Our findings suggest that women embraced the NOI's concept of "natural beauty" and the protection the organization offered them via the Fruit of Islam, a paramilitary division of the NOI for male members. Indeed, many women found these aspects of the gender ideology empowering. Yet varied interpretations of the gender ideology and dictates about co-education and marriage caused some women a significant degree of distress. Despite this, women arrived at NOI temples throughout the United States in search of solutions to their shared experiences of racial injustice and economic exploitation. Many Nation women shared Elijah Muhammad's critique of the Black church but privately questioned the NOI's theology. Nation women directed and taught classes in the Nation's independent schools, which were commonly known as the Muhammad University of Islam. They worked for and managed NOI businesses and labored together to meet the NOI's financial needs. The Nation's hierarchical structure locked women out of positions of leadership in ministry on par with their male counterparts, but they exercised agency in most aspects of the group. Women's experiences in Elijah Muhammad's NOI varied greatly. Nevertheless, their narratives reveal important commonalities of experience and provide a unique insight into what has been America's most successful and ambitious Black nationalist entity. The NOI had an enduring impact on its female members. Numerous aspects of the NOI's dietary laws, dress codes, and gender politics followed Nation women into both the Imam W. D. Mohammed community and Louis Farrakhan's Resurrected NOI.

Encountering the NOI

African American women came into contact with the NOI primarily via friends, the recruitment efforts of local temple ministers, the Fruit of Islam, and the group's growing body of propagation literature, which by 1959 included *Messenger Magazine* and *The Supreme Wisdom*. In the 1960s, *Muhammad Speaks* provided women with an opportunity to acquaint themselves with NOI teachings and gender dictates. The overwhelming majority of women encountered the group in their early twenties and thirties. Their religious backgrounds were primarily nominally Christian. Contrary to popular thought, not all of the women who arrived at the NOI's temples were poorly educated members of the proletariat. A significant number of women who joined the NOI had college degrees or were pursuing an advanced degree. Women's motives for joining the NOI varied considerably. For some women the Nation stood out as a beacon of "Black consciousness" while for others it offered the potential for "rehabilitation," "structure," and "family." Several scholars, including historian Bayyinah Jeffries, suggest that women were lured to the NOI by the prospect of securing a "good man."[2] This proposition is misinformed. Oral history narratives reveal a more complex portrait of women's motives for joining the NOI. They found the NOI's efforts to combat social ills, its do-for-self ethos, and its respect for Black women attractive attributes. Former Nation member Lynice Muhammad exemplifies this sentiment when she comments:

> The part of the Nation I found attractive was the part of them encouraging structure. . . . I liked the idea of them giving structure, giving people, at that time African Americans, the ideal of being a part of something that we could not be at that time. . . . I really liked the idea of them giving us backbone, structure and helping us to be somebody.

Lynice's remarks are telling for two reasons. They speak to the reality of Black exclusion and subjugation in the United States, and they reaffirm that the Nation's appeal lay largely in the perceived strength of its community and the sense of pride it instilled in its followers. Former Nation member Safiyyah Shahid explains that the women who joined the Nation chose to "determine their own destiny" and that of their communities. Women were also drawn to the Nation as a result of what historian Ula Taylor describes as its "rhetoric of love, protection and respect."[3] Indeed, such rhetoric helped define the NOI to women and those on the fringes of the movement as a place where Black women were treated like and commonly referred to as "queens" and the "mothers of civilization." While such rhetoric was not the primary factor propelling women's engagement with the NOI, it did offer them a powerful corrective to dominant attitudes pertaining to standards of white hegemonic beauty. Former member Shirley Morton remarks that the NOI's rhetoric of love and respect empowered her to embrace a concept of "natural beauty":

> I am proud and happy just to be Black. . . . I can proclaim to the rest of the world that through the teachings of the Honorable Elijah Muhammad, I know that I am the mother of civilization. I wear the clothes of civilized people. My dresses are far below my knees and I love it. This makes me respect myself better, but it also makes other people respect me. . . . The

Honorable Elijah Muhammad teaches us that we Black women are the most beautiful of all women.[4]

In her comments we can see that first and foremost being a part of the NOI enabled Shirley to embrace and become "proud" of her skin color. Again, this suggests that the NOI's message appealed to women primarily on the basis of its racial politics. It is important to note, however, that Shirley's remarks highlight that Nation women made the gender ideology work for them. In Shirley's case, we can see that it empowered her to appreciate herself and her Nation sisters as "the most beautiful of all women."

Nation women tend to describe their initial impression of the NOI as being very positive. NOI attire, strict search procedures for security purposes, and the segregation of male and female members within each temple ensured that those attending the Nation for the first time understood the group to be, if nothing else, organized and respectful. Former member Zubaydah Madyun comments that she came away from her first NOI meeting in Chicago in the early 1960s with the impression that they "were very nice looking, decent people." Nation women were instructed to make "sisters feel at home" during the newcomers' first NOI meeting.[5] This included embracing other women as equals regardless of their socioeconomic standing, educational background, and marital status. Thus, perhaps unsurprisingly, women recall being welcomed with open arms in the NOI.

Women usually attended weekly NOI temple meetings for around six months before their request for membership was processed and approved. This apparently lengthy process provided women with sufficient time to familiarize themselves with the NOI's teachings and, perhaps more important, to sample the life of Nation women before formally committing to the organization. Letters requesting membership in the NOI were standardized and sent directly to Elijah Muhammad in Chicago for consideration:

Dear Mr. Mohammed,
    In the name of Allah, the merciful, all holy, praise is to Allah, the lord of the world. I have been attending the teachings of Islam by one of your

Ministers, and I believe in Islam, my own religion, and I desire to claim my own. Please take away this old slave name of the devil and give me my own holy righteous name.[6]

Muhammad personally reviewed such letters meticulously. Misspellings or grammatical errors would result in a letter's being declined or returned with a request to resubmit. Former NOI member Islah Umar, who joined the Nation while working toward a master's in speech pathology and audiology, recalls that her first letter for membership was declined because the Nation wanted her "to submit . . . to make you feel you failed and that you're not all you thought you were." Islah's second letter was, however, approved. Receipt of approved letters authorized women like Islah to replace their surname with an "X," and from 1967 onward it enabled them to begin wearing the official MGT uniform.

Pursuing membership in the NOI carried with it the very real possibility of family rejection, discrimination, and marginalization in the workplace and surrounding community. Familial and societal attitudes toward the NOI were shaped by the national media and so-called moderate Negro leaders. The notion that the NOI represented a "sickness" in U.S. race relations had taken root prior to WNTA-TV's airing *The Hate That Hate Produced* in 1959. In 1957, for example, readers of the *Pittsburgh Courier* described Elijah Muhammad's occasional articles for the paper as "biased in nature, misleading as to facts and history . . . and wholly undesirable for consumption by high school students."[7] Women were cognizant of the fact that their decision to join the NOI could result in rejection by their family circle and isolation from their kinship networks given the popular portrayal of the NOI in the media as a subversive and dangerous cult. Indeed, so much was the fear surrounding the NOI that former member Amidah Salahuddin notes that her mother took out an insurance policy on her when she joined the Nation's Harlem temple in 1968. Much of the rejection that women experienced from their families stemmed not so much from a fear that the NOI was dangerous but from the fact that it was not Christian.

Former Nation women convey a common impression of being disillusioned with the Black church before attending NOI meetings. It is important to note that their dissatisfaction was not a result of theological uncertainties or questions pertaining to Christ's divinity. Indeed, in our sample of interviewees we have found that while women privately questioned whether Wallace D. Fard Muhammad could be both fully man and fully God, most never questioned Christ's divinity. Race-based concepts associated with Western Christianity troubled women, as did the perceived inability of the Christian church to speak to their concerns. The theology of the NOI, as articulated by Elijah Muhammad, rarely played a significant role in attracting women to the NOI. Many former Nation women speak of their struggles to accept the theology of the Nation and their privately questioning it. Jeanette Nu'Man, for example, notes:

> The more I studied the Bible, the more problems I had with the church itself. I began to have the same challenges with the NOI as I read the Qur'an and then saw what was happening in the NOI. . . . There is no reference to Fard Muhammad in the Qur'an. Pride in being a Black person and the history of Black people attracted me to the NOI. Fard Muhammad was not Black and he was not white; he was this Asiatic Black man. He looked Caucasian and he was supposed to be God.

Jeanette's doubts were shared by other women, although they never relayed them to their ministers or MGT captains. Moreover, not all Nation women were familiar with Qur'anic teachings or the Qur'an itself. Thus, while Jeanette's doubts resulted from Fard's absence from the Qur'an, other women expressed doubts that related to a more particular aspect of NOI theology. Former Nation member Khayriyyah Faiz describes feeling uncomfortable with the notion that all Caucasians were "devils":

> I thought about the white man being the devil and the Black man being God. That didn't quite fit in my mind set because I knew that in the nature of human beings, that there were African American people who were not necessarily pure in their thinking and in their hearts, and I knew of Caucasians who I had met who were good people. So that idea didn't fit comfortably within my paradigm, psychologically or spiritually, but at the same time, I knew that the racist society that I grew up in kind of attested to a lot of that.

Nation women found much in the organization that they liked. These positive aspects, as Zubaydah Madyun describes, often "overrode" the uncertainties that she'd had about the theology of the movement:

> I did not believe that Master Fard was God. All the other things overrode that. I just always felt that maybe he did come and do some good and get us going just like Noble Drew Ali and Marcus Garvey. I thought there was some truth in there somewhere, but I just did not believe that he was God in that person. I could not get with that.

In these narratives we can see that although the Nation's critique of white supremacy appealed to women, the intricacies of NOI theology did not. Indeed, as Jeanette's comments suggest, some women were at least partially aware of the stark differences between the NOI's teachings and Qur'an-based teachings. We have found, however, that not all Nation women based their disbelief on the fact that there was no mention of Fard Muhammad in the Qur'an. Nation women read the theology of the organization as something that was designed to get them on the road to Islam and help them to overcome the effects of pervasive ideologies of racial supremacy.

Families reacted angrily, and at times with despair, to news that their children had joined the NOI. Countless Nation women comment that their parents were horrified by their decision to join the organization. Bayyinah Abdul-Aleem registered with the NOI in Philadelphia in 1973 at the age of twenty. She recalls that while her parents were not "intensely religious," they were "nervous" about her decision to join the Nation. Similarly, Winifred Muhsinah, who joined the NOI in Miami in 1966, notes that her mother was "very upset because I had been raised a Methodist Christian. . . . My friends sort of weren't openly offensive, but they looked at me differently." The Nation assisted its members in overcoming such rejection by providing them with alternative kinship networks that were based on a reciprocal commitment to NOI ideals. New members were kept so busy within the Nation that, as Islah Umar comments, "you did not miss what you had left." Alternative kinship networks acted as surrogate families, and, perhaps more important, they promoted a concept of shared experience that trumped differences in social status and educational achievement among Nation women.

Life in the NOI

Kinship networks were developed through the Muslim Girls Training (MGT) classes that Nation women attended three evenings per week. It was through these classes that women were informally mentored and equipped to perfect the image and ideal of the Nation. The MGT served three purposes within the overall structure of the NOI. It provided women with a space in which they could exercise leadership and cultivate support networks, it educated women in domestic science, and it disciplined women for failing to adhere to the Nation's strict code of conduct. The MGT was hierarchical in structure. MGT captains ensured that women adhered to every facet of the Nation's teachings. Failure to comply with the Nation's standards would result in disciplinary action. The Nation placed its members into two different disciplinary categories depending on the severity of their transgression. A class "C" category was reserved for smaller misdemeanors such as violating the dress code and carried a ninety-day suspension from the Nation. The class "F" category was reserved for more serious offenses, such as adultery, and resulted in indefinite expulsion from the Nation.[8] Although a class "C" category may appear to have carried a minor penalty, it is important to note that its implementation was devastating for members. Nation members' activities revolved around the NOI and its schedule of weekly meetings. Moreover, many members lost contact with family members upon entering the Nation. Once suspended from the Nation, members found themselves more isolated and alone than ever.

The MGT provided women with opportunities to exercise leadership within their local temple and Nation community. MGT captains and lieutenants did not exercise authority over men, but they worked alongside their male counterparts to achieve similar aims. Former MGT captain Safiyyah Shahid describes her working relationship with the Fruit of Islam (FOI) in Atlanta:

> As captain, I often worked with the FOI captain and even with the minister. If we were trying to organize a meeting where people would come out and learn about the teachings, we worked together to do that. So in a way I was in isolation, but in another way, I worked very close with

the males, and really after a while they considered me to be one of their peers. . . . Most certainly the organizational structure seemed to favor men in terms of the hierarchy, but I think that because we developed a working relationship, over time a lot of those barriers sort of slipped away. . . . They didn't just see a female; they saw a mind.

Opportunities for leadership within the MGT were not restricted to captains and lieutenants. Captains were responsible within local chapters of the MGT for overseeing the weekly classes. However, according to Ajile Rahman, women within each temple were accorded the opportunity to teach classes on prayer, child care, health, and English grammar. Such opportunities enabled women to develop their talents and build up their confidence.[9]

Nation women's experiences in MGT classes were very much shaped by the temperament of their respective captain and lieutenants. Unannounced visits to women's homes by dictatorial captains to ensure their cleanliness became a painful and embarrassing episode for many rank-and-file women. Former Nation member Lynice Muhammad recalls:

I disliked that many times those people who were in authority would take advantage of others sometimes. We didn't have much say in how we were controlled. Like one instance, I remember they had an inspection. They would come to your home, and my mother was the mother of eleven children, and sometimes her home was not as orderly as she wanted it to be, and then they would subject you to something. So sometimes I think we took things to extremes and [did not really know] how to treat each other.

Nation women's complaints about or protests against such treatment tended to fall on deaf ears. Indeed, according to one former member, the removal of MGT captains was "unheard" of in the Nation. One exception seems to have taken place in the Nation's Philadelphia temple in 1969 when Minister Jeremiah Shabazz removed a Sister Hattie because she had been operating the MGT "as a separate entity from the rest of the community." Hattie was replaced in 1970 by a young college-educated woman, Intisar Shareef. Intisar had been a member of the

NOI's Philadelphia chapter for less than a year before being appointed by Jeremiah Shabazz as the local MGT captain. In her capacity as MGT captain, she sought to assist women in meeting the demands of their membership and rebuilding their commitment to the NOI following Hattie's exit. For example, she notes:

> The women had always had a goal of trying to raise $5,000 for what they called the [Temple] No. 2 poor fund, and that money was sent to Elijah Muhammad. . . . So in Philadelphia the sisters had always had the goal of raising $5,000—they had never done it. When I came in, I noticed that they would always run out of food at every meeting, and there were people standing in line with money in their hands waiting to buy, and there wasn't enough. I sat down with the lieutenant and said we could figure this out and get more people to donate and set up a system to rotate the sisters who are donating. So I got us the names of the sisters and contacted them and got more people to donate, and we made more money. . . . They raised the $5,000 in the first six months that I was working with the sisters.

Intisar fostered a sense of community among the women in the Philadelphia chapter. She notes that in accordance with Minister J. Shabazz's instructions, she rewarded ten of her most dedicated workers with an all-expenses-paid trip to Bermuda for a week following their efforts to raise the $5,000 for the "No. 2 poor fund." Captains such as Intisar were not uncommon. Perhaps unsurprisingly, we find that many former Nation women refer to MGT classes affectionately as the "sisters' class." It was the bond that developed between these women that kept many in the Nation during times of dissatisfaction. Former Nation member Amidah Salahuddin, for example, remarks that "the bond with sisters in the NOI kept most of us connected. It was in spite of many of the things we didn't agree with . . . but our relationship with one another was the bond that kept me there." The "bond" between Nation women was nurtured via the MGT and its structured classes, which in many cases provided women with opportunities to learn essential life skills and develop their self-confidence. Natalie,[10] for example, who was a lieutenant in the MGT in New Jersey, comments:

I was better educated because I grew up with a lot more than some of the other sisters. I saw a lot of women that were in here, and they were like welfare people . . . struggling sisters, uneducated. . . . I enjoyed that we were able to force them to read and all kinds of things to do to make them better. . . . We didn't complain so much because we had a lot to do. . . . We were at the temple all the time—three, four, or five days a week. . . . Coming out to the classes, you were learning your lessons, you were drilling . . . you were learning how to cook. . . . In MGT class, I was responsible for going over the Honorable Elijah Muhammad's lecture. . . . I would prepare [a] test. . . . We would have discussions. Sometimes I would give lectures. We were just busy, very busy. . . . MGT gave us worth, but I think it gave us something greater than that, and that is, it gave us sisterhood.

Natalie's comments about the sisterhood that developed among Nation women reveal that MGT was more than simply a militaristic forum in which women could be disciplined.

Indeed, in many instances women felt empowered by MGT classes and recall feeling a sense of unity with women from very different backgrounds. Intisar, for example, notes:

We had a sisterhood that was enlightened, and we had varied individuals, and we had an open and accepting attitude about what we did as women because we found strength in a lot of different places. . . . I was working and rubbing shoulders with brothers and sisters who had been incarcerated for murder—sisters who had been in jail for prostitution—but we all rolled up our sleeves because we were working for a common cause, and there wasn't any sense of one being better than the other, and I would never have experienced or learned that if I had not been in the NOI.

The MGT operated alongside but largely independently of the FOI. It provided women with a safe space in which to air their concerns, support one another, and help new recruits to make the transition to life in the Nation. The importance of MGT classes is encapsulated in Islah Umar's comments that they became the "community and world" of Nation women.

Nation Women's Dress

All Nation women, regardless of their rank or standing in the NOI, were expected to adhere to a strict dress code. Male members of the organization wore dark suits with bow-ties while their female counterparts wore their dresses and skirts below the knee and covered their hair. The introduction of the official MGT uniform in 1967 standardized the Nation's dress code for women and saw skirt lengths extended to two inches above the ankle.[11] According to Ajile Rahman, the NOI's dress code for women was modeled after the Motor Corp Garments of the Universal Negro Improvement Association (UNIA).[12] Clothing that in any way resembled secular fashion trends was forbidden in the Nation. *Muhammad Speaks* columnist Tynetta Deanar often accused Black women who wore such clothing of "playing the part of copycats" in the "white woman's wardrobe."[13] Makeup was similarly frowned upon. It is evident from NOI literature that makeup was considered "an extravagant financial waste to our Nation's pocket book."[14] Many Nation women saw the MGT uniform as a "protectionary" measure designed to liberate them from a mythology that construed Black women to be morally deficient and sexually promiscuous. Indeed, many women welcomed and embraced it as "a nice relief from being a piece of meat in the streets," although others found it "boring" and rigid. MGT fashion shows in numerous temples reflected a subtle resistance to the dress code and led to its eventual modernization. Women's collective efforts to revise the dress code were effective because these efforts were made via the MGT. It is important to note that Nation women were not so much disobeying the dress code through such shows as they were teaching other women ways in which they could accessorize and inject a little bit of originality into the official dress. Women were encouraged to purchase their uniforms from the NOI's clothing factory or, when possible, from their local temple. The introduction of the official uniform helped create substantial employment opportunities for Nation women. In Philadelphia, for example, Nation women operated their own sewing shop where they created garments and uniforms that adhered to the Nation's dress code.

Diet

MGT classes instructed women first and foremost to master domestic science. The home was considered the woman's sphere of influence and primary responsibility. The ability to prepare meals that adhered to the NOI's dietary laws was considered a fundamental requirement for all Nation women. Elijah Muhammad published two books that outlined the dietary laws of the NOI. The first, *How to Eat to Live*, was published in 1967. The second volume, *Book No. 2*, was published in 1973. Prior to the publication of these books, Muhammad outlined the Nation's dietary laws in articles for the *Muhammad Speaks* newspaper. Two of the most prominent features of Elijah Muhammad's dietary guidelines were his prohibition of pork and requirement that NOI members eat no more than one meal per day. In his articles for the *MS* paper, Muhammad argued that eating only one meal per day would "lengthen our lives by ridding us of the greedy desire to eat three times a day and between meals."[15] Muhammad did not support such dietary laws through reference to the Qur'an.[16] Rather, the Bible, particularly Leviticus 11: 7–8 and Isaiah 66:17, provided Muhammad with his rationale for the prohibition of pork.[17] Muhammad also prohibited consumption of collard greens, turnips, white potatoes, and peas, primarily because they had constituted a significant part of the slave diet. Nation women responded creatively and positively to the dietary laws. They regularly published recipes for meals in the *MS* newspaper and became renowned for their bean pie.

According to feminist scholar Ula Taylor, Nation women were regularly weighed and placed in a class "C" category for weight gain.[18] Oral history narratives and articles from the *MS* paper contest this notion. Former Nation women note that women of all shapes and sizes were welcomed in the NOI. Jessica Muhammad, for example, comments, "We had women who were fat, but I didn't see any difference or prejudice against them." Similarly, Islah Umar remarks that a lot of the women were "overweight" and that she ran "self-esteem workshops" with the women to build up their confidence. NOI literature also contests Taylor's assertion. In letters to the NOI's advice column author, Harriett Muhammad, women expressed concern about their weight. Harriett was notoriously tough on the women who wrote to her for advice. She married Elijah Muhammad's son Akbar in 1961, and her articles "For and About You" reinforced the organization's stringent gender ideology. In an article titled "How Will Power Will Pull Weight Down," Harriett responded to a woman who claimed to be overweight by ten pounds and unable to "control" her "eating habits." In response to the letter, Harriett remarked, "Your best weight may be as much as 10% under or 20% over the calculated standard for your height and age. . . . The best way to keep from becoming overweight is to eat sensibly, exercise reasonably and live happily."[19] It is probable, and indeed likely, that women did eat more than one meal per day. Images of Nation women in the *MS* newspaper confirm Jessica's and Islah's comments about the diversity of Nation women's bodies. More important, they contest the notion that dietary laws were rigorously enforced and that women were punished for overeating. Nonetheless, women were expected to be able to cook and prepare meals that adhered to the dietary guidelines published by Elijah Muhammad. This was considered particularly important for women seeking marriage.

Marriage

Many women entered the NOI at the behest of their husbands. However, an equal, if not greater, number of women joined the organization unattached. Nation women had little option but to marry within the organization. Marriage to Muslims outside the NOI and across racial lines was prohibited.[20] The pressure that some women experienced from their peers led them to marry men with whom they had little in common. Marriage was expected and more often than not required. Indeed, Jeanette Nu'Man notes that "being unmarried was unacceptable" in certain segments of the Nation. Much of the literature that describes the demographics of the NOI highlights the presence of ex-prisoners as composing a significant segment of the group's male membership. The NOI's first National Minister, Malcolm X, believed the NOI to be most successful with ex-prisoners because they had been "preconditioned" to hearing the "truth about the white man."[21] Not all Nation men abandoned their pre-NOI days in the way that Malcolm X did. Oral history narratives suggest that many in fact carried a criminal mentality into the NOI and into their marriages. A number of educated women described marrying ex-prisoners or other men who did not share their wives' level of professional success, which sometimes led to domestic abuse.

Narratives from some Nation women in Atlanta, New York, and Chicago illustrate that they were able to decline marriage requests from the FOI. In some cases, they were even dissuaded from marrying by their temple ministers. In these isolated cases, ministers expressed concern on the basis that they felt marriage might detract from the woman's work for the Nation. Ana Karim in Chicago and Deborah Davis in New York, for example, escaped peer pressure to marry because of their work for the Nation. However, it is clear that not all women had this experience. Nation members courted under the supervision of their regional MGT and FOI captains. The courting process was usually brief and standardized. According to some Nation women, it was expected that this process would result in marriage. Men expressed an initial interest in a woman via their FOI captain, who would in turn relay the news to the woman's MGT captain. News of a potential suitor reached a woman via her MGT captain. Women who declined the interest of men in the Nation often came under scrutiny from their peers. Former Nation member Jeanette Nu'Man, who joined the NOI in college in North Carolina, remarks:

> The NOI attempted to partner me with this man in the community, and I wiggled my way out of it by going back to Atlanta. It wasn't so easy in Atlanta. There was a process—the male would express interest in you to the captain and then the female lieutenant would approach you. . . . It was a little like being in the army. The captain would come and talk to you and say this brother is interested in you. I think if my circumstances had been different, I would have said no, but I was in a pivotal place in my life. My family had stepped away, and my mother was upset because I was not dating. I was feeling pressure from the organization because they would say, "You should be married" . . . and they would say, "What's wrong with this brother?" . . . It caused so much trouble with my family because my mother stopped talking to me . . . so I sort of did it to be rebellious.

The benefits of marriage were extolled in numerous editions of the NOI's newspaper and through MGT classes. In an article from *MS* in 1969, for example, Lolyln X exhorted:

> Sisters, we must submit to our husbands, for it is our role. . . . Your life is a reward, when you submit to your husband. . . . A Muslim marriage is everything wonderful—unity, harmony, love and patience. . . . We[,] as wives, should serve as a source of inspiration to our husbands: never allowing ourselves to hinder him in any way. Even though you are his wife, secretary, confidante, Girl-Friday, chief cook 'n' bottle washer, there is no sacrifice that you can't make to please him. You might have to bend over backwards, but in the end, it'll be worth it.[22]

Not all Nation marriages were sites of "harmony, love and patience."[23] Nation women who found themselves in loveless and unhappy marriages complained to their MGT captains and via letters to Harriett Muhammad. Letters from Harriett reveal an expectation that women set aside their concerns, fears, and aspirations in order to return to their husbands' ultimate authority in the family unit.[24] Spousal abuse and domestic violence were, however, taken seriously by the Nation in certain regions. Numerous accounts of men being physically disciplined for spousal abuse are reported by women across the NOI's chapters. Indeed, some women construed the public beating of an abusive husband as an appropriate deterrent. Sandra's[25] remarks below confirm the physical discipline that resulted from spousal abuse:

> The Nation promoted respect for your wives and making sure they were chaperoned when they were out in the community, but I do recall instances of abuse, and brothers would take on those brothers and the ministers would address them. . . . If a man took advantage, abused his wife or someone in the community, they would literally give him a thrashing, and I never saw it, but I said praise be to God.

Not all women recall feeling that domestic violence was something the NOI handled particularly well. Michelle[26] joined the NOI in Atlanta in the 1950s. She comments that domestic violence was not "dealt with very well . . . basically ignoring or taking the man's word over the woman's." The ways in which complaints that related to domestic violence were dealt with within the Nation clearly differed rather notably.

Much of the acrimony that existed within some Nation marriages arose from the way in which men interpreted the organization's gender ideology. Elijah Muhammad's writings on the need to "protect" and "control" women were read by some men as sanctioning women's subordination. This reading of the Nation's gender ideology had significant implications for women.

Education

Many women compare life in the NOI as similar to living in an "incubator." News was filtered, and the movement of members was monitored. Travel passes, chaperoning of women in the community by the FOI, and sensitivity to women's safety together restricted and effectively controlled women's movements. Such practices had a negative impact on women's pursuit of college education and advanced degrees. Many women arrived at the NOI while holding or in pursuit of an advanced or undergraduate degree. Membership in the Nation, however, often interrupted their studies. The discouragement of formal education hampered the professional and intellectual development of both male and female members. Women, however, felt the impact of this more heavily. The Nation's aversion to co-education combined with a concern about women's safety resulted in many women's discontinuing their formal education after joining the Nation. Elijah Muhammad expected his followers to be well read and versed in the literature of the organization. The education he advocated was gender segregated and racially exclusive. It is important to note, however, that he did subsidize the formal education of Nation women where and when he felt it would benefit the NOI. When he initiated plans to build hospitals and nursing homes to serve the needs of NOI members, for example, he sent a group of thirteen women to pursue a degree in nursing. Former Nation member Amidah Salahuddin recalls with pride and joy being one of the initial thirteen women selected to attend nursing school. She comments that "we were the first class to graduate . . . and God blessed me to score 100% on all tests." Elijah

Muhammad also intervened directly to ensure that one of his columnists, Ana Karim, received her degree in her Muslim name from her college in Tuskegee, Alabama:

> I registered under what we called then a slave name of Burks, and the Honorable Elijah Muhammad changed my name while I was a student there. So three years or so I continued down there under Karim, and all of a sudden here comes the assistant dean again saying, "We're not gonna give you your degree in this made up name; this is not your name." And we went back and forth and so . . . I called down to the Honorable Elijah Muhammad because he gave me the permission to call him if I met with anything, you know, extreme down there, but for them to take away my name and issue my degree to me in the name they wanted me to have, that was too much. When I talked to him, he said, "Sister, I will get back to you." He asked for the number for the college of education and the name of the dean who told me I could not have my degree in the name of Karim. So I gave him that information. Two hours later he called back at the dorm. He said, "Sister, your degree will be issued in the name that I gave you." So he said, "Congratulations on your graduation." And he said, "We look forward to you joining us here in Chicago," and that was the end of it.

Women like Ana and Amidah, however, were a minority within the Nation. Certainly, many women who wanted to pursue their educational aspirations found the discouragement of higher education difficult and disappointing. Indeed, former Nation women who made the transition to Sunni Islam in 1975 were generally overjoyed by Imam Mohammed's encouragement of formal education for both men and women. Our research findings suggest that more college-educated women entered the Nation in the 1970s.

Nation Women's Activism

The Nation of Islam's structure of nation-building solely for the Muslim community made it so that women's work and leadership were in many ways confined exclusively to the NOI. Male leaders embraced women's contributions in all forms if they advanced nation-building as shown in Safiyyah's earlier comments about her work with the FOI in Atlanta. Nation women's experiences of leadership and activism were rather different from those of their counterparts in the civil rights movement. Nation women's activism, however, was neither less nor more important than that of their counterparts in the civil rights movement. Women's activism and leadership in the civil rights movement took different forms. However, much of their leadership was confined to "bridge leadership," in which women acted as intermediaries between national civil rights movement leadership and local communities. Having coined this term, Belinda Robnett defined it as the "primary domain of Black women's leadership."[27] Not all Nation women were unfamiliar with the activism of the civil rights movement. Indeed, we find that a small number of Nation women arrived at the organization via their work in the movement. In the narratives that follow, Amidah and Ana describe their frustrations with the civil rights movement and their entry into the Nation. Amidah grew up in Harlem during the height of the civil rights movement and became the motivational youth speaker for the National Association for the Advancement of Colored People (NAACP) chapter in Harlem. Amidah's interest in the Nation developed over time. It was an encounter, however, in an NOI store and a lack of "seriousness" on the part of her peers in the NAACP youth movement that led her to join the Nation:

> I was very active in the civil rights movement, and I was the motivational speaker for the National Association for the Advancement of Colored People youth in Harlem. The headquarters was based on 125th street, and I just lived a few blocks away. I also had the opportunity to be in the circles of the Rev. Martin Luther King. I met him when I was sixteen [at] a fundraiser in Brooklyn in 1964. I attended one of the top high schools in New York City, the High School of Music and Art. In 1964 I migrated alone to . . . Miami, and when I returned in 1965 after graduating high school, I attended college and also got married at seventeen. I had a very turbulent marriage, and I had already been aware of the Nation of Islam because they were pretty much visible in the Harlem community, and my mom happened to have a friend in the NOI who converted to Sunni Islam and so I had an idea of it. . . . I was on 125th Street, and I stopped by

one of the stores owned by the Muslim brothers. I didn't know that when I went in, but I was interested in buying the bean pie because that was pretty popular in Harlem; everybody knew about the bean pie, and even if they didn't care about the [Nation] philosophy, everybody wanted the bean pie. So one of the brothers in the store looked me up and down and with this kind of arrogant look, he said, "You can't be a sister," and I was thinking, "Well, what's so special about a sister?" That was my response to him. I didn't say it out loud, but I was kind of intrigued about what was so special about a sister and why I didn't measure up. According to the standards, my bar was very high because I had a lot of principles to live by. . . . The NAACP was a forum. It gave you a platform, and I was a little strict on performance. I thought that my peers were not serious enough. I came from a strict household, and I always ended up in leadership positions. In the NAACP I was the youth activist speaker at events. Comparing to the NOI, you are dealing with a whole group of people who are responsible so you are not the only one. It was a group of people who had the same mind-set.

Similarly, former Nation member Ana Karim left the Student Non-Violent Coordinating Committee (SNCC) for the NOI in 1968. Ana left the civil rights movement for very different reasons from Amidah's. Ana immersed herself in the fieldwork of SNCC after arriving at college in Tuskegee from Ohio in 1965. She experienced the full assault of massive resistance from whites in Tuskegee. When she returned to Ohio for a short break from SNCC, Ana found a special delivery letter from Elijah Muhammad inviting her to a meeting with him in Phoenix, Arizona. It appears that Muhammad became aware of Ana's work in SNCC via the NOI's regional minister in Cincinnati, who sent Muhammad newspaper clippings of Ana and other SNCC members being beaten by police. Ana accepted Muhammad's invitation, but only because she believed she might be able to get him to help with voter registration. To her dismay, Muhammad had no interest in aiding SNCC. He wanted her to join the NOI. Ana rejected the offer and notes that Muhammad expressed concern about her safety in SNCC. His closing remarks, however, stayed with her: "Sister, if you stay down there, you are going to lose your life." When she returned to

Tuskegee, she was assigned to help with voter registration. Her experience there was to be her last active engagement with SNCC:

> As we approached one house, we heard a truck coming on the road because it was a little dusty rural road; we could see the dust in the air. . . . I hid in a cornfield maybe about sixty feet from the house. There were two Caucasian guides, one at the wheel; and two on the truck bed that were on the porch talking to an African American sister who was pregnant, and some argument or whatever—we could hear loud voices— broke out, and we saw them grab her off that porch, hang her by her feet and split her stomach open. So it was so horrendous at 19 to see something like that happen. . . . We reported this to the student leaders, the chapter leaders, the SNCC leaders on the campus. Nothing was ever done to find the people who murdered this woman. . . . We were out there still trying to get people registered to vote—George Green, another student on campus with me. We got split up and just, you know, trying to go in different areas and reach as many people as possible. We were all in a car visiting the different houses when a truckload of Caucasians with shotguns started firing at us. Speeding down that road, the car nearly overturned, and we all could have been killed either by shotgun or by a bad car accident, but luckily the car, by God's grace, stayed on its wheels, so we were able to get out of there and back to what we called the "Freedom House." So that began my thinking when the Honorable Elijah Muhammad said, "If you stay down there, you are going to lose your life." I nearly lost my life that night, and for the second time that night; the first time is if those men had caught us when we saw them kill this woman.

Ana's decision to leave SNCC was not informed solely by concerns about safety. She had become disillusioned by what she refers to as the "after hours integration" that her African American male counterparts in SNCC and white female volunteers engaged in.[28] Ana excelled as a leader in the NOI. "The Honorable Elijah Muhammad asked me to introduce Islam in Tuskegee" by contributing to the *MS* paper a column that Muhammad titled "Islam in Tuskegee." Upon her graduation, she moved to Chicago and became a secretary on his house staff. She became an ardent student of Nation teachings and spoke on

behalf of Elijah Muhammad at local temples on at least three occasions. "He sent me to Detroit, to Cincinnati, and to Dayton to deliver
his message from the pulpit, and that had never been done by any
woman. . . . He sent me to teach in areas, he said, where there was
a problem. He said the minister there is not following [his] instructions." The fact that Ana was authorized to speak on behalf of Muhammad to correct ministers illustrates that his gender dictates were not
inflexible. Ana was a high-profile, well-educated, and well-regarded
Nation woman. Her peers described her as a "no-nonsense woman"
who went on to become the MS paper's first female editor in 1975.
Ana's and Amidah's narratives highlight that Nation women were not
as far removed from the realities of civil rights activism as has been
previously thought. When they entered the Nation, they found that
their activism and leadership occurred largely within the organization's schools, businesses, and the MS printing plant.

Nation Women's Work

Nation women contributed to the maintenance of NOI schools, businesses, and the MS newspaper. Women operated with more agency and
freedom in NOI schools and small businesses than in the MS paper.
Their collective contributions to the NOI, while largely undocumented,
ensured the group's survival and its exponential growth during the tur-
bulence of the civil rights movement. Nation women worked together
to achieve the Nation's aims. Thus we find that they often speak of their
work within the NOI as a collective effort rather than as a mark of individual esteem. Nation women used their collective bargaining power to
resist and modernize numerous aspects of the NOI, especially in those
areas where they operated with greater freedom. The creation of *Jewel
Magazine*, for example, in the early 1970s in Philadelphia saw women
harness their creative and entrepreneurial talents to provide an alternative to the MS newspaper.

   Clara Muhammad hosted the NOI's first educational classes in her
home in Detroit in 1931. Despite having only a seventh-grade education,
Clara pioneered an alternative school system for the Nation's children.
The Nation's parochial schools, or Muhammad University of Islam,
as they became known, taught essential subjects, but the MUI's focus

was largely on providing a safe space in which children could enjoy an education that was void of pseudo-scientific racism and fallacious histories that relegated them to an insignificant footnote in someone else's history. Education has long been considered an important, if not fundamental, prerequisite for social mobility in the United States. Historically, African Americans have struggled to gain a formal education equal to that of their white counterparts. Clara and the Nation's early female pioneers were acutely aware of the inferiority complex that the public school system bred in children. They resolved to provide their children with an alternative education that would be independent and economically viable. The MUI school curriculum was designed by both men and women and included foreign languages such as French, Spanish, and Arabic. According to Bayyinah Jeffries, all the MUI foreign language teachers were male and foreign-born.[29] The local police department in Detroit viewed the MUI as "contributing to the delinquency" of minors and attempted to close it down several times.[30] However, it continued to operate and grew significantly. Jeffries, for example, notes that MUI schools were operational in Milwaukee, Washington, Cincinnati, Baltimore, New York, Atlanta, Boston, and San Diego between 1934 and 1955.[31]

The desegregation of the U.S. public school system in the 1950s worked to the initial disadvantage of African American children. *Brown v. Board of Education* (1954) produced minimal integration of schools. Indeed, not until the 1964 Civil Rights Act threatened to stop federal funding for segregated schools did the pace of integration quicken.[32] *Brown* produced massive resistance to forced integration across the United States. The chaos and violence that followed the 1954 ruling disproportionately worked to the disadvantage of small Black schools, teachers, and principals who found their schools closed and the prospect of securing employment at white schools almost impossible.[33] It was in this context that the MUI appeared as a beacon of stability and security. During the MUI's early years, teachers were employed on the basis of their commitment to the Nation and its ideals, although they were not all NOI members. As the organization attracted more college-educated women, the number of MUI teachers holding degrees grew. The employment of college-educated women as teachers added to the acceptance of the MUI as a credible alternative to public schools. Former member Rosalind X remarked in the *MS* newspaper in 1971:

> I am very proud to say that six of my children are attending the University of Islam, a school that they can call their own, under the guidance of a great Leader and Teacher, and the direction of a well qualified Principal, Sister Beverly 6X, who is also of our own. It is so wonderful to now have degree teachers.[34]

Clara Muhammad remained an important figure in the Nation's school system. However, as the 1960s progressed, the MUI came under the direction of Dr. Zella Prince. Prince received her bachelor of science degree from Newark State Teachers College, her master's degree from Seton Hall University, and her doctorate from Columbia University.[35] Women such as Prince were not uncommon in Nation schools. Many of the women who worked as teachers in the MUI were college educated, although not always in possession of a teaching qualification. MUI teachers were not paid on par with their counterparts in the public school system. Jeanette Nu'Man notes that while she was teaching in the MUI in Atlanta, her family was particularly annoyed that she was paid as little as $65 per week. MUI schools, however, thrived on the dedication of their teachers and principals.

Potential teachers were recruited into the Nation's school system via their local temple or when and where a position became available. College-educated women were rushed into the MUI schools. Jeanette, for example, notes that less than two days after her arrival in Atlanta from North Carolina, she began teaching in the school. Teaching in the MUI schools provided women with an outlet to harness their talents and make use of their qualifications. However, Nation schools were not the only form of paid employment that women could take advantage of in the organization. Indeed, the NOI's plethora of small businesses provided women with multiple opportunities for employment.

Elijah Muhammad's economic blueprint for the NOI was based first and foremost on the principle of self-sufficiency. In his 1965 publication

Message to the Blackman in America, Muhammad instructed his followers to "pool resources," "recognize the necessity for unity and group operation," and "give employment to your own kind."[36] Nation members were expected to be resourceful and entrepreneurial. The Nation's economy was financed via mandatory donations from members, profits from small businesses, and, from the 1970s, international investment from Libya.[37] Women took great pride in the Nation's ability to erect and sustain small business enterprises. Former member Mary Muhammad,[38] for example, notes that the NOI "offered members a future, it offered members to see themselves self-sufficient in business and seeing a society that was controlled and operated by African Americans." For women eager to start their own businesses, Islah Umar notes that "the NOI gave a lot of support and pointers for doing for yourself, how to make a business out of nothing and knowing that you could do it and you had to do it." The businesses that women owned were small, and some were operated from home. However, whether via their own creation or through work in the Nation's businesses, women contributed to the Nation's model of Black entrepreneurship. Women's businesses and employment opportunities for women were a regular feature of the *MS* newspaper. The "Shirt Hospital" by Sister Ida 4X Gidas and home-baked delicacies by a Sister Meda are two of the most often advertised businesses in the paper. The Nation's business model provided inspiration not only to its members but also to their neighbors and associates in the larger community. In 1975, for example, the *Chicago Defender* noted, "At a period in history when the whole fabric of Black economic and social welfare is becoming threadbare due to the wear and tear imposed upon it by the white establishment, the vast majority of Blacks look upon the success of the Nation of Islam with pride. Indeed, it is becoming more and more a role model for Black entrepreneurship."[39]

Nation women maintained a visible presence in the *MS* newspaper from its founding in 1960 to its transformation in 1975 under the direction of Imam W. D. Mohammed. Prior to the creation of the *MS* newspaper, the NOI had promoted itself via irregular articles in a number of newspapers, including the *Los Angeles Herald Dispatch* and the *Pittsburgh Courier.* The latter featured Elijah Muhammad's articles from

June 1956 until August 1959 under the title "Mr. Muhammad Speaks." The "Mr. Muhammad Speaks" column was thereafter published by the *Los Angeles Herald Dispatch.*[40] Muhammad contributed irregular articles for *The New York Amsterdam News, The New Jersey Herald,* and the *Afro-American* in an effort to enunciate the NOI's program. The NOI self-published pamphlets, including *The Supreme Wisdom* and *Messenger Magazine.* Women featured heavily in *Messenger Magazine.* Indeed, several pages of the magazine displayed images of women at various events and bazaars. These images show Nation women to be creative, industrious, and engaged in the production of various items, including towels, clothes, pillowcases, and other goods.[41] However, according to E. U. Essien-Udom, publications such as these had proved costly. The idea for a national newspaper came from Malcolm X, who had been appointed by Muhammad as the Nation's national spokesperson in 1960. Initially, the *MS* newspaper employed Dan Burley as its editor. Burley set out to give the paper a professional look. His tenure as editor, however, was brief. He was replaced by Richard Durham during the 1960s. Following Durham's departure from the paper, John Woodford and later Leon Forrest took over. In 1973 Forrest was replaced by Askia Muhammad, who currently writes for *The Final Call* newspaper. The content of the paper was approved by its editor and by Elijah Muhammad. Women featured in and contributed to every issue of the paper. Tynetta Muhammad's column, titled "The Woman in Islam," was featured in the paper beginning in May 1960.[42] Regular columnists and writers for the paper included Ana Karim, Tynetta Muhammad, Harriett Muhammad, Margary Hassain, and Bayyinah Sharieff. Women also provided testimonies of their journeys to the NOI in a column entitled "What Islam Has Done for Me." Clearly, the content of the *MS* paper was very much controlled. Its primary purpose was propagation of NOI teachings. However, the content of the paper provides some insight into women's divergent experiences and agency in the group. The articles penned by Harriett and Tynetta in particular reveal an unflinching commitment to Elijah Muhammad and his gender dictates. Both used their space in the paper to encourage women to submit themselves to their husbands and ultimately to the NOI. Tynetta Muhammad's writings for the paper proved to be particularly

interesting to the FBI. Although the Bureau rarely attached any importance or significance to Nation women, Tynetta proved an exception.
Her writings for the paper and, more important, her relationship with
Elijah Muhammad intrigued investigative agents at the Bureau who
under the direction of J. Edgar Hoover were eager to find any evidence
to discredit Muhammad and his movement. In their surveillance of
Tynetta, for example, they noted:

> Tynetta Deaner, in late 1959, was a young, light-skinned, unmarried
> Negro girl who became a secretary to Elijah Muhammad and soon
> began writing a column entitled "Women in Islam [sic]." In her col-
> umn, Tynetta forcefully echoes Elijah's teaching that the Negro woman
> should completely disassociate [sic] herself from the customs and
> practices of the white woman, that the white race is "the real enemy
> of our people," and that the Black people must develop strong "racial
> pride and solidarity." What Tynetta advocates, however, is not what
> Tynetta practices. Since serving as a secretary to Elijah she has taken
> two vacations, once traveling to Cincinnati in 1960, where she gave
> birth to a baby girl, and again to Albuquerque in 1964 where she gave
> birth to a baby boy. This young Negro columnist, who so strongly
> advocates pride of race, listed on the girl's birth certificate that the
> baby was white, that she herself was white, and that the alleged father
> was white.[43]

Nation women in Philadelphia worked to create a glossy alternative
to *MS* for women in the 1970s. The result of their creative efforts was the
birth of *Jewel Magazine*. *Jewel* was overseen by the NOI's MGT captain
Intisar Shareef and approved by the regional temple minister, Jeremiah
Shabazz. *Jewel Magazine* promoted a revised and modernized version
of the MGT dress code for women. Intisar describes the magazine as
being less concerned with the "religious" aspects of the NOI; however,
the magazine did not violate NOI dictates:

> *Jewel Magazine* was an outgrowth of the MGT class. It was a class we
> had on Saturdays for the sisters; we taught them all the things that
> Elijah Muhammad said we needed to know: how to take care of our

children, how to take care of our home, how to cook, sew, etc. . . . There were several sisters in our mosque who designed clothing and fashions and so forth, and as a result of that, they were sewing different variations of this uniform, and so we started having fashion shows in our class, and we were also at that point buying jewelry wholesale, and so I had one lieutenant who [was] a former airline stewardess, and she had a very, very good eye and so she would buy the jewelry wholesale, and we would sell it in class and make a profit. . . . We were able to accessorize garments, and we got really excited and had several fashion shows, and as a result of that, the sisters wanted to come together, and we had some sisters who were writing poetry, writing stories and so forth, so the energy around what was going on in class was something folks wanted documented and put into a magazine form because there wasn't any magazine for Muslim women. I think it was around the time of *Essence* magazine, but there wasn't any real magazine that spoke to us. So the sisters decided that they could in fact—with fashion being the cornerstone of it—they could in fact come together to create a magazine. We published several editions, one of which interviewed Sammy Davis Jr., so they had an opportunity to meet people in the entertainment world, educational field and advertise our look as modest but attractive; we did things about weight loss and child care. It became a very all-encompassing voice for our community. . . . We were very careful about what we put in that magazine because we knew we were up for scrutiny. . . . I think we might have published about maybe eight issues or less than a dozen because it was expensive, and then when Elijah Muhammad died, our financial situation really changed significantly.

Jewel Magazine was not officially circulated outside the Philadelphia temple. However, the magazine found its way into the homes of Nation women throughout the United States via informal networks and Nation women's journeys outside Philadelphia. Nation women recall being impressed by *Jewel*. Indeed, one former Nation woman described it as similar to the popular American Muslim women's magazine *Azizah*. It appears that no copies of *Jewel Magazine* have survived. It is important to note, however, that the magazine inspired and led to the creation of a women's magazine in Farrakhan's NOI, *Virtue Today*. Current NOI member Audrey Muhammad founded *Virtue Today* after having been introduced to *Jewel Magazine* while under the tutelage of Professor Intisar Shareef at Contra Costa College in California.

Women's Work outside the NOI

Paid employment within the confines of the Nation protected women from unwelcome encounters with Muhammad's critics. However, not all women were able to or wanted to work within their Nation community. Women who worked outside the community often encountered some form of discrimination. These women recall discrimination not from whites but from members of their surrounding African American communities. Women were immediately identifiable as followers of Elijah Muhammad because of their uniforms. They thus became targets for opponents of the NOI's mandate, as expressed by Safiyyah Shahid:

> Probably most of the discrimination I sensed and felt came from people in the African American community who did not really believe in the idea of separation. I think there was some discrimination in the company I worked in . . . in terms of my moving forward toward management in the company.

For women like Safiyyah, discrimination in the public sphere was a temporary discomfort. She comments that "a lot of our life was internalized to the Muslim community that we were a part of. . . . [W]e just didn't have a whole lot of public contact outside the NOI." Ideally, the Nation preferred that its female cohort remain first and foremost in the domestic sphere. Indeed, Elijah Muhammad regularly commented that "the teachings of Islam does [sic] not force the woman in no way to go out and work. It is her job to stay at home and rear her children."[44] According to NOI columnist Margary Hassain, a woman who journeyed outside her home was likely to be or become a "tale bearer":

> Messenger Muhammad teaches the woman in Islam to stay in her own home and care for her husband, herself, her children and her

home. Staying in one's own home, keeps the peace. When the woman is allowed to constantly visit from house to house she is an idler and a trouble-maker. She is a tale bearer bringing in news and out the news.[45]

Yet opting out of paid employment was not something all Nation women could afford or wanted to do. Socioeconomic realities often meant that women had to work in order to ensure the economic well-being of their family units and themselves. Jessica Muhammad, for example, whom we introduced at the outset of the chapter, continued to work while she was in the Nation, as did several of the other women. E. U. Essien-Udom recognized that economic realities often meant that Nation women had to work. Nation women who worked outside the group did so largely because they wanted to. These women subscribed to the belief that a woman's first commitment was to her home, but they did not interpret the home as their exclusive sphere of influence, as is evidenced in Alia's[46] comments:

I just didn't embrace gender roles, restrictive in the Nation of Islam. I just didn't embrace them. I knew I was going to grad school. That was not a question; I didn't ever question whether or not I would only have children and stay at home. I knew that I had other things that I wanted to do with my life, and that having a profession was one of them. And so I didn't think that I couldn't have [a profession].

Some women did welcome and embrace the NOI's emphasis on traditional gender roles. They understood it to be a corrective measure designed not only to halt the proliferation of female-headed households but also to liberate women from the demands of balancing work and family commitments. Islah Umar exemplifies this sentiment, commenting that:

Men were meant to go out and take care of the family. . . . That also attracted me that women were not being directed to go out and take care of the family, and when you are in a hard-hitting setting, you are definitely being prepared to take care of yourself and work side by side with a man. But you don't want to have to do that if you don't have to, so the

NOI offered an option that women should be able to stay at home, and men were supposed to work. So in our ethnic group that was like what we wanted to hear.

Oral history narratives suggest that place and time mattered when it came to women's decisions to work. Narratives from women who joined the Atlanta temple in the 1970s, for example, suggest that they were not required to do a lot of "MGT stuff" if they were in paid employment or school. Nation women, whether in paid employment or at home, were required to be resourceful, manage their time well, and contribute to the overarching goals of the organization. As Safiyyah highlights above, much time was spent within the Nation. Yet, despite the fact that women spent much of their time within their organization, they were not always aware of the internal politics within the group.

Clara Muhammad and the Secretaries

Nation politics were kept, by and large, from women and from rank-and-file members more generally. Unsurprisingly, their narratives indicate that they were largely unaware of the problems and power struggles that occurred within the group and particularly within its Chicago headquarters. Malcolm X's exodus from the Nation in March 1964 was widely publicized and upset many women. However, the events that led to Malcolm's exit were unknown to many women in the movement. Malcolm's exit from the NOI in March 1964 was a result of power struggles in the Nation's headquarters. When explaining his exit from the movement to the national media, however, Malcolm divulged a wealth of information concerning Elijah Muhammad's domestic life. Elijah Muhammad engaged in a series of sexual relationships with women who worked for him as personal secretaries. According to Malcolm X, rumors of this behavior had arisen as early as 1955.[47] Malcolm's revelations to the national media were dismissed by many Nation women. Many refused to believe the comments, considered them "misinformed," or concluded that the press was attempting to create disunity and confusion among members. Islah Umar, for example, notes,

"Anything that Malcolm said was not honored and Elijah Muhammad was considered divinely guided, so no one talked about him." Over time, however, Nation women came to the realization that their leader and teacher had fathered children with women other than his wife, Clara. Karen Muhammad,[48] for example, notes, "It was a disappointment when I learned of it. I kind of really didn't want to believe it, but it was a disappointment, especially when I saw his wife and the contributions she had made to the Nation." Nation women revered Clara Muhammad. For them, she was a role model and someone they aspired to emulate. Public exposure of her husband's behavior caused Clara significant distress, as noted by Ajile Rahman:

> Sister Clara's personal tragedy was great. It is one thing for a woman to know of her husband's unfaithfulness—but quite another for the world to know it. . . . Clara Muhammad felt betrayed by her husband and by Malcolm, whom she considered a son, because he helped publicly expose the matter. Her response to Malcolm's public acknowledgment of what she considered a private matter was, "I never thought he would do it."[49]

Elijah Muhammad's domestic problems were known to the Federal Bureau of Investigation from the early 1960s. In a 1962 memo, for example, one investigative officer noted:

> Elijah Muhammad is engaging in extramarital activities with at least five female members of the Nation of Islam (NOI). This information indicates Muhammad has fathered some children by these women and that his wife, Clara, has become aware of his infidelity which has resulted in domestic strife. . . . He wields absolute power in the hegemony of the NOI and any successful attack on his character or reputation might be disastrous to the NOI. . . . Chicago and Phoenix should make recommendations concerning the use of information thus obtained to discredit Elijah Muhammad with his followers. This could be handled through the use of carefully selected informants planting the seeds of dissension through anonymous letters and/or telephone calls.[50]

As outlined in the FBI's memo, Clara had indeed become aware of her husband's infidelity. Her response to news reports of Muhammad's affairs was private. On June 25, 1962, Clara left the United States to spend time with her son Akbar in Cairo, Egypt. According to Clara's FBI file, "no return reservations" were made for her journey back to Chicago.[51] She did, however, return to Chicago on October 17, 1962, to confront Muhammad privately. Muhammad's relationships with several of his secretaries continued after Clara's death in 1972. The *MS* newspaper gave extensive coverage to Clara's death in the August 1972 edition of the paper. *MS* editor Leon Forrest noted in the paper, "Sister Clara Muhammad in her deeply moving, quiet way set a sterling, ringing national standard for all Black women to follow."[52] Clara's death occurred at a time when members were beginning to witness changes in Elijah Muhammad's rhetoric, especially as it related to his attitude toward whites. Nowhere was this evident more than at the 1974 Saviour's Day convention. During his annual address, Muhammad instructed his followers to "thank" the whites and to "stop putting the blame on the slave owner."[53] Nation women construed these comments as signaling a "moderation" in the NOI's mandate. Safiyyah, for example, comments that "more and more toward the end he talked about not pointing the finger at the white man for our ills and that was different from his tone from his earlier years; he even said study the white man, so that was a big shift." Elijah Muhammad's efforts to moderate or relax NOI teachings manifested themselves in other aspects of the organization. In the MGT in Atlanta, for example, women were not tested on or instructed to memorize NOI teachings after 1974. Jessica Muhammad notes:

> There were rumors that the Hon. Elijah Muhammad was dying, so things were changing. His son Warith Deen was being groomed for succession so I don't think those lessons were as important as they once were. I wasn't really involved in too many MGT meetings because I was guarding the door to keep the white man from coming in.

Jessica's and Safiyyah's comments reveal the extent to which women noticed subtle changes in the direction of the organization.

Jessica's comments in particular highlight that the Nation's direction was changing partially in response to concerns about Elijah Muhammad's health. Muhammad suffered chronic health problems throughout the early 1970s. Indeed, at the 1972 Saviour's Day convention he appeared to be so unwell that his children momentarily pleaded with him to sit down. Yet, despite his ailing health, Muhammad refused to publicly appoint a successor. Inside his family, it had long been accepted that Wallace Muhammad would inherit and lead the Nation.

Elijah Muhammad suffered congestive heart failure and passed away on February 25, 1975. Many Nation women were in a state of disbelief. Indeed, it appears that in some temples, news of Muhammad's death was dismissed as untrue. Jessica Muhammad notes that in the Atlanta chapter weeks after Elijah Muhammad's death, "there were all kinds of rumors that he was not really dead and that he was going to show up again." Wallace Muhammad was named as his father's successor at the 1975 Saviour's Day convention. It was under Wallace's guidance that many of the women were to make the transition to Sunni Islam. As we will see in the next chapter, however, aspects of the NOI followed these women into Sunni Islam.

The women presented in this chapter each experienced the NOI differently. Not all of their experiences were positive, and many questioned and resisted aspects of the organization. By 1975 many women were ready and eager to embrace Sunni Islam. Many women joined the Nation independently of their families and suffered some degree of familial rejection or disapproval as a result. Nation women's encounters and lives in the Black Muslim movement illustrate that they were neither passive nor silent within the organization. Women were instrumental in creating and supporting the NOI structures. Clara Muhammad's efforts to pioneer the MUI in the 1930s and to ensure the group's survival during her husband's incarceration demonstrate the extent to which women supported and upheld the NOI structures. Nation women found ways to navigate NOI norms and in some cases moderate them to their liking. Contrary to popular opinion, Nation women were not drawn to the organization primarily by the prospect of marriage. Rather, they were drawn to the Nation primarily because they shared the NOI's vision for progressive communities and solutions to pressing problems. Nation women contributed to the organization at almost every level with the exception of ministry. Their Nation experience, as we will see, affected how they embraced, resisted, and understood the teachings of Imam W. D. Mohammed when he assumed leadership of the Nation in February 1975.

2

"Thank God It Changed!"

Women's Transition to Sunni Islam, 1975–80

I had questioned things privately to my husband and my brother. . . . All of us had been educated in school, so when W. D. Mohammed came on the scene and gave us a lot of avenues for discovering and exploration, it was like giving water to people who had been in the desert because we had wanted for a long time and our thirst had not been quenched.
—Intisar Shareef

Imam W. D. Mohammed was decades ahead by bringing women to the forefront and declaring in one of his lectures, "I will follow any qualified woman." He said, "What God instills in her to bring about change and human excellence among our people, I will follow."
—Ana Karim

Imam W. D. Mohammed is most known for bringing the NOI community into the fold of Sunni Islam. He assumed leadership of the NOI upon the death of his father, Elijah Muhammad, in 1975 and immediately taught from the Qur'an, replacing the Nation's concept of "God in the Person" with the universal Islamic understanding of a transcendent God. In the first year, he invited whites to join his following, instructed his community to participate in the Sunni Ramadan fast and five daily prayers, began dismantling the Fruit of Islam and the Muslim Girls Training, and changed the name of the community's national newspaper from *Muhammad Speaks* to the *Bilalian News*. Imam Mohammed began using the term "Bilalian" to refer to Black Americans, connecting them to the legacy of Bilal ibn Rabah, the enslaved African who converted to Islam in Mecca, whereupon a fellow convert bought his freedom. Bilal became a close companion of the Prophet Muhammad and the first man to perform the Islamic call to prayer. Explaining why he coined the term "Bilalian," Imam Mohammed stated, "I think there's more dignity in identifying with an ancient ancestor than in identifying with skin color. When I say I am a Bilalian, I'm saying that I am a man like Bilal."[1] By 1977, Imam Mohammed had changed the name of the group from the Nation of Islam to the World Community of Al-Islam in the West (WCIW), redesignated temples as mosques and then as *masjids* and ministers as imams, and sold dozens of NOI properties to settle debt acquired through the Nation's vast business empire. Imam Mohammed also revised the Nation's approach to Black liberation with a new political stance toward America, whose ideals of freedom, justice, and equality he emphasized. Promoting participation with, not separation from, society, he encouraged his following to participate in Fourth of July celebrations in 1977, the same time that he placed the American flag on the cover of the *Bilalian News*.[2] The new ideology and changes in the organizational structure of the Nation brought new opportunities for women.

Embracing Minister Wallace

NOI officials and ordinary followers of Elijah Muhammad committed their undying support and loyalty to Wallace as he was declared the Supreme Minister of the NOI at the 1975 Saviour's Day convention, the day after Elijah's death. Elijah Muhammad never publicly appointed a successor. According to some reports, members of the "royal family" selected Wallace immediately after Elijah's death. Because Wallace had openly disagreed with his father, outsiders have been curious about his selection. In his book on the transition, Clifton Marsh notes that "the appointment of Wallace D. Muhammad astonished the general public." At the same time, Marsh suggests that within the Nation, the selection of Wallace was expected. This view is partially correct. Indeed, some Sunni women were surprised, particularly some in Louis Farrakhan's temple in Harlem, given Farrakhan's charismatic persona and ascendance in the organization. Several scholars writing about the transition describe disillusioned followers leaving the group and rejoining when Farrakhan reestablished the Nation, although there are no clear numbers as to how many.[3] Imam Mohammed's community, however, is the larger of the two.

The Sunni women interviewed here recognize the hardship of this time but mostly express an overriding ease. Safiyyah Shahid, of Atlanta, was in disbelief at first, as were many, upon hearing of Elijah's death, but her feelings of sorrow and confusion immediately transformed into calm and certainty upon hearing Wallace's inaugural address. "He assured all of these thousands of people who had come that the work of his father was going to be carried forward." Jessica Muhammad, also of Atlanta, similarly recalls her confusion. "I just couldn't see how most folks could say that they believed in what Elijah Muhammad was talking one day in terms of the Black man being God and the white man's the devil . . . and then the leader dies, and then the next day we are saying something that was just the opposite." Nonetheless, Jessica successfully made the transition. "It was the natural path for my community. Also, my friends and my husband at the time were excited about [Wallace]." Jeanette Nu'Man, also from Atlanta, recalls, "People were not happy, people were confused. People wanted to cling to the things that [Wallace] was dismantling." Yet speaking for herself, Jeanette states, "Imam Mohammed was a relief to me. I felt like I could breathe. I found it exciting to learn how to be a Muslim, and to learn the history of Islam and learn about the Prophet." Several women note that Elijah was a man like any other and that they dealt well with his passing. In general, Sunni women's accounts show that the selection of Wallace as leader strengthened a host of members' dedication to NOI leadership during a trying time.

The legend of Wallace's prophesied succession made his selection relatively easy to embrace for many women. "The fact that he had been chosen for the mission was something that was expressed quite openly and quite frequently," Khayriyyah Faiz, of Atlanta, notes. Fareedah Pasha, who joined the Nation in the 1950s in Harlem, had never heard the story of Wallace's special destiny until she moved to Chicago in the 1960s. "It would come up in conversation: 'Oh, Wallace is very special.' We were taught that he had these special gifts in the sense that he was born after Fard Muhammad left, and the name that was left for him, and then the picture that is very popular with him and his dad holding [the] Qur'an, so we were being prepared."[4]

Fareedah is referring to the NOI legend which states that when Wallace's mother was pregnant with him, Fard predicted that her child would be a son, wrote the name Wallace on the back of a door in Elijah's home, and prophesized that he would be a "helper to his father."[5] This legend was brought to life by the famous portrait Fareedah mentioned: Elijah and Wallace posed in front of a life-size portrait of Fard standing and reading a book, understood to be the Qur'an. In the father-and-son pose, Wallace stood with one hand extending a Qur'an and the other hand placed firmly on the shoulder of his father. As Fareedah suggests, the portrait supported the idea that Fard expected Wallace to teach the Qur'an.

Wallace's Path to Dissent

Wallace's preparation to teach the Qur'an began in childhood. He attended the Muhammad University of Islam, where he gained distinction among his peers in the study of Arabic. Elijah's determination "to teach Arabic in our school," recalled Wallace, certainly sprang from Fard Muhammad, who had impressed upon Elijah the relationship between studying Arabic and understanding the Qur'an. Shortly before Fard's disappearance, he gave Elijah two copies of the Qur'an, one with the Arabic text only and the other with both the Arabic and English translation, which Fard followed with the instruction "to learn Arabic."[6]

Not surprisingly, the two sons of Elijah who advanced in the Arabic language would eventually move toward a Qur'an-guided understanding of Islam. Akbar Muhammad's turn to Sunni Islam was more expected given that beyond the University of Islam, he studied Arabic and traditional Islamic sciences at a world-renowned Islamic university, Al-Azhar in Cairo. Wallace's new understanding emerged more gradually, for which he gave special recognition to Jamil Diab, his Arabic teacher for most of his years at the University of Islam. Employed by Elijah, Jamil Diab, a Palestinian Muslim, never taught against NOI theology but did, according to Wallace, hold "private conversations" with him regularly and in "a very clever way" attempted to show him and other students that "the Qur'an is a book that presents the best logic." His instruction under Diab had such an impact on Wallace's rejection of his father's teachings that he later reiterated, "[It was] Diab's influence, and especially the Arabic. Arabic was the key, I think."[7]

Still, Wallace's early Arabic education did not change his thinking immediately or independently. His father, ironically, was a major influence as he taught Wallace, and many other followers, to study and examine, "don't just look at the surface. Study it. There are answers that Allah wants us to get." As early as age fifteen, Wallace "started to wonder why this man looking so white was supposed to be Black and a Black god." He compared Fard's portrayal to that of Jesus in Christianity. He concluded, "It seems to me that we are saying the same thing and got it more confused." Recalling this revelation years later, he noted, "Maybe the Qur'an had started to influence my thinking without me knowing."[8]

Wallace had not yet questioned Nation theology openly, but his ongoing independent study of the Qur'an and Arabic set him apart as he became known as the person to seek out for "the religious side of the Honorable Elijah Muhammad's teachings." In 1958 his father appointed Wallace, then twenty-five years old, to lead as minister of Temple No. 12 in Philadelphia. Women who lived in Philadelphia at that time describe Wallace as bringing "knowledge about things that we didn't really understand." Barbara Hyman, who joined in 1953, explains, "He came to let us know about Prophet Muhammad. . . . Everybody else didn't know about that stuff." Saafie Karim, who joined in 1955, recalls, "I was sitting here once, talking to my husband, and said, 'Wait a minute, I think he's not teaching like his father.'" For Saafie, it was Wallace's attitude toward whites that made her realize that "his language was different. You know, you're waiting for this punch line, you're waiting for it," but never did he call "the white folks the devil." Several women recall that he taught members to pray, read the Qur'an, and study Arabic. According to Della Shabazz, whom Wallace appointed as the sister captain of the Philadelphia temple, he even began to challenge some of the organizational dictates of the Nation. Officially, local Muslim Girls Training (MGT) captains carried out instructions from the supreme sister captain, who reported directly to Elijah. However, according to Della, "[Wallace] said the local temple should be in charge of what's going on. We shouldn't have Chicago coming in and taking over." When Nation officials came to Philadelphia to inspect the temple, "Sister Ethel [supreme MGT captain] started changing things and having people doing things, and I said, 'No, we are not going to do that.' She said, 'Well who are you?'"

Della laughs as she recalls telling Sister Ethel that her noncompliance was based on instructions from Minister Wallace.[9]

Wallace's late-1950s lectures included elements of Sunni Islamic creed, enough so that his father accused him of teaching more of the "true Mohammedan religion," but he did not yet reject Fard's divinity.[10] This changed, however, after his time in prison for draft evasion between 1961 and 1963 and a critical conversation with his mother, Clara Muhammad. At Sandstone, Minnesota, Correctional Institution, separated from his family and community, Wallace was better able to contemplate his own thoughts and closely analyze the Bible and the Qur'an. He made up his mind never to teach the idea of Fard's divinity upon his return to the community. He shared his dissenting thoughts with close relatives, which led to his first suspension in 1964. His mother asked Wallace to go back to his father and accept his teachings. He responded, "Momma, who did Mr. Fard tell you all he was? Did he tell you all he was God?" She answered, "No."[11]

Wallace was not the only one dissenting at this time. As we have seen, the controversy surrounding Elijah's relationships with several secretaries sparked Malcolm X's dissent in 1964. A grandson of Elijah, Hassan Sharrieff, also sided with Wallace and spoke publicly to the *Chicago Defender* in July 1964 about corruption in the Nation hierarchy. Describing his grandfather as a "fake and a fraud," Sharrieff said corruption was wrought by "Mr. Muhammad and his whole staff." Wallace agreed, telling the newspaper, "Not only are [Sharrieff's accusations] true, they are mild." Later that year, in November 1964, Elijah's son Akbar visited the United States from Cairo, and he too went public with his criticism of his father, telling a New York newspaper that his father's version of Islam was "a homemade one with its own tight rules and regulations that tend to stifle any criticism of its leaders."[12]

Doubt and dissent occurred also among rank-and-file members. Barbara Hyman was put out of the temple in Philadelphia because she refused to separate from her husband, who had traveled with a small group of men to Chicago in 1964 to "find out" Wallace's plans and support him. It is possible that these men had heard news of Wallace's new organization, the Afro-Descendant Upliftment Society, established during his first suspension in 1964. The organization gained meager support, and by the time of the Saviour's Day convention in 1965, Wallace had been accepted back into the Nation, his acceptance prompted by the assassination of Malcolm X and the threats against Wallace's life throughout his suspension. Elijah certainly must have issued the orders that Wallace remain safe, suggests Ajile Rahman, who highlights the role that Clara Muhammad played in securing Wallace's safety: "It was his mother who told Elijah Muhammad, 'Don't touch him. Don't lay a hand on him.'"[13] The few dissident members who supported Wallace were disillusioned when he returned to the organization.[14] Barbara's husband never went back, although Barbara did five years later. "I knew that Islam was a beautiful and righteous thing, so I thought, 'I won't be able to come to the *masjid* [the temple] because of him and I wanna go to the *masjid*.' So, I left him."

Responses to the New Leader's Dissent

Wallace was suspended again shortly after his return in 1965. This pattern of suspension and reacceptance lasted until the early 1970s, when Wallace was accepted back for good. It was not until 1974 that Elijah allowed Wallace to return to preaching, which included his regularly teaching in the Chicago temple, alternating with Minister Yusuf Shah. "I would say things I know were different from some of the things the people had been taught under the leadership of Elijah Muhammad. . . . I would test what the Honorable Elijah Muhammad would accept." Various reports suggest that Elijah acknowledged the opposing teachings of his son and encouraged him. Wallace reported that officers of the FOI brought one of his taped lectures to Elijah with the aim of exposing his Sunni teachings. Elijah played the recording in the presence of Wallace and several officials. "He jumped up out of his seat and applauded and said, 'My son's got it! . . . My son can go anywhere on earth and preach.'" On another occasion, Yusuf Shah reported that when he brought one of Wallace's taped lectures to Elijah, he said, "I thank Allah for my son. This is what we . . . prayed for."[15]

Amatullah Um'rani was a member of the Chicago temple during the period in which Elijah gradually offered his support for Wallace to teach Islam. She explains how the opportunity to hear aspects of the new teachings before 1975 helped her to embrace the new leadership and direction:

[Wallace] conveyed that he had a great love of, and knowledge of, the Qur'an. What he did at that time, during that year and a half of giving the main lecture at the weekday temple meetings, was to establish himself clearly as a leader, in terms of a person who had something that appealed to the soul. . . . The speech that he gave on Saviour's Day was an extension of what he had been giving the community already except that he now accepted the leadership of the Nation as a whole. The fire that he had—it wasn't emotional, but it was a fire of conviction: "I really have a mission; I have something to give and it's been burning within me because I've observed this for years, but I've been patient out of respect for my father."

Many women were like Amatullah Um'rani and describe the immediate satisfaction of the new teachings. Wallace's longstanding protest resonated with many who had long felt dissatisfaction with NOI officials whom they saw as power-hungry. Others, like Hanunah Sabur, of Atlanta, had begun studying the Qur'an for themselves before Elijah's death. "Knowing he had defied his father" convinced Hanunah that he was the right leader, "because his mind was on what I was reading in the Qur'an." Others, however, found the transition difficult in the beginning—for example, Maryum Sabree, who joined the Nation in Harlem in 1959. To go from NOI teachings to the teachings of Sunni Islam was not a simple thing, Maryum notes. "But I never said I wasn't going to be a Muslim. That never crossed my mind not to be a Muslim and not to believe in Allah." When speaking about Allah here, Maryum is not referring to Fard. "I never believed Allah was a man. I just believed He was somebody watching over us. I never believed Jesus was God because he was a man." Women's expressions of faith in God, not Fard, as the key to weathering this challenging period are not uncommon. Amidah Salahuddin, of Harlem, had her problems with NOI doctrine but still acknowledges the immense faith needed to follow Wallace:

And what made me stay? I can only say Allah because I can't say that there was anything else in me that could have connected me to this new way of life that I was about to embark on. There was nothing outside of [the transition to Sunni Islam] that attracted me, for one thing, even though many people that I knew had emotional breakdowns. Some just left, some went back to Christianity, some went to drugs, some of them went back to behaviors that they had left behind at one point. But I just know that that was one of the miracles in my life, the ability to hold on and to have the patience to be taught and to learn this new way of life that I was waiting for.

Similarly, Fareedah Pasha comments, "The new teachings, that took a moment. I never doubted necessarily, because I think as a believer, when you believe in God, when you believe in Allah, even though you don't know how everything is going, you have that trust that this is the right thing." But how could Fareedah attribute her successful transition to a belief in Allah as understood in Sunni Islam when she had been taught to believe that God was a man? To this question, Fareedah responds:

When I look back on it, I really believe that we had that belief even though we had that picture with the *shirk* [Qur'anic term for worshipping a being other than God]. . . . We believed in Allah because I don't think we could have been able to make that transition without a lot of trauma. But if you have this belief in God, then you realize [the Nation of Islam] was just a period that we're going through to get me to [Sunni Islam] because look how You saved me, look how You helped me. This was no accident when you look back.

Respect for the Old Leadership

Chief Minister Wallace, who had become Imam W. D. Mohammed by 1977, taught Fareedah's sentiments precisely: that the Nation of Islam, and now the transition to Sunni Islam, was no accident. A significant part of his initial teaching as the new leader consisted of offering meaning to the Nation of Islam's historiography and mythology in ways that presented his leadership and transition to Sunni Islam as the natural evolution of the NOI desired by both his father and Fard. He made both men central in the process. Several women remarked on the way in which Imam Mohammed "respected" and never "criticized" his father in the process of transition, helping them along the journey.

Imam Mohammed was profoundly aware of the fundamental challenge in moving the community forward; members "want to follow me
as their leader but they also are appreciative [of] and feel indebted to my
father." This problem extended to Fard. How could Imam Mohammed
separate these highly regarded figures, to whom members remained
attached, from their teachings, which had to be abandoned? Imam
Mohammed soon realized that reconciling the error of the teachings
with the excellence of the teachers was not a problem but a solution. He
realized this solution when he began to see evidence that the intent of
Fard's strange lessons was to bring followers to Sunni Islam gradually.
Unlocking the mysteries of Fard's lessons and emphasizing the sincerity
of Elijah Muhammad served as vital keys to bringing the community to
Sunni Islam.[16]

Imam Mohammed taught that Fard "came with reverse psychology,"
presenting himself as a "saint" to liberate a people who were severely
afflicted with an inferiority complex. "I am convinced that he himself
never told anyone that he was God in the flesh, but I strongly believe
that he hinted intentionally so that others would say that he was God
in the flesh." The Honorable Elijah Muhammad, an aspiring student
of scripture and son of a Baptist preacher, fulfilled Fard's intention
when he deduced that Fard was "the second coming of Christ" and
then later decided, after Fard's departure, that Fard was "Allah, God
Manifest."[17]

Elijah Muhammad came to this conclusion after reading the Qur'an
and other books that Fard left behind and urged him to read: "When
I began to read I have detected, especially after reading Koran care-
fully, that Fard was Allah himself incarnated. The more I read the more
I become sure about this fact." Imam Mohammed explained that this
error was expected of a man of the Bible:

> So I saw his sincerity in his expression, "I am the messenger of
> Allah." . . . He was speaking from Bible knowledge because the Bible says
> the shepherd is the messenger of God, so he was saying that I am the
> shepherd, I am the preacher . . . so I am a messenger of God. That was
> his reasoning. He knew the Bible but he didn't know the Holy Qur'an. In
> fact, he told you that I would teach you the Holy Qur'an.

Despite Elijah's conclusion that Fard was Allah, Imam Mohammed believed that Fard planned for his teachings, imbued with Muslim and Qur'anic symbols and references, to ultimately lead Elijah and his following to Sunni Islam.[18]

To Imam Mohammed, it appeared that Fard deliberately drew attention to the Qur'an: "I looked at the picture of this teacher. The only picture he left to be available to us is a picture of him holding the Qur'an. And he is looking down in it . . . very piously with great respect." Also, in one of Fard's mystical lessons in which he presented mathematical problems, the reward for the correct answer was a Qur'an. "I don't think that man if he wanted his doctrine to survive would have attracted us [to the Qur'an] or whet our tongues, our thirst for the Quran."[19]

In his Weberian analysis of the transition, religious studies scholar Lawrence Mamiya argues that the rising socioeconomic and educational status of the NOI membership necessitated that leaders of the movement soften their rhetoric against whites, as members were too intelligent to accept such racial claims. Indeed, Imam Mohammed was highly aware that the social class of his community had changed, a fact he often highlighted when explaining why Fard taught as he had and why people believed. "This man played on the simple minds of the Bilalian (African-American) people and gave them something that they had no knowledge of and couldn't question. But, if we had been educated . . . we would have deciphered much of that a long time ago and wouldn't have bought it from the very start."

Remaining sensitive to the intelligence of his father and other early followers, Imam Mohammed spoke to later followers who were attracted to the Nation for its community-building program but never believed that whites were the devil. Referring to the lesson which taught that the "Colored man" was in fact "the so-called white man," Imam Mohammed noted, "I don't think any of us ever digested that to our satisfaction. We couldn't understand how the white man became a colored man." The imam explained this lesson in a way that made it more palatable to educated people. "Well, to color something means to slant it or present it in a false way. And the white man is responsible for slanting truth. . . . He colors everything." But beyond providing a rational explanation, Imam Mohammed's goal was to impart that Fard's lessons should not be taken at face value but rather understood as part of a scheme to lead to higher understanding.[20]

Imam Mohammed pointed his community away from the shallow concept of "colored" as referring to skin and to the higher concept of "colored" as a mentality, which Imam Mohammed called a "Caucasian mentality." "'Whiteness' is a mental falsehood that has been formed in the minds of not only physical white people, but people all over the world." As a religious scholar, Imam Mohammed particularly brought attention to the impact of religious ideas as indoctrinated by white supremacist Christianity. "Everything that you find in this world has the plague of grafted, Caucasian mentality. . . . [Most religious ideas] came from babies in scriptural knowledge up out of pagan ignorance and savagery in Europe. They got the divine wisdom of the Bible in their hands and began to read it with their raw, unformed selves. They came up with all kinds of weird interpretations." In the first year of the transition, Imam Mohammed continued to speak of and condemn the "Caucasian mentality" and its influence on religious concepts. Correcting biblical notions formed part and parcel of his work as his followers were transitioning not only from the Nation of Islam but also from the biblical interpretations that affected both their former Christian lives and Nation of Islam teachings. We will see this approach in the way in which Imam Mohammed brought a new gender ideology to the Nation of Islam community.[21]

Imam Mohammed's View of Women, Early Influences

"I'm trying to promote women's lib and at the same time save society," Imam Mohammed stated in a 1977 lecture.[22] Sunni women readily describe the period of Imam Mohammed's leadership favorably, evoking terms of liberation: "I experienced religious freedom that I had never experienced before, and it has never gone away," W. Muhsinah Abdullah, of Miami, describes. "To use our own minds, to make decisions. It was true freedom," Shafeeqah Abdullah, of Detroit, recalls. Women felt liberated on multiple levels as Imam Mohammed changed the direction of the NOI in terms of religious belief, race philosophy, and gender ideology. Most scholars who wrote about Imam Mohammed's transition credited his new outlook on race and religion to the

demands of Sunni Islam, notes Mamiya. He, however, highlights the
socioeconomic demands on the leadership, as noted earlier.[23]

Imam Mohammed's more progressive positions stemmed from a
combination of factors, including shifts in American cultural views
and social policies on race and gender progress as reflected in the education and skill sets of Nation women. In other words, Imam Mohammed was influenced by civil rights policies such as affirmative action
and women's rights policies ushered in by the feminist movement as he
witnessed the NOI grow with college-educated and working women
who benefited from these events. As we will see, he highly regarded
and promoted such women in restructuring the organization and
therefore moved in relative concert with liberal American cultural
ideals of gender inclusion. At the same time, under the imam's leadership, parts of the NOI gender ideology and practices were upheld,
placing the community at times against the grain of popular American
notions of women's advancement. Imam Mohammed's thought was
thus affected by, but not guided by, ideals of women's liberation in the
larger culture; rather, his gender ideology was guided by his understanding of Islamic sources, some of which happened to overlap with
gender ideas in the Nation, such as the role of men to provide for the
family and the expectation that women dress modestly. Likewise, the
fact that his opinions and practices did not always conform to popular
positions among contemporary Muslim scholars, in the United States
and abroad, demonstrates that they did not guide his understanding or
approach.

As we have seen, officials tried on numerous occasions to expose
Minister Wallace for preaching against his father's teachings. Author
Michael Saahir provides a detailed account of one of these episodes,
based on the recollection of Minister Yusuf Shah, the assisting minister in the Chicago temple in 1974. In Shah's account, we discover what
Imam Mohammed actually taught, and, surprisingly, it was a dissenting
statement about *gender*, and not race:

> He began to play the tape. . . . [Imam Mohammed] said, "I know what
> my father taught you all about the Black man being first, the Maker and
> the Owner and all that." He said, "The Black man is not first, the woman
> is first." Everybody looked right down to . . . the Honorable Elijah

Muhammad. . . . They were looking for him to jump on Imam Mohammed. . . . The Honorable Elijah Muhammad dropped his head. We were
still waiting. He said, "Well, that's right."[24]

Given this one account, it is hard to know if Shah's statement captures
Imam Mohammed's exact words. And we can only speculate about his
explanation of why "the woman is first" based on later commentary
made by the imam. What is clear is that Imam Mohammed spoke favorable words about women while in the Nation, and his protest against
NOI teachings carried a distinctly gender-sensitive dimension.

Imam Mohammed's double resistance to the Nation's gender ideology and race theology comes across in a story that also incorporates a
fond memory of his mother, Sister Clara Muhammad:

My mother was an excellent cook. . . . I would sit in the kitchen and
watch her. So I became a cook and a manager of the restaurant at the
same time. These brothers and sisters are coming in to the restaurant
one day, and this big 6 foot 2, heavy, muscular brother walked in . . . and
said, "Sister, serve the god." Oh boy, did he anger me. This big old Black
man could crush me with one swipe, and I would be through. But I went
up in his face and said, "Look, you don't come up in here talking like
that. You are not my god. You look like you just came from work. You
are struggling to stay alive and working hard. You are not my god." Then
I went back into the kitchen and left him there. He looked like he was
ashamed.[25]

Malikah Omar was a waitress at the restaurant that Imam Mohammed managed, possibly the woman for whom he stood up. Malikah
wrote an article in the *Bilalian News* in 1976 praising the new leader.
She recalls her time working under Minister Wallace and how she had
expected the son of Elijah Muhammad to "throw his weight around"
and give her orders:

I asked him one day, "Why don't you give me some orders as to how you
want things done?" He said to me, "Sis. Queenie, I would just as soon
try and order Ma around as to order you around. . . . Just treat me as if

I were your son. I'd rather be in the kitchen as your dishwasher than as your manager."[26]

Imam Mohammed's sensitivity and courage to stand up for women was certainly influenced by the high regard he had for his mother and his close relationship with her. Enduring poverty in Black Chicago during the Great Depression, Imam Mohammed had to have been enamored of his mother as she demonstrated "remarkable patience and courage" in carrying the Nation of Islam while raising eight children during Elijah's time in prison. Those who interviewed Imam Mohammed note that he would show "unreserved admiration and warmth" when asked about her.[27] Many of his followers were also touched by the love and respect the imam demonstrated for his mother. Maryum Sabree states, "He talked about her so beautifully all the time, and all she had done, and how she had helped him. . . . [As a boy], he'd sit wherever she was doing something and observe what she was doing. . . . I guess I'd love anybody who talked so lovely about their mother."

Ayesha K. Mustafa, editor of the *Muslim Journal*, attests that Imam Mohammed's love of and appreciation for women was most "prominent when it came to [his] discussing his mother. I think everything emanated from her; his appreciation for sisters could always be referred back to his appreciation for his mother. He spoke of her in such glowing terms . . . how she was never disrespectful to herself as a woman." Imam Mohammed was particularly impressed that his mother was the one who introduced her father to Fard. As described earlier, there are varying accounts of the story, but Clara narrated to Imam Mohammed the version in which she was responsible for the life-transforming encounter between the two leaders. Imam Mohammed would later recount this story to his following on numerous occasions. Notice in his narration how many times he reminds them of her role. Imam Mohammed begins with his mother's words to him:

My girlfriend told me there's a man who's saying some things about our people, said we didn't always dress like we dress. We once dressed in long flowing cloth and we were royal. . . . My girlfriend said, "I'm going to hear him [again]. . . . Will you go with me?" She [Clara] said, "Son, I thought about it. I said, 'Well maybe this might help my husband.'" So she took him. *She took my father.* Now *she took my father.* That's *very important that my mother actually took my father*, upon information *from her girlfriend, took my father* to see the one they call the Saviour, Master Fard. *Took my father to see him for the first time. . . . My mother was with him. My mother went with him. . . .* When the meeting was over, as they were walking out, my father told my mother, "Clara, when you go back home, we gon' have to throw all the pork out of the ice box." Now that's what one lecture, one speech did.[28]

It appears that the contribution Sister Clara Muhammad made in the Nation's very beginning and later as the first teacher in the University of Islam and mentor to hundreds of women via the MGT network significantly influenced Imam Mohammed's view of women, that women can and must contribute to the larger society but without neglecting their role in the family as supportive wives and educated mothers. Sister Clara Muhammad epitomized this ideal as she contributed to the NOI community while remaining a devoted wife and mother. As we will see, Imam Mohammed especially used the concept of mother to frame women's needed contribution to society. Perhaps the clearest indication of his regard for his mother as an example of women's impact on society is his changing the name of the NOI school system from Muhammad University of Islam to Clara Muhammad Elementary and Secondary School, whose mission, as defined by Imam Mohammed, mirrors Sister Clara's legacy as a mother educator: "To produce a product that will be a contribution to America and to the world."[29]

Imam Mohammed's Gender Ideology

Several women describe Imam Mohammed's gender philosophy as a defining feature of his new leadership. Daiyah Akbar, of Newark, states, "I could feel more free. In the old days, sisters really were kept on the back burner. We were like the last to speak. [With Imam Mohammed,] we could voice our opinions, our minds. It wasn't really, really bad, but you could see the difference and the change when Imam Mohammed came on the scene." The way in which women describe a clear shift in gender attitudes with Imam Mohammed indicates that the experiences

of women were at the center, and not the periphery, of Imam Mohammed's thought. Womanist scholars note that when the everyday experiences of Black women form the basis of theological inquiry and
exploration, the liberating theologies that result are ones that speak to
Black women's multiple oppressions—particularly the intersection of
racism and sexism in Black women's lives.[30] Given the influence of his
mother, Clara, and his personal repugnance toward sexist attitudes in
the Nation, it is not surprising that Imam Mohammed's religious interpretations often took on a womanist quality as they sought to challenge
detrimental gender constructs alongside harmful racial ones. Part of
correcting the idea that Black men were gods was correcting the idea
that Black women should be subservient to them. Moreover, his views
on women and their roles took into consideration African American
women's race and class struggles. But while Black women's experiences
and the contexts of their lives influenced his thought, unlike womanist theology, they were not the basis of his gender ideology. Rather, the
Qur'an and Sunnah (the example of the Prophet Muhammad) were the
primary sources and criteria of Imam Mohammed's gender thought.

Imam Mohammed summarized his underlying view on women in
a 1979 interview with Clifton Marsh. After "reexamining" Islam's position on women in light of the Qur'an and the Prophet Muhammad,
he noted, "The rights of women to equal education were protected by
Islam during the days of prophet Muhammad [sic]":

> I have come to the conclusion that actually in our religion, we cannot
> make any distinction between man and woman in terms of intelligence,
> spirituality or nature. Morally and intellectually speaking, women are
> equal with men and they are not to be treated any differently. They are
> to engage in business, to own wealth, to own property. They are to be
> allowed to excel in academic pursuits. If women are given freedom to
> excel in academic pursuits, how can we tell them to stay home? What is
> all this education for? You can't keep [women] at home to nurse babies.[31]

While many of Imam Mohammed's views of women were in agreement with those pursuing equal rights for women, advancing the status
of women was not his exclusive concern. As noted earlier, he once commented, "I'm trying to promote women's lib and at the same time save

society." As we will see, Imam Mohammed's comments on women were almost always tied to consideration of the whole society, community, and family.

For a Muslim theologian whose primary source was the Qur'an, Imam Mohammed paid exceptional attention to the Bible and dealt with its treatment of women considerably. He felt compelled to study the Bible, first, because his father's following was mostly raised in the church. "I certainly owed it to those who . . . when they walk into the temple and have a seat, I tell them . . . that they need to join the Nation of Islam. How do I know they need to join the Nation of Islam, and I don't know what they already are?" Second, he engaged the Bible because of his regard for his mother:

> And I owed it to my mother, to learn what produced her, what made her such a beautiful mother. Some of you say, "Oh, [it is because of] the Nation of Islam." No. My mother . . . didn't use drugs, she didn't smoke, she didn't drink liquors, and she wore long dresses . . . she didn't make any vulgar or indecent display of herself—*before* she became a follower of the Honorable Elijah Muhammad. She was a decent church woman who believed strongly in God and prayed and sang. We woke up to her voice. . . . She'd be singing songs of praise to God that she learned in the church.[32]

Imam Mohammed's engagement with the Bible led him to correct anti-women interpretations.

In the previous chapter, we saw how women resisted attitudes and structures in the Nation of Islam that attempted to limit women's role to the home. Although most Nation women favored MGT and embraced the idea that women's role in the home be honored and cultivated, they did not always want to be, and most were not, restricted there. It is as though Imam Mohammed understood and spoke to this sentiment among women as he laid out his gender philosophy. W. Muhsinah Abdullah states, "We were encouraged not only to be mothers and wives [by Imam Mohammed] but to be mothers to the broader community. There was a greater contribution. *Mothers to society*, that was his term. There was a greater contribution that we could provide to the world by going out and involving ourselves in the community."

Imam Mohammed introduced the concept of "mother leadership": "To be a mother is to be a leader over the life when it first comes. The woman is the first shaper of the human life or the human society," a male writer quotes Imam Mohammed in a 1977 issue of the *Bilalian News*. The issue was devoted to the status of women and featured a cover story, "Women: Equals? Inferiors? or Superiors?" The writer notes that according to the imam, women have a leadership role to contribute to society even if they do not bear children physically. This meant that the imam's idea of women as the first to develop and influence life did not limit them to contributing to society only by raising wholesome, productive citizens. Women were leaders by actually participating in the world. Their unique capacity as mothers—that is, as shapers and nurturers—however, offered a unique benefit to society. "Society is suffering right now, not because we don't have male leadership, but because we don't have mother leadership. . . . We need a mother's voice to be heard in the society today. . . . We want to hear . . . mother sentiments, some mother-concern. Then we want to see the strength of that strong sentiment that God formed in mothers by paying labor pains, etc., manifest in society."[33]

Although Imam Mohammed did not view women as different from men in their intellectual and spiritual capacity, he did see them as having distinct, though equally regarded, natures. In the 1979 interview with Marsh, Imam Mohammed stated that "in our religion, we cannot make any distinction between man and woman in terms of intelligence, spirituality or nature." Given the writings and lectures of Imam Mohammed and women's interpretations of them, it is more likely he meant that the Qur'an does not present men's and women's natures as different in terms of their propensity toward good or evil, not that women and men do not have distinct inclinations toward certain divine and human traits. For example, he wrote:

In the two powerful Attributes "Al-Rahman" and "Al-Rahim," Allah reminds us that He is not a male-sex or a female-sex God. He is a Benefactor (a Giver of Graces) like the man, the father, and He is also the greatest Bestower of Mercy and Compassion, like the female, the mother. Allah is not male or female, but He is the Source of Excellence of the male and the female and He is the Originator of everything.

It is also possible that what Imam Mohammed meant by no distinction in nature is the Qur'anic concept that men and women originate from a single, common soul, or *nafs*.[34]

Within this understanding of different natures, Imam Mohammed presented his criticism of popular feminism: "'Women's lib' is not an accident. It is a divine thing but women have to rise above the 'lib' to understand that we want more than just lip. We want mothers who have mothers' hearts. We want to hear some hearts, some mother sentiments." Here is where Imam Mohammed made clear that his pro-women concerns were informed not by trends in society but by a desire to better society, that his pro-women concerns were also pro-family, pro-community, and pro-men:

> In Islam . . . we are respecting the role of women by not allowing ourselves to step back and allow women to share everything equally. Some things a man can do and it's his natural role to do those things. If you (women) will admit the truth you know that it's not in you to jump up and go out and fight a physical enemy. It's not in your nature. God didn't put that in your nature. Your nature is love. You want to protect your home life. You want to protect those fine elements that [humanity] has been able to establish over centuries, over generations, thousands of years, in the home, in the fabric of human development, in the fabric of society. You want to protect those things. I'm trying to promote women's lib and at the same time save society.[35]

Women were fine with the idea that some roles were gender specific if it brought balance to families and communities. Jeanette Nu'Man states, "He talked about equity. Men and women were not equal, but equitable, meaning it's a balance. . . . They have different things on the scale, but those things are of equal value." Sandra El-Amin, of Atlanta, shares this same concept, which she embraced at the time because it made sense as part of God's natural design:

> Role definition grew out of what's a direct result of biological imperatives. So women nurtured life in their bodies, women suckled babies, and women were the first teachers. . . . So it made sense to me that women had a primary responsibility for homemaking and rearing children,

training children, even in terms of establishing schools. . . . The way I understood that is . . . that was a high honor, but that certain Western cultural development had kind of devalued that role. . . . I also could understand that [because of] the fact that the man had [greater] physical strength, he was in a position to provide support and protection for the woman.

The gender specificity of roles was similar to that promoted in the Nation, but Sandra clarified the difference with Imam Mohammed:

Imam Mohammed sort of kicked the men off of the pedestal that they were little gods, and he focused more on the equity in terms of the role definition and the complementary status. And [he taught] that in terms of intelligence and talent, there was no superiority, and also the idea that in God's sight, piety or good conduct was something that elevated one person in rank over another, but not gender.

We gain a sense of how women re-projected Imam Mohammed's gender teachings at that time from the issue of the *Bilalian News* covering the status of women. An article by a respected woman writer, Hafeezah N. Kashif, interprets Imam Mohammed's teachings: "As Emam [the early spelling that Imam Mohammed used for his title and name] Muhammad states, the moral voice of mothers can change society. We, as mothers . . . must begin to instill in our children (our society) the love of the creator, the love of truth, the love of pure, high morals. . . . We must begin to speak out in the society . . . [and] join in unity, whether Bilalian, Caucasian, brown, yellow, or whatever." At the same time that the woman's role as mother is stressed, we find a new emphasis on women's "speaking out" in settings beyond the home. The imam used the language of the Qur'an to support the link between women and society. Imam Mohammed noted that the Qur'anic Arabic word for community, *ummah*, stems from the root word from which is also derived the Arabic word for mother, *umm*.[36]

But the concept that is most recalled is one original to Imam Mohammed: "man means mind." It was important to Sandra El-Amin because she had felt that the "Black supremacist ideology of the Nation of Islam was as detrimental as white supremacist doctrine."

"Man means mind" meant "in my thinking . . . that what separated man from all other creatures is his intellect. A person's thinking is what really determined . . . who a person ultimately was morally or socially." Imam Mohammed made clear that when he used the term "man," he was "not referring to the male-sex."[37] "Man means mind" then lent itself to interpretations that promoted not only racial equality but also gender equality. "If 'man means mind,' then the male is no different from the female other than in terms of the physiological differences," Muhsinah concludes. In other words, anatomical distinctions between women and men could not be overlooked, but if intellect is what defines human beings, and "women had minds, in that way they were equal," Sandra explains. At the same time, Imam Mohammed did in fact take into consideration anatomical differences in a very deliberate way. Ayesha Mustafa notes, "A lot of people quote the imam as saying 'man means mind' but they forget that he also said 'woman means womb of mind.'" This could have been what Imam Mohammed was referring to when he made the dissenting statement in 1974 that the Black man was not the original maker, but that the woman was first, that she was the first to affect and shape human life and intellect.

Imam Mohammed conscientiously used the core concept of "man means mind" to resist Western white supremacist notions of race and gender and to inspire personal spiritual growth. In 1976, Imam Mohammed published *The Man and the WoMan in Islam*. In the first chapter, "Man," he described the "kindergarten mentality" of "Western world" people: "They do not see mind, they see human flesh colors." "A great knowledge" that will correct this mentality is "that 'man' (in the symbolic language of scripture) means 'mind' and that words make people." When "ancient wise people" used the concept man, "they were not talking about your flesh, they were talking about your mental makeup." Our higher state is reached when words help us to gain "self-mastery" over the physical realm, and the highest words are from scripture. "The Divine Word of Almighty Allah unlocks the mind, turns the light on in our being, and makes a spiritual sun to rise within us. . . . It causes us to take on form in the likeness of Divine Word."[38]

In the second chapter, "Woman," he continued to provide a critique of Western thought, evoking Nation of Islam language while transcending it. The enemy is no longer Caucasian skin but Caucasian mentality, "the childish understanding that has been given to you by Western Caucasian minds." This false understanding "is the ancient pagan Western Church language" from which we have inherited "the meaning of woman as 'woe unto man' or 'woe unto mind' (divine mind). . . . The Church treated women as beings that did not have a soul like the man had a soul. The Church treated woman as a tempter to tempt the man to sin because of the picture of woman in the Genesis scripture of the Bible." The imam went on to provide the correct understanding:

> The original meaning of the word "woman" is womb of mind. "Wo" stands for womb and "man" means mind. The female, as a sex being, mates with the opposite sex to reproduce the human species. . . . The female was called "womb of mind" because every mind is born out of the womb of a woman whether it is a male body or a female body.

Imam Mohammed introduced the concept of womb, a correction to "woe," to provide a more ennobling definition of the word "woman." He also connected the word "woman" to the concept of mind. In no way was he reducing woman to womb or prioritizing womb over mind, but rather he was making a correction: "a false description, a false nature, and a false form were given to the woman that naturally separated the woman from the mind. They said that the woman was a separate and distinct creation from the man." "They" refers to Christian writers and interpreters of the Bible whom Imam Mohammed exposed in many lectures for shrouding the Bible in pagan ideas.[39] He gave particular attention to the treatment of women in the Bible:

> The Bible goes on to say that the first mother was made from the rib of our first father. . . . I'm giving it to you in this language so you can see the kind of childish ideas that we grown-ups have been holding on to. It says, He took a rib—one rib—from the man. . . . He put the flesh that was taken out, back in its place—just a patch-up job . . . and then made the woman with this rib. What does that make the woman? It makes her a different creation from the man. . . . So if this woman is made from one bone[,] she doesn't have the full value, the full human worth of the man.

Right from the beginning the woman is put in an inferior image. . . . [K]
eep reading about the woman as her story is told from Genesis to Revelation. She becomes more and more ugly, inferior and wicked. . . . These
destructive concepts in human ideas or in human minds are still hurting
human development. . . . God gives us the most beautiful concept of the
man that He creates. The man that He creates is a mind, . . . a rational and compassionate human mind; and from that mind is born, not a
woman, but society.[40]

That Imam Mohammed was more interested in correcting negative
conceptions of the woman and connecting her to the concept of mind,
and therefore society, than in defining her role in the home is demonstrated also in how he used Qur'anic language to ennoble women.
In his book's chapter "Marriage in Islam," he stated the responsibility
that the Qur'an outlines for men, "to provide the material needs for his
household," but did not preclude women from this "burden," which if
she chooses to share with him, it "is to be considered as a gift from her,"
but never an obligation. Interestingly, as Islamic studies scholar Amina
Wadud notes, while the Qur'an enjoins men to care for their families
financially, it does not enjoin women to be the traditional caretakers
of children. Indeed, child bearing is an obvious responsibility that the
majority of women naturally assume, and men could never share in this
function. When the Qur'an does bring attention to this role in its chapter "Women," it commands a special regard for this female-only capacity, and Imam Mohammed highlighted this injunction as a correction
to traditional Christian thought:

The Holy Quran says that we should revere God but that we should also
[revere] the womb of the female. Many men tend to look down upon the
woman as a producer or as a child bearer. Even many so-called great religious orders have regarded this physiological function of the female as
something to be despised or as something evil. [The] Prophet Muhammad said that women should not be despised because God has placed an
abundance of good in them.

After making this correction and then noting that children are a natural and expected outcome of marriage, Imam Mohammed returned

to language that linked women as mothers to society. "Society begins growing in the womb of the mother. . . . In one of his sayings, [the] Prophet Muhammad tells us in plain words that the future heaven of the society depends upon how the mother raises the little children that are at her feet."[41]

As Ayesha Mustafa notes, most women remember "man means mind," forgetting that the imam also taught "woman means womb of mind." The concept of woman as mind, not simply womb, is what women most cherished and claimed. The concept of mind was the part of the equation that had been omitted until now, and women used it to support education and work outside the home. In the 1975 documentary *Nation of Islam: A Portrait*, Sonia Sanchez, who was in the Nation of Islam between 1971 and 1975, speaks passionately about the concept in the first year of the transition:

The Honorable Wallace D. Mohammed has said that man is mind and woman is mind, and by saying this, he's saying that woman is mind housed in a female body. . . . Women do give birth to children. He is saying that that is not a priority, that's a natural thing . . . that we do. . . . But he's saying too that the woman has a mind, and it's only because the woman has not dealt with her mind, or man has not dealt with the woman's mind in this country, that she's been relegated to the kitchen. And he says, I don't relegate . . . Muslim women to the kitchen at all. She must be about doing other things. A nation needs the strength and the work of a man and a woman. He says the Western countries have dealt with the women on a very negative level, that's why we have a woman's liberation movement today moving around. And because he said those simple words, we saw ourselves differently. So of course then I can be co-director of the Office of Human Development.

Sonia Sanchez left the Nation in December 1975 because her political views began to shift in ways more radical than allowed for in the new direction of the NOI. Her new position was influenced by feminist critiques of Black social movements. Such critiques noted the disconnect between claims of women's equal participation and the actual division of labor in social justice groups. But what is more important, Sonia Sanchez's identification with the Black feminist movement and her conflicts with the Nation of Islam now led by Imam Mohammed highlight divergence between Imam Mohammed's views and those of feminists. In his chapter "The Responsibility of Motherhood," Imam Mohammed made comments that clearly go against the grain of feminism: "No father should take over the rearing of his children from the mother, especially when they are under the age of 12 years. Their nature during this period is to be fed by mother and not by father. . . . In designing this creation, the Almighty Creator gave mind first to the female so that she could do her job and then release it to the world of the males." The way in which Imam Mohammed dichotomized social realms by gender, and his reference to "the world of the males" in particular, contradicted his overall message of the importance of women's participating in society. Like Sonia Sanchez, Sunni women focused on his primary message, which was the emphasis on mind. "Remember, Sisters, that every female is a man (mind) just as every male is a mind," he re-stated soon after his comment about "the world of the males."[42] Unlike Sonia Sanchez, Sunni women spoke to the crucial role of mothering but always in ways that empowered women to cultivate their intellects and to contribute to society. We can see this expressed in different ways by two women. Deborah Davis comments:

> I remember [Imam Mohammed's] saying that the mother's job is to excite the mental appetite of the child, and that was another level of freedom for me. I thought about it, and I said, "Wait a minute now, if the mother's job is to excite the mental appetite of a child, then the mother's mental appetite has to be excited. And my mental appetite is definitely not excited if my hand is in the toilet everyday and cleaning, cleaning, cleaning. I've got to get up and study. . . . I have to be educated.

Mary Hamidullah[43] states:

> I remember my mind just being completely blown away when Imam Mohammed said man means mind and woman means womb of mind. It just was completely a game changer for me, and for a lot of people, because I think those words to me—although womb of mind could put you in the light of the woman role being the mother role, which is something I have always accepted—womb of mind to me was more expansive

than just staying at home and raising children. And so for me, I think that opened up a lot of possibilities for thinking about a woman's work within our community, and it definitely made room for those women who were seeking professional lives within the community and outside of the community. . . . He talked in terms of human beings, and not so much gender related. But he also talked about how even though we might be a male, we have a female identity, and even though we are female, we have a male identity. . . . So we began to see ourselves as spiritual beings. We are spiritual beings in this life in male or female form—and man means mind and woman means womb of mind—but you were still a mind in your female self, and there is an aspect of the womb of mind in your male self . . . and so you see yourself in a much more expanded way, and I identified with that a great deal.

"The female–male self" is an important Qur'anic term that Imam Mohammed used to correct the biblical interpretation that woman was created from man. "The Holy Quran says that God created you from one 'nafs'. . . . God created [humanity] from one soul, and He created a mate from that soul," Imam Mohammed stated in a 1976 *Bilalian News* article in which he interpreted the verse (Qur'an 4:1) as follows: "He [God] . . . produce[d] something that would have the ability to reproduce its mate out of itself." This primordial soul, therefore, possesses the essence of its mate and has the ability to function as both a male and a female. At several "Sisters' Meetings" in the early 1990s, Imam Mohammed further explained why this original soul was neither male nor female, "but a combination of the two," and he used Arabic grammar to discredit any idea that woman originated after or from man, showing instead that woman originated from this female–male soul. The Arabic term for this original soul in the Qur'an is *nafs wahidah*, a single soul. In "'nafs wahidah,' the *wahidah* is feminine, so it couldn't be talking about a man person. The man as a man is not feminine. But *nafs*, the word for soul, or person, or self, in the Qur'an, referring to this one that God created the woman from, or man and woman from, it is feminine. Grammatically speaking, it is feminine." This detail in the grammar, however, does not mean that the original soul is a woman. Imam Mohammed explained, "And certain things in the description of males and females [in terms of their origins] are masculine, other things are feminine. The *ruh*, the spirit [which God breathed into the human being], is [grammatically] masculine. . . . But *nafs*, the soul, the *nafs* is feminine." Because "the soul is the reservoir of all the energies of and possibilities for the human life," it must possess feminine and masculine qualities. "All of it comes out of the soul. That's why God, in the Qur'an, mentions the soul and its needs. Its needs for *taqwa*, regardfulness, and its needs for enlightenment." This broad capacity of the soul within every human being is what Mary found expansive. The woman, therefore, is not the first in creation, but she is the first to shape the generations of humanity in the womb and in the world.[44]

The way in which Imam Mohammed understood the Qur'anic female–male self as the beginning of human creation complements the way in which he saw himself advancing women's place in society while also saving society. He was not interested in the rights of women foremost and at any cost, the way in which he understood the goal of the women's liberation movement, but he was interested in contributing to the collective success of his racial group, which required men and women together working to establish wholesome families and communities. In the last chapter of his book on gender, "Challenge to the Bilalian Community," he wrote:

The union of man and woman as husband and wife is moving the man up to be a greater provider. . . . If a man had nothing to work for but himself, he would stay a small thing in the earth. . . . [T]his world of grafted [reference to NOI description of the Caucasian devil], unnatural mentality . . . makes us think that we do not need each other and that every man and every woman is an individual. That is the kind of ignorant thinking that they feed the masses of the people, but they teach their own class of people that . . . they should live together and die together. . . . Brothers and sisters, hold on to the great truth that we have been blessed to receive from God. . . . We have the opportunity to be the moral leaders of the world tomorrow. . . . But, first, it is my desire to see us just become good housekeepers, good parents, good husbands and wives, good fathers and mothers, and good providers. I would like to see us do things the way that the Holy Quran says that all parents are obligated to do them: clothe your children, feed your children, and give them an education. . . . I want to see my own people stop acting like single people when they are married and stop acting like childish parents when they have millions of children all over the world.[45]

That Imam Mohammed ended his book on gender with a challenge to the African American *community* reaffirms the way in which his gender thought considered the well-being of women, men, and children. As anthropologist Carolyn Rouse notes from her study of women who followed Imam Mohammed into Sunni Islam, "Womanists and Muslim women share a desire to empower both genders." Although many womanists would not espouse the type of gender role definition that Imam Mohammed did, they might acknowledge that for many Black women, "there are alternative ways to view the importance of women, and that maybe the model of men and women performing the same roles is not the best way to organize a family or society."[46]

MGT, CERWIS, and the First Female Minister

Leading a national community from Chicago, Imam Mohammed implemented changes that positively affected women on a national scale, putting his new gender ideology into action. His weekly Sunday lectures, known to have lasted anywhere from four to ten hours, were broadcast at local temples, and excerpts were published as the centerfold in the weekly newspaper. He made it immediately clear that the community should no longer see itself as isolated but part of the broader American society and Muslim community. Teaching against the mentality of shunning "the white man's work" or "the white man's education," Imam Mohammed encouraged education and work in the broader community for women and men. Over and over again Sunni women describe going back to school, returning to work, or doing both soon after Imam Mohammed became leader. The structural change in the Nation of Islam that most advanced this attitude toward education and work was the transitioning of the MGT.

In the very beginning of the transition, MGT classes and officer positions continued, but the nature of officers' authority changed as Imam Mohammed did away with strict codes of conduct. These included women's requiring a male escort when traveling at night or across cities, women's staying at home—not even attending the temple for classes—during pregnancy, and the most prominent one, women's wearing the official MGT uniform. NOI laws that were also decreed in Sunni Islam, such as prohibitions against extramarital sex, alcohol and drug use, and pork consumption, remained, but the policing and disciplining of members who committed transgressions ended. According to Fareedah Pasha, Imam Mohammed discussed this change within the framework of his interpretation that the NOI was a natural progression to Sunni Islam: "In the Nation, they had people who would come by and inspect your house . . . but the imam said we're not babies anymore; that was baby thinking. . . . So [by] 1975 it was time, he said, to be responsible." Safiyyah Shahid, an MGT captain in Atlanta, describes the far-reaching impact that this new responsibility had on members' lives:

> You're not just doing something because you were told that if you don't do it, you'll be out of the community for thirty days. Now you've got to make some decisions for your own life and that was liberating. . . . In the Nation of Islam, it was so structured that individually, you might not have been able to realize your potential. Under Imam Mohammed's leadership, women were doing all kinds of things. Some became more politically aware, . . . many women became writers, and it just really spread out to whatever you chose.[47]

Sometime between July 1975 and March 1976, Imam Mohammed changed the name of MGT to the Muslim Women Development Class (MWDC).[48] According to Ayesha Mustafa, "The first thing he said was, 'You're not girls anymore.'" Initially, these classes continued to teach topics in MGT. Between the end of 1976 and early 1977, the position of captain had totally ended.[49] Opportunities for women's leadership expanded as the responsibility to lead MWDC classes opened to other women, a leadership structure that varied across cities as *masjids* demonstrated greater autonomy while under Imam Mohammed's general guidance.

At the same time that MGT was transitioning, parallel movements opened doors for women beyond the MWDC, and this also led to varying levels of popularity of the MWDC by city and the eventual ending of this class in most if not all cities in the 1980s. The new development that most signaled the imam's goal to enhance women's lives and make use of their talents and contributions was appointing the NOI's first sister minister, Amatullah Um'rani. It was not a position that women had lobbied for—Um'rani even describes herself as "a reluctant leader"—but Imam Mohammed made the appointment "within weeks of the passing of the Honorable Elijah Muhammad. I was already a sister minister in April [1975]."

Amatullah Um'rani joined the Nation in 1972 with a master's in social work from Rutgers University. Told that she should be working for her own Nation, not for the devil, she left a teaching position at Southern University to teach at the University of Islam in Chicago. Her prominence in the Chicago temple grew as she frequently wrote articles of personal reflection published in *Muhammad Speaks*, starting with her contribution to the column "What Islam Has Done for Me." An officer in training under Chicago's National Sister Captain Portia Pasha, Um'rani was also heavily involved in the activities of MGT. Such a rare set of accomplishments had not gone unnoticed by Imam Mohammed. He surprised Um'rani by asking her to stand in front of the entire congregation during one of the main Sunday meetings, most likely in March 1975. Um'rani recalls, "It was amazing. He said, 'I've been observing the work of this sister and I'm going to appoint her to work as a sister minister.' Even then, I was like, 'No, it couldn't be me.' Even though I had many experiences . . . I lacked self-confidence." Lacking confidence, however, was not how others saw Um'rani.

In a letter written to Sister Captain Pasha, dated May 9, 1975, Imam Mohammed stated that Sis. Sharolyn X (Um'rani's previous name) would start "a regular column in [the] *Muhammad Speaks* newspaper entitled 'Minister Sharolyn.'" He also requested that the sister captain "make available to her approximately fifteen to twenty minutes at each MGT/GCC Class Meeting for her to present a spiritual message to the Sisters." He ended the letter by noting, "We expect a great deal of good efforts to come from the Sisters in the future." Um'rani had the autonomy and flexibility to design aspects of her position. She gave herself the title National Coordinator of Women, and in this role as a "religious teacher" she traveled across the country to give lectures and regularly corresponded in writing with both MGT captains and sister ministers, which means that both positions existed at the same time,

MUḥAMMAÒ'S TEMPLE NO.2

7351 SOUTH STONY ISLAND AVENUE   CHICAGO, ILLINOIS 60649   (312) 667-6800

May 9, 1975

In the Name of Allah, The Beneficent, The Merciful; Peace
and Blessings upon His Servant and His Messenger, Muhammad,
forever. Amen.

As-Salaam-Alaikum

Dear Sis. Captain Pasha:

Sis. Sharolyn X has been doing quite a bit of study in the
Ministerial area. Her background and her progress are very
good.

Very soon she will start what we hope to be a regular
column in Muhammad Speaks Newspaper entitled "Minister
Sharolyn."

I would like for you to make available to her approximately fifteen to twenty minutes at each MGT/GCC Class
Meeting for her to present a spiritual message to the Sisters.

I hope that her example will encourage the Class to study
and use their talents in this area.

We expect a great deal of good efforts to come from the
Sisters in the future.

As-Salaam-Alaikum

W. D. Muhammad
The Honorable W. D. Muhammad
Supreme Minister

WDM:fs

cc: Sis. Sharolyn X

Imam Mohammed's letter presenting Amatullah Um'rani as a minister, 1975

varying by local temple, soon to be called mosque. Most Sunni women
interviewed did not recall the sister minister position, although the
Bilalian News featured Um'rani's regular column with the byline "Minister Amatullah Um'rani" throughout 1976 and 1977. There are a couple
of reports of sister ministers in cities outside Chicago. In an interview
with Sultana Ali from the Brooklyn temple, she describes herself as one
of several sister ministers appointed by the local minister. According to

Sultana, the sisters' ministry was limited to teaching Islam to women in prison: "We taught them how to eat and about modesty." In Atlanta, Sandra El-Amin recalls Sister Minister Carolyn, who was appointed by the local minister. "Her main function was to instruct women on the new religious concepts." The sister captain in Atlanta, Safiyyah Shahid, could not recall the exact structure of Sister Minister Carolyn's classes except that she had "very close contact with her" and that Sister Minister Carolyn taught "deeper understanding and appreciation of the religion," even the "metaphysical aspect." Carolyn Cordell, age eighty at the time of our interview, describes herself as the "first sister minister in the Southeast" but could not recall any exact dates although she describes giving presentations to the women during MGT class. This corresponds with Imam Mohammed's instructions to the national sister captain in Chicago regarding the duties of the sister minister.

Although local temples may have attempted to model Imam Mohammed's initiatives in Chicago, the outcome was not always the same. Other than in Chicago, community members were mainly reliant on local ministers to disseminate information to the congregations. Um'rani remembers being flooded with correspondence by mail and phone as women attempted to gain information about each change, especially those directly affecting them. It is clear that the role of sister minister varied by city and is likely to have not existed at all in most cities, or for only a very brief period. In Chicago, for example, the title was replaced with "instructress in religion," and the role expanded to include women's ministry to men. By summer 1977, Imam Mohammed had changed the title of "minister" to "imam," around the same time that he replaced the term "mosque" with "*masjid*."[50] Because the purpose of the sister minister position was to create opportunities for women to study and teach religious knowledge to the same extent as male ministers—in other words, to create a women's counterpart of the traditional minister role—when the title of "minister" was replaced with "imam," an alternative title was also needed for women ministers. As Ayesha notes, "Women could not be called imams" in Sunni Islam. The title "imam" is reserved for men only, not because it entails religious preaching, which women have always done in the Islamic tradition, but because it also includes leading men in the ritual prayer, a leadership role from which women have been prohibited in the Islamic tradition. The term that Imam Mohammed chose for women teachers was "instructress," a title that had been used previously in the Nation. In a 1979 interview, Imam Mohammed stated, "We have women in key positions in the Masjid. We don't call them Imams, we call them 'Instructress.' They teach the religion, they propagate just like we do."[51]

In Chicago, alongside the imams' classes where men were trained in religious knowledge, Islam classes for women were led by instructresses considered advanced in their study of Islam. Ayesha Mustafa, Amatullah Um'rani, and Amidah Akram were the first women teaching this class in Chicago. Um'rani describes this period as a time of "transformation" in which women were "active all over the place, and not just doing searches and not just teaching women," as in MGT. "We were actually able to get up and give speeches before the whole congregation." During the main Sunday meeting, a "brother" would normally open up the meeting with a short message before the minister's sermon. Now with female teachers, women "would rotate to open up the meetings," according to Ayesha. But also, beyond the *masjid*, Imam Mohammed "wanted the sisters to teach and get out in the community as instructresses of Islam. He wanted us to mobilize in the community." The women teachers made up part of a propagation team consisting of males and females. "We had marches," recalls Um'rani. "We set up tents and talked to people in the communities on the megaphone. We went to the schools; we went to churches. We went into prisons." Um'rani made clear that there was "no women's propagation team," that the women worked alongside the "brothers."

Masjid communities outside Chicago also used the title "instructress" for female religious authorities. An August 1977 issue of the *Bilalian News* carried an article titled, "Woman: Her Identity and Her Role," by Hafeezah N. Kashif, Instructress, Masjid Muhammad, Washington, D.C. In Atlanta, however, it is likely that this position did not exist, as women did not mention it in their interviews, but Sandra recalls similar developments there that she associated with progress for women in the new leadership: "I can't remember if they were called the minister classes or imam classes, but [Imam Mohammed] opened that up to women."

In Chicago, the Muslim Women Development Class (MWDC) eventually "faded" or was "merged" into the instructresses' class, according to Ayesha. In Durham, North Carolina, the MWDC also had a short stay. Durham's Sister Captain Rhonda Muhammad does not recall classes beyond 1976. Instead, she remembers that most of the efforts of women in the community was redirected toward reopening the Sister Clara Muhammad School, which had closed because of financial problems. Similarly, women in Atlanta make no mention of MWDC in their accounts of the transition experience, but several of them were greatly affected by CERWIS, the Committee to Enhance the Role of Women in Society. Imam Mohammed established this committee between 1977 and 1978.[52]

CERWIS came about because the instructresses' class was "somewhat contained," describes Ayesha. Initially Imam Mohammed selectively appointed the instructresses in Chicago and dedicated time to do special lecture sessions for the women. As more women became interested and expressed ideas beyond what Imam Mohammed initially envisioned, he saw the need to create a structure in which women could "organize and do more things" independently. More so than the instructresses' class, CERWIS developed on a national level. Local chapters had the autonomy to focus on activities as they chose. One of the first chapters opened in Atlanta, where Khayriyyah Faiz was chairperson. Khayriyyah states, "I thought that it was a wonderful, strategic move to energize our sisters and empower them." While the "Nation of Islam was about enhancing the role of women at home," Sandra notes, "CERWIS was an important concept that went along with the transition" and its new attitude toward women.

Mary Muhammad describes what made CERWIS better than MGT:

Imam Mohammed wanted us to come out of that womb that we were in, that was just for the Muslim women, and to go out to the broader community and bring what the Qur'an was giving us and the great example of our Prophet . . . to be able to move out in the society and work with other faith-based groups also and be intelligent enough to speak on a level that they can understand.

Mary found not only CERWIS's content of study and mobilization far more favorable for women but also its organizational structure. At Mary's Jersey City *masjid*, the local imam would select the women to serve as instructors for MWDC based on their skills and service in the community, retaining the old Nation structure in which a top official selected the local sister captain.[53] Mary was "elated" when this practice stopped with the advent of CERWIS. A voting process was established in which women nominated and voted in leaders for themselves.

At various moments between 1976 and 1980, these new developments away from MGT—MWDC, sister ministers, instructresses, and CERWIS—existed at the same time in various capacities across *masjid* communities, but for the most part, they were associated with the transition and represent the early stages of organized opportunities to expand women's leadership and work in their community and the larger society. Except for a couple of CERWIS chapters—one in Charlotte, North Carolina, led by Mary, and another in Columbia, South Carolina—these titles and organizations no longer operate in the WDM community. The reason CERWIS was not sustained in most cities, if a chapter ever existed at all, is not entirely clear. Amatullah Um'rani speculates that the lack of sustainability had to do with the fact that "the corresponding changes in the *masajid* [*masjids*] were numerous and dramatic as compared to the earlier procedures and practices prior to 1975. There were changes in leadership, physical locations, and understanding of, or loyalties to, the new leadership of Imam Mohammed." Despite Imam Mohammed's recommendations, imams in some cities were not interested in establishing a CERWIS chapter. Other factors leading to CERWIS's disappearance included women's efforts' expanding in different directions, often personal. Amatullah Um'rani, for example, left her position as National Coordinator for Women in 1979 to attend naprapathy school at night, while continuing to be employed as a full-time psychiatric social worker, although she continued to participate in various activities within the WCIW. Personal aspirations aside, there were other efforts in the *masjid* communities to which women dedicated themselves, including the various committees that Imam Mohammed established as part of maintaining activism in the community, including the Child Interest Committee, the Fairness Committee, and the Protection of the Aged Committee. In Chicago, women chaired or participated in numerous committees. Muni'imah Muwwakkil led a group that sponsored New World Patriotism Day parades, which highlighted Imam Mohammed's patriotic vision. Also, women adopted the concept of CERWIS and founded service organizations of their own. In 1981, women co-founded the International League of Muslim Women. The organization has placed a special emphasis on providing counseling, food, and other forms of assistance to women and families in need. The organization has several chapters today.[54]

The First Female Editor and Men's Resistance

Imam Mohammed appointed not only the first female minister of the NOI but also the first female editor-in-chief of *Muhammad Speaks*, Ana Karim, the former SNCC member introduced earlier. Soon after Imam Mohammed took leadership, he sent Ana to the *Muhammad Speaks* newspaper plant to work as a journalist. The environment at the plant "brought out memories of what happened in Lowndes County," Alabama, where Ana witnessed atrocities during her voter registration work. Ana describes the leadership of John Ali, plant manager and former national secretary of the NOI, as "harsh." "The manner in which he spoke to the staff, the way in which he dismissed many of the intelligent ideas reporters offered, was reminiscent of the hardcore racist and ruthless rule of southern whites in Alabama during the civil rights struggle." Ana called members of the entire staff of the *Muhammad Speaks* printing plant and rallied them to stand up for themselves. Eventually, "it got to a point where John Ali was run out of that plant, so it was then that the Honorable Imam W. D. Mohammed asked if I would become the head of that plant and that's how I began."

As editor, Ana led the newspaper in the direction that Imam Mohammed instructed and applied her discretion accordingly. She ran into difficulty, however, because a few at the newspaper "were not on board with the Honorable Imam W. D. Mohammed and wanted the paper to remain, or the name to remain, *Muhammad Speaks*." *Bilalian News*, the name Imam Mohammed introduced, was meant to positively influence African Americans of all faiths. "The imam wanted us to be a beacon or harbinger to the future generations to reach for excellence." The *Bilalian News*, he instructed her, should feature developments within the new Muslim community, including his lectures, as well as positive news about the larger African American community. A few reporters on the paper, however, "wanted to report on things that the imam had given me specific instructions not to put in the paper." Ana calls them "closet socialists." "I didn't want communist influence in Cuba or anywhere else dominating the stories in that paper; they were putting it on the front page. I would tell them, 'It is *Bilalian News*. What are you reporting on socialism and communism for on the front page?'" They would respond with condescending remarks, "Sister, you just don't understand how the paper is run." Ana would reply, "Maybe not, but I do know what I heard the imam say, so I would appreciate it if you would comply."

Muhammad Speaks had a strong international component. Within Ana's staff, the attempted focus on communism and oppressed people around the world reflected resistance to the new leadership and "a very subtle attempt to turn the paper away from the imam. . . . Our paper, the *Bilalian News*, would have been covering all kinds of issues related to other cultures had I not said to them, 'You have to focus on the Bilalian community.'" International news was important, Ana told them, "but it cannot dominate this paper. It cannot." Fighting the "renegades" on the newspaper staff would have been difficult for any editor given the task to lead the paper in a new direction, but Ana understood that her gender amplified the fight:

> The militant, commanding FOI, . . . they were the dominant force of our community in terms of visibility. . . . So here comes a woman saying that you have to follow the agenda of Imam W. D. Mohammed. This didn't sit well with them. . . . But it didn't matter. "You either do it or else," [I told them]. [I was prepared for this type of defiance] because I assumed the hardship of the civil rights movement.

Ana's testimony strikingly captures the parallel struggles of Black Christian women: Black women fighting alongside their men for civil rights but fighting some of their men for respect and leadership as women. Although Ana met this resistance, she thought it important to convey that in both the Nation and in the new community, she positively witnessed among most of the "brothers" the desire to "lead and take responsibility for themselves, their families, and their communities."

The influence of female leadership was evident in the *Bilalian News*. Women reporters regularly contributed articles, and entire issues were devoted to raising awareness about the treatment of women. Most interesting was a January 1978 issue with the cover story "Wife Beaters: Incidents and Solutions Explored," by Rhena Muslim Muhammad. The cover graphics were quite striking with a drawing of a house inlaid with the word wife and cracks breaking through the house to signal its falling apart. In a 1979 issue there appeared a "special" to the *Bilalian News* titled "Family Life" by Mildred El-Amin. In it, she drew from Imam Mohammed's Qur'an-based gender teachings: "The Holy Quran teaches us that creation of the species began with a single being. That single being was made from two beings, male and female, that came together to form the human family. The close relationship of man and woman must be made strong—it is the foundation of the strength of the society." El-Amin penned her column for the next decade and compiled her columns in a book titled *Family Roots: The Qur'anic View of Family Life* in 1991.[55]

In a September 1976 issue there appeared a striking photograph of an elderly woman brandishing a *Bilalian News* newspaper in her right hand and holding down to her side a small stack of papers in her left. Below the photograph, the caption reads, "Sister Varnada, age 90[,] of Detroit, sells 80 *Bilalian News* papers per week." This photo and caption by themselves reveal the marked change in women's roles under the leadership of Imam Mohammed. One of the public images most associated with the Nation was of the FOI selling papers on the streets. This was not the domain of women. Under Imam Mohammed, however, many women became top paper sellers. A 1977 *Bilalian News* article reports:

> Mr. Hasan and Mr. Muhammad along with Sisters Earline Muhammad and Nasirah Muhammad will be joining many other American Muslims on the annual pilgrimage to the Holy City of Mecca, Saudi Arabia. Emam Wallace D. Muhammad . . . is sponsoring the four as reward for their dedicated efforts to help propagate Al-Islam as diligent *Bilalian News* salespeople. The two sisters each sells 300 copies of *BN* per week, and each of the two brothers sells 800 copies per week. All four are well-known and deeply loved by WCIW members and many others who see them busily propagating Al-Islam on the streets of Chicago.[56]

"Because the imam talked so much on education," Ana left the paper in 1978 to pursue a second bachelor's degree in her childhood interest, agronomy, and continued on to complete her master's. Another woman, Dorothy Ghallab, followed her in the editor position. Three men followed Ghallab until Ayesha Mustafa, the current editor, began her tenure in 1988. Since Ana's time, the name of the paper has been changed to the *Muslim Journal*, and its staff is majority female.

Fighting Resistance from Local Imams

> Under the Honorable Elijah Muhammad, women were leaders within the ranks of the women, but the imam brought the leadership of women over men as well as women. And he said many times—because he knew the mentality of some of our brothers coming out from under the leadership of the Honorable Elijah Muhammad—"I will follow a woman, any qualified sister; I will follow her because that is the way of [the] Prophet Muhammad. . . . Brothers, God has given the tools of creativity and leadership to both men and women."

Ana Karim, quoted above, was not the only one fighting the entrenched attitudes that carried over from the Nation. Women in their local mosques were too. Ana, however, was fortunate to work directly with Imam Mohammed and witnessed firsthand the structural changes he made to implement his gender philosophy. Other women report a different experience: "Imam Mohammed pushed the envelope, and women were seen as partners in the world. . . . I got that from him philosophically, but I never really saw it operationalized. That doesn't mean it didn't happen, but [I did not see his philosophy actualized] from where I sat, being several layers removed from Imam Mohammed."[57] The woman quoted here had never heard that Imam Mohammed had appointed a sister minister. It was the local imams who were largely responsible for this disconnect between Imam Mohammed's philosophy and its actual implementation in some *masjids*. Ana Karim recalls an imam board that "would help oversee community activities." She states, "I found the difficulty was with the imam board." Several women shared sentiments like Ana's. Represented below, these women lived in various locations on the East Coast and in the South.

Although Imam Mohammed desired that women attain the religious knowledge of imams and created opportunities for them to teach, he essentially carried over the power structure of the Nation of Islam in that imams remained the organizational leaders of their *masjids*. Imam Mohammed described the leadership structure of his community in a 1979 interview:

> The central leadership is still in myself, but it's not an absolute leadership. The power is shared with a council of Imams and about 17 advisors to that council. Many others not named [are] in the body of advisors. We try to share the leadership. The Imams' meeting going on right now is supervised by Brother Imam Fatah; he has a free hand to do that. The business, real estate, and other capital holdings throughout the country—we look to the people who are over those regions to make the best decisions for the interest of the community.[58]

The WCIW was divided into regions with organizational heads who also appear to have been imams. Imam Mohammed mentioned in the interview that "Dr. G. Haleen Shabazz is the imam over the Midwest region," further indicating an organizational structure led by men, even outside the confines of the *masjid*. However, Ana points out that "women held many positions within the economic entities of the community." It is unclear as to whether women were included among the advisors to the council of imams. Ana says that she "sat on the imam board and recorded their decisions. It was obvious that some of them were not supportive of Imam W. Deen Mohammed's democratic approach to leadership. The statements I recorded and sent to the imam kept him informed of this mentality." In this way, a woman was influential in moving the community toward the "model of [the] Prophet Muhammad," which the imam was attempting to emulate through the imam board, according to Ana, in which there was "input from all community members."

Indeed, the new structure of the WCIW pushed toward this ideal of collective input as it gave women the freedom to address their concerns directly to the imam and the freedom to speak their minds in front of men in public. They no longer had to go to the sister captain as a go-between the women and the patriarchal power structure. Daiyah Akbar recalls that letters of concern were given to a "sister officer," who would in turn give them to a "brother officer," who would ultimately deliver them to Elijah Muhammad. "The difference with Imam Mohammed was we were able to walk upfront and hold our heads up and speak even in the brothers' presence in the same room when Imam Mohammed opened the Sunday meetings up for questions and answers." Daiyah also gives examples of Imam Mohammed's setting aside time to speak to everyday women one-on-one in a restaurant.

Women also describe having the newfound freedom to publicly teach other women ideas that may not have been supported by their local imam, especially imams not ready to abandon the teachings of Elijah Muhammad. Women were no longer threatened by penalties under MGT that prevented them from openly disagreeing with their ministers. Before the transition, Patricia Muhammad[59] was married to the minister of her temple, who was extremely chauvinistic. His attitude was, "You're just supposed to follow my lead and do what I tell you; you're not supposed to think." During the transition, Patricia was excited about the changes, and because she was the minister's wife, women often looked up to her for knowledge and explanation of Imam Mohammed's teachings. "I can remember him telling me, 'I don't want you spoiling what I've already set down here for the sisters, [the ideas] that *I teach*.' It was like, 'I don't want you to set a bad example.'"

Patricia's comments suggest that women not only felt freer to express themselves but also felt empowered by the fact that they were not beholden to any particular interpretation of religious concepts by any given imam. Naomi Rahman[60] recalls, "There was this thirst [for knowledge] now that the floodgates had been opened, because in the Nation of Islam, what you should read was restricted. When Imam Mohammed came, he opened up a world of Islamic literature, and I couldn't wait to get warmed up." Women found some autonomy to interpret these newfound sources. "Imam Mohammed came on the set and said, 'You're a free person. This is how Allah created you, and this is your capacity. I'm gonna provide you with guidance, but I'm not gonna tell you minute to minute, day to day, what you're supposed to be doing.'"

Like Naomi, Jennifer Lewis[61] embraced the imam's focus on independent thinking. Jennifer left a mosque in one city that she describes as relatively gender progressive for a mosque in a different city that was the exact opposite. She spoke up about the domestic violence there. "Their husbands didn't want them to hang with me because I was a troublemaker. . . . I was telling them, 'You have to accept Islam for yourselves, you have to study, you have to read. . . . If the interpretation comes from your husband or from the imam, that's one interpretation. You can have another when you're looking at it.'" Women's freedom and confidence to study, interpret, and apply the new religious knowledge coupled with their ability to freely share their ideas with imams or fellow mosque members meant that women had greater agency. But they also felt greater resistance from men, as backward-thinking imams found themselves confronted with women's perspectives. Naomi participated in a study group in which women from various African American *masjids* in her city came together to discuss readings on Islamic topics. The women came up with the idea of a united *'Eid* (Islamic holiday) prayer in which all of the *masjids* would pray together. When she brought the idea to her imam, it was rejected. Women from the other *masjids*, not a part of the WCIW, also came back with negative responses from their imams. "They basically all said, No." Ten years later these same imams decided to organize a united *'Eid*. Naomi felt that an otherwise great idea had been rejected because it was proposed initially by women.

Hasanah Ali[62] describes the space in which women found themselves. "The freedom was there. It was still a struggle, but at least the earth had kind of cracked open a little bit. The seedlings were coming up albeit there was a culture that was also competing to let things go back to business as usual." Hasanah was the chairperson of her local CERWIS chapter, where the participating women put emphasis on programs to nurture stronger families as a corrective to the Nation culture, in which men were "too busy" selling newspapers with the result that they did not properly nurture "family life and marriage." The dichotomy between women's work in the home and men's work in the public domain was softened when Imam Mohammed removed sales quotas and encouraged men to help their wives with housework.

According to Hasanah, "There were sisters here and in other cities who were really hungering for an organized effort to enrich family life." Hasanah used CERWIS as the platform for this effort but indirectly met resistance from imams who "didn't necessarily want to see CERWIS flourish." Hasanah's CERWIS chapter organized family days at the mosque, where workshops were held on the topic of improving marriages. "We were trying to spark change, but we had to use delicate and real diplomacy because the brothers did not necessarily want to see those changes." Because Imam Mohammed had established CERWIS, the committee escaped outright resistance. "Here is Imam Mohammed's model, so who can [openly] come against it. That was Allah's way of buttressing it." Instead of any direct resistance from imams, Hasanah observed a pattern in which "every time CERWIS was putting on a program, believe it or not, the *masjid* would plan something at the same time to force the community to not support the CERWIS event. So it wasn't so much the community, but there was a germ that did not want to see the healing worked on anyway."

Hasanah's CERWIS chapter did not last beyond the early 1980s. However, as Hasanah puts it, "at least the earth had kind of cracked open a little bit." The new gender philosophy and the concrete actions Imam Mohammed made to implement the philosophy ultimately set in motion increased opportunities for women to influence and lead their communities on a national and local scale. As mentioned previously, other Muslim women's groups later emerged that were founded by women. Women learned to organize and sponsor events outside the *masjid* to circumvent any resistance. However, the people participating in these events were members of the *masjid* community. This continuity in audience allowed women to continue to serve, teach, and influence their religious communities. But even within the *masjids* led by imams who initially did not support CERWIS, over time women took on major leadership roles. Women's growing influence, participation, and leadership were inevitable because of several factors, including Imam Mohammed's model; his mainstreaming of the group, which meant that community members reassumed gender roles and attitudes favorable to women in the larger society; and his building upon women's legacy of leadership and work in the NOI. The men were busy Nation building in public but so were the women in MGT. With the creation of national WCIW committees and efforts such as Sister Clara Muhammad School that depended on women's and men's participation on the local level, women could not be prevented from continuing their legacy of activism in their *masjid* communities.

Women Worshippers: Dress and the Practices of Sunni Islam

Within the first year of the transition, Imam Mohammed introduced the five pillars of Islam: testimony of faith (*shahadah*), prayer (*salat*), fasting (*sawm*), charity (*zakat*), and the pilgrimage to Mecca (*hajj*). The Nation community previously observed its month of fasting every December, but in 1975, the community would fast a few months earlier. In that year, the month of Ramadan occurred in the summer. Joining Sunni Muslims who fasted during this sacred month on the Islamic lunar calendar, Nation members observed their first summer fast, which required longer hours of fasting in the heat, and demonstrated their commitment to new Islamic practices only six months after the passing of Elijah Muhammad.

Generally, Sunni women adjusted favorably to the five pillars of Islam as well as to the Qur'an, the Prophet Muhammad, and women's dress. The charity requirement, 2.5 percent of one's wealth after expenses, proved no hardship for most. As for the pilgrimage to Mecca, the overwhelming majority did not make the *hajj* until after 1980, although Imam Mohammed led a delegation of 300 from his community in 1977, at that time the largest group to travel from the United States. Ayesha Mustafa was a part of this group.[63] Women who made the *hajj*, then or later, speak about it in glowing terms as an affirmation of faith. "Hajj was wonderful," describes one woman. "I think that's what made my roots deeper into Islam."

Women scarcely express any hardship with reading the Qur'an. Although reading the Qur'an was not encouraged in the Nation, as noted earlier, some had already read parts of it before the transition. One woman describes, "The perception of what you were reading was through a lens of Nation of Islam teaching, so now you have to put on a lens totally inclusive of all humanity." Also, reading the Qur'an in its entirety was something most had not done until the transition. A few expressed some hardship with the Qur'an in the beginning, like the woman who says that she was "disappointed" that it did not have the narrative style of the Bible.

Rarely do women state that they had a difficult time with the Qur'an's controversial verses related to women, for example the verse (Qur'an 4:34) that outlines steps for a husband to address a wife who severely jeopardizes the marital union. Women describe coming to an "understanding" of such difficult verses, offering common explanations found in American Muslim discourses or feminist readings of the Qur'an. Referring to the verse permitting polygyny, Fareedah Pasha says that the "understanding" made "it a lot easier" to accept. "If you say you're a Muslim, you accept everything in the Book, but it's getting to that level of understanding too that allows you to accept it. . . . So I do thank Allah for that because [polygyny] was a kind of tough one."

Women generally describe in positive terms learning about the Prophet Muhammad. Fareedah provides historical detail on the imam's gradual introduction of the Prophet Muhammad during the early stages of the transition:

We used to say, "In the name of Allah . . . ," and then we'd thank Him for His messenger, the Honorable Elijah Muhammad. But now when Imam Mohammed would open up . . . when he came to [the word] messenger, he would say, "His messenger Muhammad," and then after a few times he would say, "And I mean the Prophet Muhammad ibn Abdullah," and then everybody would say, "Aaahh."

Jessica Muhammad's sentiments of initial hesitation in embracing the Prophet Muhammad are unique and interesting. "There was a little bit, just a little bit, of my baggage [based on] my love for Africa. There was some tendency in me to want everything to be Black, and just a little hard at first in the beginning to get into the Prophet, but of course I fell in love with him [when I did]." Imam Mohammed recommended that community members read the biography *Life of the Prophet* by Muhammad Haykal. It was the biography of the Prophet and not so much collections of *hadith* (statements made by or about the Prophet Muhammad) that women studied early on. Some state that they "were more into the Qur'an than the *hadith*."

The two pillars on which women comment the most are prayer and fasting. The hardest one by far, though not necessarily hard for everyone, was prayer. Women note that prayer was introduced in the Nation of Islam, but it was more akin to prayer in Christianity in which parts of the Qur'an were recited, but only in the standing position, and only in the morning and night or when having a meal or congregating at the temple. With *salat*, there was bowing and prostrating. The prayer had to be recited in Arabic, although Imam Mohammed stressed learning the English meaning to gain the greatest benefit. It was the *salat* "times"— that is, the requirement to pray five times a day during specific intervals of the day—that made prayer a hardship for some women. One woman notes, "The biggest issue with the prayers was figuring out how to get them all in. Doing a formal thing five times a day was different and it did have its challenges." Working women especially found it difficult as it was not easy to find a private location to worship while on the job or to carve time out for it. But even for women at home with children, the new obligation could be trying. A mother at home states, "The excuse of having children and being bogged down with everyday chores was big enough for me to keep from establishing my five prayers." It took her fifteen years to gain the conviction to do it. "I decided that I was going to pray no matter what and that meant stopping on the highway and getting out on the side of the road." Other women found a sense of satisfaction with the new prayers from the very beginning. Another mother at home states, "By the time you get moving around and doing this and that and the other, and you don't focus as much on Allah as you *could*, and when it's time to stop and pray, you go right back to thinking about Allah."

Most women found fasting in the month of Ramadan easy to get used to because the Nation had already prepared them for fasting. There were three types of fasting in the Nation as described in Elijah Muhammad's *How to Eat to Live*. The first type was eating one meal a day. The second type was fasting over an extended period once every month, "three days, four days, or for whatever length of time you are able to go without harming yourself." Water and coffee, the latter without or with very little sugar and cream, were allowable during both of these fasts. Both were associated with medicinal, healing, or life-extending purposes, whereas the third type of fast, the December fast meant to diminish Nation members' attachment to the Christmas holiday season, had an explicitly spiritual component. Elijah Muhammad wrote, "Waste not your earnings in such ways as worshipping and feasting as the Christians do. . . . In this month of fasting, we should keep our minds and hearts clean. . . . In this month we should keep our minds on Allah. . . . Keep up prayer. . . . And during this month, let there be no quarrelling and disputing in our homes or abroad."[64] With Imam Mohammed, the spiritual dimension was enhanced as women strove to read the Qur'an in its completion, a Ramadan goal that the imam encouraged as though it were mandatory. Also like Ramadan, the December fast was a daily fast for a month. However, several women considered the Ramadan fast to be easier because the December fast as they practiced it did not include *suhur*, a meal taken before dawn. Women recall simply waking up in the morning and not eating or drinking until dark. Also, the time to break the fast in the evening was unclear. Women describe guessing the time at which it was no longer daylight. This aspect also made the Ramadan fast easier because women now knew exactly when to eat—at sunset.[65]

Dress is the most apparent dimension of women's Islamic practice. In the Western media, Muslim women's dress has been depicted as a symbol of their oppression. However, when asked about the new dress as Sunni Muslims, constantly women use terms of liberation: "I felt free," or "It was freedom," or "It was a relief." Of course, most Sunni women speak favorably about the new dress requirements because they are comparing them with their Nation uniforms. Deborah Davis's comments demonstrate women's affinity for the uniform, some women's opposition to the change, and her personal reason for embracing the change: "When we were in uniform, we were respected in New York, very well respected. So we're out of uniform now, and people don't necessarily know why. Some people were very upset about that. Oh my God, they were so upset. But it didn't bother me because you have freedom now in expressing yourself. It was freedom."

Amatullah Um'rani even describes the uniforms as oppressive, but not in the sense that Muslim women's dress is customarily imagined so: "I remember my hair being completely wet because of the headpieces [the fez in particular]. Somebody thought that the plastic, inner lining held the shape really well, and it did look nice, but some of the uniforms were oppressive." In contrast to imagined notions of Muslim women's oppression in popular culture based on portrayals of Muslim women as gloomy and solemn in black garments, the oppression that Um'rani describes is analogous to that of women's wearing high heels for fashion and beauty. Nation women viewed the uniforms, particularly the

Marjorie Karim, of Atlanta,
in MGT uniform, 1975

Jeanette Nu'Man, MGT lieutenant in Atlanta, wearing uniform with cape for security
duty, 1974

The Vanguard, the drill team unit of MGT, in pant-skirt uniform, Harlem, 1971

fez style, as quite fashionable and beautiful. As Fareedah recalls, "I couldn't wait to get into mine when I was a pre-teen." But even the more glamorous sides of the uniforms—the eye-catching colors, including white, pink, lavender, lime, and yellow, and the coordination between color and occasion, that is, a specific color for a particular event, day, or entire week depending on the temple and the time period—"could become expensive," notes Fareedah. "It was a relief for me not to have to try to keep up with it."

Women's positive comments about dress also result from the way in which Imam Mohammed introduced the change. The move away from the uniform reinforced one of the defining values characterizing his new teachings: the value of the human intellect. Ana remembers the imam's saying, "Wearing a uniform is not the essence of the human being." Safiyyah Shahid recalls a similar emphasis on the God-given capacity of the intellect:

> Initially that was a big thing for us, how we were going to express our-
> selves when so many of those shackles so to speak had been taken off. In

the Nation of Islam it was defined. You wore this. . . . But [now what was emphasized was] your ability to express how you did that; that you were free to come to your own interpretation. So, [Imam Mohammed] didn't give you a garment. He didn't say you couldn't wear makeup. He didn't even say you had to wear a scarf.

Modesty was still emphasized as an Islamic value, but women could now wear mainstream clothes. Women were happy to design new styles or shop at the store. Amidah Salahuddin notes, "Imam W. D. Mohammed eliminated the garments in the Nation of Islam [as part of] transitioning us to become more Americanized so that we would fit into American society and in our workplace and not seem as though we were different."

Women in the WCIW developed a unique form of dress that continues to set them apart as women under the leadership of Imam Mohammed. This distinction results from the challenge he left for women to figure out for themselves how to create a uniquely American or African American Muslim style. This was very different from other Sunni African American Muslims at that time, who simply adopted the dress styles of other Muslim cultures. "The challenge," Jeanette Nu'Man describes, "was trying to figure out what to wear that was appropriate and understanding the Qur'anic guidelines in terms of what modesty really means." Fashion shows became popular in the community, recalls Fareedah, as Imam Mohammed invited fashion designers to "come forward with some ideas." The two *hijab* styles that evolved and most set this community apart were the "scarf," a square scarf folded into a triangle and tied around the back, and the "headwrap," or *gele*. Early on, some women wore the scarf loosely tied with bangs slipping through the front. Eventually more women adopted the headwrap, which Jessica describes as a peculiar trend in which women went from the very conservative uniform headpiece to a more relaxed version—that is, the lightly tied scarf—to a more conservative form in which women again covered all of their hair in the headwrap or the scarf. Here is why she moved to the headwrap: "For many of us, it was getting back to a personal identification or expression of our covering. For instance, a lot of us were Afrocentric and chose to use more African ways of covering versus looking at Chicago [namely, the *Bilalian News*] for our style.

And then the fashion started kicking in and we saw different ways of expressing our modesty." Jeanette also chose the headwrap because she had worn Afrocentric clothing in college prior to joining the Nation. While Jessica and Jeanette were embracing their African heritage in Atlanta, Amidah observed women in the WCIW being influenced by a variety of ethnic Muslim groups in the more cosmopolitan setting of Harlem:

> We had the Senegalese sisters with all their headwear on. And then we had a lot of the immigrant sisters from Pakistan . . . and Egypt. So the *khimar* [a *hijab* with the material draped beyond the neck, either to the back or the front] came in and sisters were doing that beautifully. . . . We had so many influences that you could pretty much [come up with any style]. And then we had sisters like Lubna, African American sisters who were designers coming up and developing their own fashion wear for sisters of African American background, so that they have their own expression.

American clothes, either store-bought or handmade, eventually predominated as the style that came to characterize women in Imam Mohammed's community, but because of modesty requirements, even the American clothes took on a uniquely African American Muslim expression. "Short dresses over pants," recalls Fareedah, were an example. "They were very attractive." On top of such modest arrangement of garments, the headwrap mostly, but also other *hijab* styles, would unmistakably mark these women as Muslim, which most women desired.

To be certain, women who chose to wear a *hijab*, the case for the majority of those in our interview sample, chose for themselves. Imam Mohammed did not demand the wearing of the *hijab*, though his community of women followers has mixed reports about this fact. Several women state that the imam never said that women did *not* have to wear a *hijab*. Several others report that he absolutely did relax the requirement. Islah Umar states, "I remember that being said [that women did not have to wear a hair covering]. Now everybody had their own theory as to what he was getting at, but that was expressed by him." Islah's report is confirmed by recorded lectures of Imam Mohammed: "I suggest that when you come to prayer in the mosque, that sisters cover their hair. . . . But when you're out in the public . . . you're going shopping or something like that, in my opinion, it's no big deal. . . . Just be decent and modest."[66] Here is a clear example of how Imam Mohammed was independent in his thought, not always guided by traditional, mainstream Islamic views. Allowing women to uncover their hair in public is certainly a minority position among Muslim scholars. Interestingly, how women responded to Imam Mohammed's allowance proves that he had succeeded in his goal to see his followers interpret the religion for themselves. Fareedah's words support Islah's suggestion that people came to their own conclusions as to the broader message that Imam Mohammed was sending when he did not enforce the wearing of the *hijab*:

> I think there was a small controversy about that, but it [not covering] was not really observed . . . because we had the school, and we're trying to teach the children to cover. . . . And he wasn't saying anything [different from what] . . . we already know as Muslims, that there's nothing compulsory. Allah says he didn't make this [religion] as a burden on us. . . . So, I think from that standpoint, he was giving an understanding: don't make it a burden on yourself, and don't try to prove to someone else that you are Muslim by wearing the headpiece. Start with here [pointing to her heart] first. . . . Don't get so tied up into the dress; get the other part first; the rest will follow.

Interestingly, when Sunni women describe the new approach to dress as "freedom," it does not necessarily mean that they were waiting for the moment to take off their scarves. Judith Saleem[67] states that the imam's changes on dress provided "a sense of independence that I could make up my own mind." She chose, however, to hold fast to the practice of covering. "I don't know what they are thinking," she says, referring to women who no longer wear the *hijab*. "But I still feel that part of my religion from the First [the old Nation of Islam]. I still cover completely when I go out. . . . The hair attracts men [and] . . . I don't want nobody looking at me."

Of course, a large number of women decided not to commit to the practice of wearing the *hijab*, during the transition or in later years.

Jessica explains her choice, saying, "I understand my Muslim dress to be more about *taqwa* [God-consciousness] than external dress":

> Imam Mohammed made it plain that there was no compulsion in the *din* [religion], and that we had freedom to express ourselves, and that we would be judged for where we are, and that we weren't going to be thrown out of the community for not having the same views, and so, that was all I needed [to make my decision] because I believed in . . . the need for me to be self-expressed in order to be healthy. . . . So when Imam Mohammed explained that *taqwa* was our dress, [that was freeing for me].

As we have seen, it was the foundation which the Nation of Islam laid for its women followers that made the transition generally easy and positive for many. An important part of this foundation was the NOI legend suggesting that Wallace was chosen to continue his father's work. Sandra Shabazz, of Jacksonville, Florida, states very simply that following Imam Mohammed was easy because "we were taught to respect leadership." Although Imam Mohammed strove to make his followers independent thinkers, their old Nation disposition to follow a leader whom they felt to be divinely selected aided him in the transformation. And certainly, he was transformative in ushering in a new gender philosophy and practice, but this transformation was built on what these women had already achieved and represented. Essentially, he built upon what women like Ana Karim, Amatullah Um'rani, Ayesha K. Mustafa, Khayriyyah Faiz, and Jeanette Nu'Man brought in terms of education and experience, but also he spoke to the sentiments and strengths of the countless Nation women who interpreted and actualized for themselves the Nation gender ideology as we saw in the previous chapter, not leaving it to their husbands, ministers, or sister captains always to set terms for them. At the same time, Imam Mohammed's lifting certain gender structures of the Nation and teaching against certain gender attitudes provided women with greater agency and power to truly see a transformation. Similarly, the general ease that women had transitioning to the five pillars of Islamic practice is partly attributed to their Nation foundation. Even the hair covering of Sunni Islam, often hard to wear in American society, was a breeze for many who had previously worn an uncomfortable fez. As scholar of the NOI Edward Curtis states, "Discipline, ritual, and purification were essential elements of practicing Islam for many believers associated with the NOI in the 1970s. In fact, for some Muslims, the focus on a disciplined religious practice even preceded their conversion to Islam."[68] In the next chapter, we turn to the women who did not follow Imam Mohammed but joined Minister Louis Farrakhan in his Resurrected Nation. Based on women's accounts and their contributions to the Resurrected Nation, we also discover transformation, but again, built upon the legacy of the old Nation of Islam dedicated to bringing better opportunities and conditions for African American women and other women of color in America.

3

Resurrecting the Nation

Women in Louis Farrakhan's Nation of Islam

I have never seen men treat women with such respect prior to coming into the NOI. I didn't have a healthy concept of men before coming into the NOI and I certainly didn't have a healthy concept of myself as a woman. . . . Because of what I know now and what I have been taught about the roles and the nature of male and female, . . . I have come to fall in love with myself as a woman and to fall in love with the man that I was to marry.
—Khaleelah Muhammad, J.D.

It gave me joy to get to be a "woman" for once. Not to worry about having to be "strong" as we are taught from an early age as Black women in our communities. The Nation teaches that men are the keepers of women. For the first time I was able to lean on a man, while being a woman. . . . Since my husband was responsible for the bills, I didn't have to figure things out. As time passed I was able to pursue more education and develop my interests and talents.
—JayVon Muhammad

A Woman shall rise as high as her God-given gifts and talents allow her in her own interest and in the interest of her Nation within the framework of the laws of Islam. Any action, inaction or course of conduct on the part of any Registered Muslim, which impedes or opposes the provisions of this Article, shall be considered an offense against the purposes of the Muhammad Mosque.
—Mosque Constitution

My wife is a really good example of being a Muslim and a counselor. . . . My biggest struggle that I overcame was not being so militant as it relates to home life. I had to work [at] not trying to have my wife as my "first officer" and my children as "squad leaders." My wife was hurt and cried a lot and I didn't understand. I had to realize that this was not FOI class. . . . That was my biggest problem. . . . So she graduated from saluting me to giving me hugs . . . . We are teammates. We are to help each other become one with Allah.
—Minister Nuri Muhammad

Khaleelah is a passionate community activist who negotiates her working day between the NOI and managing a community project at St. Sabina's Catholic Church on the South Side of Chicago. Khaleelah's journey to the NOI is atypical in that she left Sunni Islam for the NOI. She took her *shahadah* (confession of faith) while in college and practiced Sunni Islam for just over a year at the Central Illinois Mosque before joining the NOI at the age of nineteen. Khaleelah comments that while at the mosque she often felt like a "third wheel" and was kept at arm's length by her immigrant Muslim sisters. She came to the conclusion that the "ladies did not want to pray" beside her because of her skin color. In Louis Farrakhan's NOI, Khaleelah found an organization that spoke to the realities of her experience as an African American woman. For Khaleelah, however, the NOI was also a space in which her talents and passion for community work could be used effectively. Khaleelah is currently active in the Inner-City Muslim Action Network (IMAN), as are several NOI members. Their work for the nonprofit organization forms part of the Nation's outreach and social activism, which cuts across racial and religious lines. The Nation's female membership consists of professionals, entrepreneurs, stay-at-home mothers, educators, artists, and writers. Nation women in Minister Louis Farrakhan's group exercise considerable influence and authority at both the local and national level. Their elevation to positions of leadership within the group is a result of their collective efforts to break down barriers of exclusion through local chapters of the MGT. Equally, however, it reflects Minister Farrakhan's willingness to revise the NOI's gender norms in order to make the Nation more appealing to women. Nation members are encouraged to perform traditional gender roles, as evidenced by JayVon's comments at the start of this chapter. However, the Nation's gender dictates, dress code, and dietary laws are not rigorously enforced. Nation women's rights are enshrined in the Mosque Constitution. It is important to note that this has enabled women to hold controversial and influential positions, including that of mosque minister. Farrakhan's gender ideology contains a heavy dose of patriarchy that appears tempered by a commitment to gender equality. Yet men's interpretations of patriarchy can still leave Nation women vulnerable, as evidenced by Minister Nuri Muhammad's comments. The NOI is officially led by

Minister Farrakhan, but its day-to-day operations for the past several years have been managed by a two-tier executive board. The executive board, or Council of Laborers as it is known within the NOI, is made up of both men and women. These women will prove fundamental in nominating a successor to Minister Farrakhan and in the power struggles that may follow. The promotion of women to ministerial and managerial positions within the Nation should not be read as evidence that they are represented in equal number to their male counterparts. Indeed, from the perspective of current Nation women, the need to have more women involved in ministry remains paramount.

Rebuilding the Work of the Honorable Elijah Muhammad

Susan[1] was fifteen years old when the Honorable Elijah Muhammad passed away. The NOI had been her "world" and "way of life." Susan attached particular pride to the Nation's dress code and business acumen. The theological and structural changes that Imam Mohammed implemented devastated Susan. The demilitarization of the FOI and the removal of penalties that had previously regulated her father's behavior resulted in the breakdown of her family unit. Susan describes how the changes that Imam Mohammed implemented affected her and other Nation families:

> There was an effect on all the families. We all as young women used to wear our little uniforms to school and be at the mosque all the time. Then all of a sudden we became a part of the world in general, and I remember we would go to the skating rink and skate in Atlanta, and we went from wearing our pantaloons to wearing tight jeans overnight because we were told to take off the garment. I saw in my own family just the breakdown of the family unit. My father went back to his old ways for a couple of years because he was basically a street guy. It was a process that took some years, but what had held the families together was the strong restrictions that Muslims had in the NOI to keep them balanced, and without the restrictions, they became imbalanced again. . . . At one point I really hated what Wallace had done. It was a very emotional time for me as a young woman. I was off at college, and I was just looking at the deterioration going on with all my friends and family, and at that

point, I really began to hate what he was doing. It went from not [only] his dismantling of the teachings of the Honorable Elijah Muhammad but [his] dismantling all of the work that the believers had built up over the years and [his] dismantling and closing down all the businesses. All of the things that we had worked so hard for were just all gone; all of our farm land was taken away for taxes in Georgia and Alabama. There were restaurants and bakeries all through the Black community where Black people could feel like at least somebody is doing something in our community, and all [of] that was sold off and given away. . . . There are scars that I have regarding Wallace because it was real ugly for a while. I remember being in the mosque after Wallace came and a lot of ugliness started to develop. I remember being fifteen and a fight breaking out in the mosque I was in because of this difference in ideology, and so at one point, my brother was still following Wallace, and I wrote him a letter and I told him I would never [set] my foot into a *masjid* ever again.

As we have seen, many women welcomed and readily embraced the changes that Imam Mohammed introduced. Yet for Susan, her family, and indeed many of her friends, the changes were upsetting and resulted in fractured family units. Her brother's conversion to Sunni Islam under Imam Mohammed's tutelage drove a wedge between him and family members who refused to accept Sunni Islam. Of particular note, in Susan's narrative we can see that much of the anger she felt for Imam Mohammed was spurred by the collapse of the Nation's structures and the breakdown in the relationship with her brother. Susan construed the liquidation of the Nation's businesses as an attempt to erode the visible gains the Nation had made under Elijah Muhammad. Outside observers also expressed a feeling of regret at the liquidation of NOI businesses. *New York Times* reporter Paul Delaney quoted one onlooker in 1978 as commenting, "The printing plant and presses should not have been sold. There are very few Blacks who own that kind of equipment. They could've pooled resources with some of the Black publications to keep it under Black control."[2] Similarly, in 1975 the *Chicago Defender* reported, "The vast majority of Blacks look upon the success of the Nation of Islam with pride. Indeed, it is becoming more and more a role model for Black entrepreneurship."[3] Conversations with families like Susan's convinced Minister Louis Farrakhan that he would have sufficient support in his efforts to rebuild the original Nation. Susan comments, for example, that when Minister Farrakhan visited her family to discuss rebuilding the Nation, her first response was, "What took you so long?" Farrakhan's reasons for defecting from the WCIW in 1977 included dissatisfaction with the theological and structural changes that swept through the organization and a lingering suspicion as to the role that external forces may have played in promoting the demise of the Nation.

Minister Farrakhan emerged as a high-profile minister in the Nation in the early 1960s in Boston, where he presided over Temple No. 11. According to Farrakhan's biographer, Arthur Magida, the Boston temple grew exponentially under Farrakhan's leadership and included more college-educated members than any other temple.[4] Farrakhan joined the Nation in 1955 with his wife, Betsy (Khadijah). Prior to entering the Nation, he had been employed as an entertainer under the stage name "The Charmer." Farrakhan's career in the Nation continued to blossom following Malcolm X's assassination. Elijah Muhammad positioned Farrakhan as Malcolm's successor. Indeed, he inherited a number of Malcolm's jobs, including managing Temple No. 7 in Harlem and the post of National Minister. Farrakhan's high profile in the Nation convinced many that he would become Elijah Muhammad's successor.[5] Imam Mohammed's succession ended Farrakhan's prospects in the Nation. Shortly after assuming office, Mohammed transferred Farrakhan from his power base in Harlem to Chicago, where an administrative job awaited him. Mohammed explained Farrakhan's move to Chicago as an attempt to separate him from "negative influences" in New York.[6]

There can be little doubt that the demotion upset Minister Farrakhan. The embarrassment he suffered as a result of the demotion was further exacerbated when Mohammed instructed him to publicly orchestrate the renaming of Temple No. 7 in Harlem in honor of Malcolm X. Farrakhan was not displeased with all of the changes that Mohammed introduced. In interviews with *Africa Overseas Magazine* in 1975, for example, he commended Wallace for what he described as a "profound teaching on women in general."[7] Nevertheless, Farrakhan defected from the WCIW in late 1977. In explaining his defection from the WCIW and Imam Mohammed, he later noted, "I told him that I would serve him, as I served his father, as long as I could see that he remain faithful to his father. . . . Thirty months later, I came to the conclusion that that was not best for me."[8] Farrakhan's early efforts to rebuild the NOI proved futile, and it was not until his liaison with Rev. Jesse Jackson in 1984 that he received any kind of mass media exposure.[9] A series of controversial college lectures, speaking tours, and propagation literature helped Farrakhan reintroduce the NOI to a new generation. However, it was ultimately the publicity surrounding the Million Man March in 1995 that helped Farrakhan to market the NOI to women and audiences beyond America's borders.

Farrakhan: Gender Ideology

Louis Farrakhan secured his place in history when he led the Million Man March in Washington, D.C., on October 16, 1995. The MMM witnessed the largest gathering of African American men in the history of the United States. For many, however, the most noticeable and contentious aspect of the March was the absence of Black women. The MMM was initiated by Farrakhan and organized by a broad coalition of the NOI, Christian clergy, and secular Black nationalist groups. It was Farrakhan, however, who made the decision to ban women from the March. In his address at the March, Farrakhan called on Black men to "atone" for their mistreatment of Black women. To his critics, the exclusion of women reaffirmed and added legitimacy to their charges that Farrakhan was a "blatant sexist."[10] The exclusion of women from the MMM shaped popular perceptions of Farrakhan and the NOI's gender norms. Missing from the avalanche of press reports covering the March was a serious attempt to consider the complexities of Farrakhan's gender ideology and, more important, its appeal to women. Farrakhan's gender ideology is informed by the protectionary ethos that was characteristic of Elijah Muhammad's NOI. However, a commitment to gender equality is evident within Farrakhan's discourse on male–female relationships and gender spheres. In his book *A Torchlight for America* (1993), Farrakhan comments, "We must respect and honor women if the nation is to be great. When we do not have a proper appreciation for women, this is reflected in women's roles in society. Women should be active in every field of endeavor except those that degrade them."[11] Farrakhan's ideas about the types of employment that degrade women have evolved since the publication of his book. His granddaughter's success in the modeling industry in particular seems to have helped revise his views on the profession.[12] Similarly, his adopted daughter's music career has also played some role in reshaping his rhetoric on women in the entertainment industry more generally. Farrakhan's rhetoric on the value of women enables him to promote an essentially patriarchal organization as a viable and attractive option for women. Unlike Elijah Muhammad, Farrakhan tends to address women directly and in gender-segregated settings:

> You are so valuable that a man should never have you just to have you. He's got to be worthy of you or he's not worth having you! [said the Minister]. There is hardly a man out here that's worthy of you giving away yourself to him. Now there are some out there worthy, but if you are not looking for worthy you will get what you get and you do not look for somebody worthy of you because you have no self-worth—so any man that looks or talks good gets you to lie down with him.[13]

Farrakhan's empathy for women is informed largely by the close relationship he shared with his mother, Sarah Mae Manning. Indeed, he often tells the story of how his mother tried to abort him no less than three times when he criticizes men for abandoning their pregnant spouses and when explaining that he is both pro-life and pro-choice.[14] In his writings, Farrakhan notes that women resort to abortion as a result of being abandoned by men. He comments, "She puts the thought of murder in her womb in response to your callous treatment of her and her pregnancy."[15] Undoubtedly, Farrakhan's gender ideology is informed by a deep-seated belief that social ills in Black communities and the exponential growth of matrifocal families can be reversed via the promotion of men fulfilling the traditional role of family provider. In his numerous lectures addressing gender spheres and what he construes to be "proper" gender roles, he comments that women are incapable of respecting men if they have to provide for them:

> There are many women today who are taking care of men because they oft-times have better paying jobs. Women are better trained and

oft-times better qualified. They have nice cars, homes or apartments, nice furniture, but, the thing that is missing in the home or apartment is a responsible man who is a provider and maintainer. So, some women go looking for a man and oft-times [are] taking care of him. There is no woman who could honor and respect a man that she is caring for. To her, he is like her little boy.[16]

This quotation hints at Farrakhan's belief that the breakdown of relationships between Black men and women results from a predicament wherein men are not able or willing to fulfill the role of family provider. In a 1994 lecture, this becomes clearer:

Brothers, what does it do to you as a man with your wife making more money than you? What does that do to your esteem, when you don't have a job and you've got to go to your girlfriend and beg to borrow money, or her car? You become like her grown child and her voice is not soft and sweet when she talks to you. . . . After a while, you ease out of the house; and you're down on the corner with the other brothers who are not working either. You're in the barber shop or in the pool room, talking stuff. You want to be a man, but you get to the point when you lose all hope. You get to the point when you don't expect anything better than what you already have. You live in a project house, where your mother lived, and your grandmother lived, so you say, "Aww man! I'm not going to get out of this." You don't even expect to get out of the condition that you're in. You've lost hope, and you've become so angry, so bitter, so filled with self-hate that a man can come in your community and sell you a gun. God did say that He would give you power, but when you put that gun in your hand, it gives you a false sense of power. And that sense of power, because of the condition of your mind, causes you to commit murder.[17]

We can see that Minister Farrakhan attributes family desertion directly to economic security and the failure to fulfill the role of family provider. According to Farrakhan's critique, these factors emasculate men and result in feelings of hopelessness and eventually to a life of crime. Farrakhan subscribes to a form of patriarchy that equates the performance of traditional gender roles with stable and productive family units. The number of African American female-headed house-holds grew significantly alongside the restructuring of the U.S. economy under the Reagan–Bush administrations. Indeed, this was also a time when the NOI began to grow quite considerably. According to religious studies scholars Mamiya and Lincoln, 22.4 percent of Black families were headed by a female in 1960. By 1983 this number had risen to 42 percent.[18] Lincoln and Mamiya explain this dramatic rise as occurring simultaneously with high rates of Black male unemployment. In 1984, for example, only 37 percent of Black men aged sixteen to twenty-four were employed, compared with 63 percent of white men.[19] Farrakhan's critique is informed by a realization of the unique challenges that insti-tutional racism and America's changing economy present Black men. His critique is one that speaks to the realities of contemporary Black life. Essentially this aids the Nation and its leader in making their mes-sage relevant to both men and women.

Implementing Gender Norms and Revising Boundaries

Minister Farrakhan's NOI encourages men and women to perform tra-ditional gender roles via MGT and FOI classes much in the same way that they did during Elijah Muhammad's reign. Propagation literature, including the NOI's newspaper *The Final Call*, encourages such gender roles but not to the extent that the *Muhammad Speaks* newspaper did.[20] However, there are important but often overlooked differences between Farrakhan's NOI and Elijah Muhammad's NOI, especially as the former relates to women. First, women are no longer required to wear the tra-ditional MGT uniform and hair covering at all times.[21] Second, while women are encouraged to marry within the NOI, they are no longer penalized for marrying outside the group or across racial lines. Indeed, Farrakhan acknowledges in his own writings that love "transcends race and color."[22] Third, attendance at MGT classes is no longer manda-tory and penalties are not rigorously enforced. Nation mosques oper-ate in New York, Chicago, Dallas, Philadelphia, Washington, Atlanta, and beyond. However, many Nation members are unable to engage regularly with one another because an NOI mosque may not oper-ate in their vicinity. For these members, attendance at MGT classes is almost impossible, and thus their interaction with the Nation tends to take place online and via irregular trips to NOI mosques in large cities.[23] Fourth, dietary laws are not enforced. Finally, the Nation's recruiting efforts are not directed solely at African American women. Native American women and Latinas form an important demographic within the Nation. These alterations can be read as evidence of a more progressive gender ideology. Equally, however, they also reflect the fact that Minister Farrakhan cannot enforce unpopular penalties and dictates on his followers in the same way that Elijah Muhammad did.

Why Do Women Join the NOI?

As noted previously, women were attracted to Elijah Muhammad's NOI primarily because it offered what they construed to be practical solutions to their shared experiences of racial discrimination and economic exploitation. The Nation's stringent gender ideology was rarely the foremost factor attracting women to the organization. The narratives of current Nation women reveal that their motives for joining Minister Farrakhan's NOI are very different. Their narratives show that they consider the gender ideology appealing. These women are attracted to the Nation particularly because of the protection and respect that they allege women are afforded within the group. NOI member Lorraine Muhammad, for example, notes:

> The value that the Nation put on women, I have not found that anywhere else. The minister talks about the value of the woman and the value of your womb and to hear that come from a man—it's one thing to hear that from a woman but to hear that from a man—is different. There is continual upliftment. Sometimes you find it hard to believe how valuable you are. It's overwhelming to believe how powerful we are as individuals.

Nation women like Lorraine tend to embrace and draw comfort from the gender ideals of the Nation. The opening remarks to this chapter by Khaleelah and JayVon illustrate that for these women the gender ideology is empowering. While it places their innate values as women on a pedestal, it does not confine or restrict them because of those very same values. In other words, the rhetoric of love and protection that the Nation espouses does not result in women's movements or opportunities being restricted or controlled in the same way that it did in Elijah Muhammad's NOI. Further, Nation women comment that the emphasis on men's fulfilling the role of family provider tends to free them from the burden of worrying about bills as evidenced by JayVon's earlier comments. It is important to note that the Nation's efforts to promote progressive patriarchal communities have not resulted in their female members' fleeing the job market. We find that the overwhelming majority of Nation women are either employed, in education, employed by the Nation, or self-employed. Today's Nation women are encouraged to pursue education and their entrepreneurial talents. Many of the women interviewed commented that they either entered education as a result of joining the Nation or pursued advanced degrees after joining. NOI member Theresa X notes:

> Today, I give all the credit to God and the teachings of the Honorable Elijah Muhammad as taught by the Honorable Minister Louis Farrakhan for what I have become and the fact that I was able to raise my children without becoming a statistic. I work in Corporate America for a Fortune 500 company; I completed an A.S. in Liberal Studies in 1999, a B.S. degree in Organizational Behavior in 2001 at the University of San Francisco (USF), and a master's in Organizational Development in 2004 also at USF.

The foregoing narratives highlight why women are attracted to Farrakhan's NOI. While we can see important differences between current and former Nation women, it is worth noting that these women do share some similarities, especially as these similarities relate to their position on the NOI's theology and do-for-self ethos. Women in Minister Farrakhan's NOI are much more familiar with Sunni Islam than their predecessors. Thus, when considering entering the Nation, many women are cognizant of the fact that the NOI's line of faith differs from that of their Sunni Muslim counterparts, as evidenced by Khaleelah's comments at the beginning of the chapter. Nation women consider these differences to be rather minimal and a matter of interpretation. The NOI's theology is rarely the primary motive prompting women to join the Nation. Like their predecessors, they consider the theology to be of secondary importance while attaching particular importance to the Nation's do-for-self ethos. The NOI's theology, like its gender ideology, has evolved. Whites are no longer routinely castigated as "white blue-eyed devils," and racial separation is not considered a primary goal, although it is something the Nation discusses at times of increased racial tension. Since the 1990s, Farrakhan has shied away from the "white devil" rhetoric of Elijah Muhammad. Indeed, he has often commented that Elijah Muhammad instructed him to stop using "the term devil" in the 1970s and instead to refer to whites as "the enemy" or "the slave master's children."[24] In interviews with NOI theologian Jabril Muhammad, Minister Farrakhan comments that a deeper study of Elijah Muhammad's teachings led him to the conclusion that "white people could be our brothers and sisters in faith, though not by nature."[25] It appears that the NOI's working relationship with Father Michael Pfleger at St. Sabina's Catholic Church has also helped to revise the group's critique of whites and Christianity. Father Pfleger has been and remains one of Farrakhan's strongest advocates in Chicago. The fact that he is Caucasian seems not to have caused concern among NOI members. Indeed, NOI members, and Farrakhan himself, refer to Pfleger as a "friend" and "brother." Farrakhan tends to explain Elijah Muhammad's teachings to the outside world as a kind of "Black theology" aimed at equipping African Americans to overcome the psychological effects of white supremacy.[26] Minister Farrakhan has made efforts over the course of the past two decades to integrate the NOI more fully into the American Muslim community and introduce Qur'an-based teachings. However, more often than not, he has reverted to the NOI's old theological teachings, thus failing to fully amend the NOI's theology. In 1994 Farrakhan reached out to the Islamic Society of North America (ISNA) for Islamic literature and advised that he would instruct his followers to observe Ramadan. ISNA later helped facilitate reconciliation between the NOI and the WDM community in February 2000 at the annual Saviours' Day convention. The relationship between the NOI and ISNA, however, remains strained as a result of Farrakhan's failure to bring the NOI fully in line with Sunni Islam.[27] Farrakhan's relationship with the American Muslim community may be strained, but his working relationship with Chicago's Black churches is by any measure quite positive. He is a regular speaker at Trinity United Church of Christ (TUCC), which until recently was led by Dr. Jeremiah Wright, and St. Sabina's Catholic

Church, which is led by Father Pfleger. The close relationship among the NOI, TUCC, and St. Sabina has resulted in some women's leaving TUCC for the NOI or the NOI for St. Sabina or TUCC. The relationship between the NOI and its Christian counterparts is based on a shared commitment to community development and "social issues" as highlighted in Father Pfleger's comments:

> I've been working with the Nation for the past 25 years or more. We work primarily on social justice issues, community development and building empowerment in the community, especially with African American males. We have workshops and different things in the church. Minister Farrakhan is one of my closest friends and mentors. He is somebody who is a great friend of mine, and I have great respect for his integrity, his passion and his courage. . . . I've had a couple of members join the NOI and I've had someone from the Nation join here. I don't see us as competing. I see us as committed to the same causes. We have some different religious beliefs, but beyond that there is not a contest between us.

While only a small number of women leave either of the aforementioned churches for the NOI, the relationship between the organizations is important. Not only does it broaden Farrakhan's support base, but it also prevents the NOI from operating in isolation as it did during Elijah Muhammad's reign. Many women who join the Nation are nominally Christian. Not all of these women abandon their Christian faith upon entering the Nation. Current NOI member A. Muhammad, for example, comments that she finds her "Christian beliefs" compatible with NOI teachings:

> I was a college student when I decided to submit my Will to do the Will of God. I had always attended church and then would visit the study group. I realized that Islam was a way of life and in no way conflicted with my Christian beliefs; it just supported them and gave me tools to actively carry them out into my life. The Honorable Minister Louis Farrakhan said that a "good Christian and a good Muslim" is one [and] the same. A Woman of God is a Woman of God. For example, if you look at the pictures of Mary the Mother of Jesus, she always is wearing a *hijab* or

head covering; nuns wear head coverings; Muslims wear head coverings. What do they all have in common? They are all striving to live lives in submission to God. In that case, I still consider myself a Christian who practices a peaceful way of life.

These comments may at first appear rather surprising. Yet they are telling for a number of reasons. They highlight that Nation women tend to synchronize their Christian faith with elements of NOI theology, thus dispelling the myth that Nation women are indoctrinated by the organization. They also illustrate the extent to which NOI theology and culture remain closer to Christianity than to Sunni Islam. And perhaps most important, A. Muhammad's comments, when compared with those of other Nation women, reveal that their religious beliefs differ rather strikingly. The religious beliefs of Nation women differ across and within regional boundaries. For while A. Muhammad describes herself as both Christian and Muslim, other Nation women hold fast to the belief that Fard Muhammad was Allah incarnate while others express beliefs that are more attuned to Sunni Islam. This suggests an important difference between Elijah Muhammad's NOI and Farrakhan's NOI. Women in Elijah Muhammad's NOI may have privately questioned the theology, but nevertheless the official line of faith was consistent. In Farrakhan's NOI, a consistent line of faith appears to be absent. Minister Farrakhan promotes himself as a Sunni Muslim when in dialogue with the Muslim world. Yet while lecturing from the NOI headquarters at Mosque Maryam, he presents a theology that is similar to old NOI teachings. Further, when speaking at surrounding Black churches in Chicago, he is at ease with basing his teachings almost exclusively on the Bible. The constant oscillation among NOI teachings, Sunni Islam, and Christianity has resulted in quite a diverse set of belief systems among NOI members. This pattern seems to result in women's having some degree of freedom to interpret and present their beliefs differently. The oscillation between Sunni Islam and Christianity opens opportunities for Nation women to work across racial and religious lines. Khaleelah, for example, is employed on a full-time basis at St. Sabina as a project manager. Her work at the church is a direct result of her connection to the NOI, as she explains:

My base is here at the faith community of St. Sabina. I'm here more than at the mosque. I reached out to Father Pfleger some years ago when we moved back to Chicago, and when I finished law school, I spent a year trying to figure out how to approach the violence issue in Chicago, and I had a hard time getting people on board, and then I thought about Father Pfleger whose name is synonymous with the Peace Movement, and so I emailed Father Pfleger and he said he would be glad for me to partner with him. He had been friends with Minister Farrakhan for a long time and in partnership with the Nation, and he wanted to include me in that partnership, and so I saw the Ministry of Justice in the NOI as a way to strengthen that partnership. I did not expect it to culminate in me working at St. Sabina.

Few Nation women engage in any meaningful way with their Sunni Muslim counterparts. Yet, the nonprofit Inner-City Muslim Action Network (IMAN) seems to be an exception. IMAN works at a grass-roots level to tackle social issues in urban communities. Most of the individuals who contribute to IMAN and work within the organization are Muslim. However, the organization welcomes involvement from non-Muslim volunteers and works across religious lines. According to its director, Rami Nashashibi, NOI members engage with IMAN because it does not require them to "check their faith at the door." NOI members consider IMAN to be an organization that works for "freedom, justice and equality."[28] It is on this basis that they engage with the organization.

Opportunities for Nation women to engage with different faith groups has expanded over recent years and more so since 2011, when Minister Farrakhan instructed his followers to embrace his newfound relationship with the Church of Scientology (COS) and in particular the practice of Dianetics. In recent years, Nation members have undertaken training in Dianetic Therapy from the COS. To date, more than 1,000 NOI members have gone through Dianetic training and have received a Gold Seal (certificate of completion) from the COS.[29] Auditing has become so widespread within the Nation that it is now a common feature of its annual retreats. Nation women appear to have embraced Dianetic Therapy. NOI member Amani Muhammad notes that the therapy is used to "assist" members to overcome "painfully stored emotion" and that it contributes to one's "finding oneself."[30] Yet, undoubtedly the NOI's recent flirtation with the COS will only widen the existing parameters in which NOI theology is understood and presented. While a general freedom to interpret and present the theology of the NOI alongside a more progressive gender ideology may attract women to the organization, there remain aspects of the group with which they feel some discomfort.

Nation Women's Dress

There remain numerous aspects of the NOI that women find less appealing and unattractive. The NOI uniform, male chauvinism, and the small number of women in ministry are features of the group that Nation women have been actively addressing and challenging. During the early years of the Resurrected NOI, and indeed even after the MMM in 1995, the MGT uniform and mandate that women cover their hair remained largely unchanged. A diverse set of opinions exists from women on the uniform. While some "love" the uniform and regard it as "directly from the mind of Allah," others find it restrictive.[31] NOI member Akilah Muhammad[32] joined the NOI in 1995. Her interest in the Nation developed over time after reading Malcolm X's autobiography and watching the MMM on television. With regard to the NOI's dress code, she comments that adopting the uniform is something that women struggle with and that others find unattractive:

> Automatically, initially, having to cover up—because of not knowing what that means and not knowing how to cover up—that's the number one thing [that is difficult]; we have to take these skinny jeans off. They want [you] to cover up the goodies. . . . It's not in your best interest safety wise [to wear revealing clothes]. It just doesn't register [at first] that this society is so ill, that men and women are so ill, and that if they can see you, they're going to want you and they are going to take you. These are protectionary measures.

Hair covering remained a distinguishable feature of the NOI's dress code during its early years, though it has become less common today. Nation women comment that covering their hair is something that they grow to accept. NOI member and founder of *Modesty International Magazine* Tamorah Muhammad remarks:

> Before I came into the NOI, I used to see the sisters with their head coverings, and I would say, "That's not me; I'm not going to be covering my head," and strangely enough, I [now] love the dress code. It's so modest, and it sets us apart from the world, and so many of us as sisters [Black women who are not Muslim] think that wearing shorts and tank tops is a way of modesty. . . . When I read what the dress code really represented, I was excited about it, and I can accessorize my garments with earrings and things of that nature.

Tamorah's and Akilah's comments illustrate that some women have been hesitant to embrace the full NOI dress code, which includes hair covering. Indeed, it is something that many Nation women comment "takes some getting used to." Nevertheless, they find their dress code more attractive than that of other Muslim women. Sarah Muhammad[33] exemplifies this sentiment when she notes, "We have a different form of dressing from orthodox Muslims so I would say that our dress is more attractive to women; we don't cover our face. We don't dress all in black." It is important to note that Sarah's comparison here is not with women in the WDM community. Hair covering is something the NOI encourages, but it is no longer rigorously enforced. It is not clear when rules surrounding the issue were relaxed or what part the MGT may have played in bringing about the relaxing of the dress code. Today's Nation women are regularly photographed without their hair covered. In a recent edition of *The Final Call* newspaper, Farrakhan's wife, Khadijah, was photographed with several Nation women advertising a selection of fashions that did not include hair covering. Indeed, only two out of the ten women pictured in the photograph had their hair covered.[34] Nation women's literature encourages hair covering. However, contemporary fashions for Nation women as advertised in Nation magazines often challenge the traditional dress code. NOI member Zenzile Muhammad outlines her struggle to keep her hair covered:

> I, as [a] Black [woman] in America, have honestly found it difficult at times to be consistent in keeping my hair covered because of fear of

rejection, feeling that I won't be accepted by my family or peers. This gradually lessened with time, study of the Word of God, assessing my own thoughts and experiences day-to-day. I am more resolved in living what I know to be true in His Word to His Divine Servants because by my seeking *His* Protection, Guidance, and Pleasure alone, I'm still sane, loved, healthy, and still here. You can say I'm more comfortable in the skin and veil I'm in.[35]

The demand for clothing that is modest but fashionable has over recent years led a small number of Nation women to venture into the fashion business. Khadijah Farrakhan's clothing line, Newell Apparel, has operated for some time, but only recently has it gained momentum. Newell Apparel tends to create clothing that is current and trendy but loose-fitting. The designs for the fashion line are created by Khadijah and NOI member Carmin Muhammad. The clothing line is based in Chicago, where it sells traditional MGT uniforms that are now available in several different colors. Newell Apparel is just one of many fashion outlets for Nation women. Queen Aminah's Clothing and Kameelah's Closet are two of the better-known designers for Nation women. Kameelah's Closet is designed by NOI member Valerie Muhammad and aims to let "a little girl be a little girl."[36] The clothing line was inspired by Valerie's struggle to find suitably modest clothes for her young daughter. Kameelah's Closet designs are featured regularly in Nation women's magazines. The Nation's fashion designers benefit exponentially from a preexisting consumer base and market. New designs have helped diversify the style and range of clothes that Nation women are encouraged to purchase. These fashions help challenge traditional dress codes that limited women to MGT uniforms, albeit in different colors. However, new fashions as advertised in Nation women's literature tend not to be easily identified as Nation clothing. Thus, unlike that of their predecessors, the clothing of contemporary Nation women does not immediately identify women with the organization. Nation women have been successful in revising the NOI dress code through their collective creativity. However, other aspects of the NOI have proven more difficult to challenge.

Interpreting Patriarchy and Challenging Sexism

The Nation has remained an essentially patriarchal organization. Women's opportunities in the Nation exceed those of their predecessors, but nevertheless men's interpretation of patriarchy can differ quite significantly and leave some women rather vulnerable as a result. Sexism manifests itself within the Nation in the form of women's being challenged or criticized when they assume a position of leadership or an unconventional role in the organization. For his part, Minister Farrakhan has attempted to counter more militant interpretations of patriarchy by promoting women to high-profile and controversial positions within the Nation. In 1998 he appointed NOI member and lawyer Dr. Ava Muhammad as an NOI minister in Atlanta. Ava may have been the Resurrected NOI's first female minister, but she was not to be the last. Farrakhan's daughter Donna Farrakhan Muhammad was also appointed as an NOI minister shortly after Ava's appointment. Further, Claudette Marie Muhammad was appointed as the NOI Director of Protocol and Public Relations in 1984.[37] Ava is a graduate of Georgetown University and a member of the New York Bar Association. She joined the NOI in the early 1980s while recovering from breast cancer. Ava appears to have shared a close relationship with Minister Farrakhan during her early years in the NOI. He explained Ava's appointment in *Closing the Gap* (2006) as the "will of Allah":

> Sister Ava Muhammad's appointment as a Minister over a mosque to head the mosque in teaching and administration is a sign that it is becoming time now for the female to come out into Allah's (God's) new world as well as to master the home to bring forth a brand new civilization. It is also a sign of the irreversible will of Allah (God) that nothing Satan can do will alter the establishment of Allah's (God's) will.[38]

Not all NOI members accepted Ava's appointment. Many current Nation women note with pride Ava's position, but they hesitantly admit that she "caught hell" from some Nation members as a result. Interestingly, when discussing the backlash against her appointment, Ava notes that much of the opposition came from other Nation women. In an interview with Ebony Muhammad for *Hurt 2 Healing Magazine*, Ava reflected:

> I faced tremendous difficulties in the post, as the appointment brought to the surface just how pervasive sexism is in the Nation of Islam as well as the Christian Church. One Pastor in Mississippi withdrew an invitation for me to speak at his church when he learned that Minister Farrakhan's Southern Representative was a woman. I don't know that I prevailed; the liberation of the female is a process. One of the greatest impediments to my ministry came from the women. Someone once said that members of oppressed groups often lead their own opposition. I found that to be true.[39]

Nation women regard opposition to Ava's appointment as coming largely from men. Mary Muhammad[40] comments below that Ava's treatment by men in Atlanta helped expose male chauvinism in the Nation:

> Male chauvinism exists but it's not meant to be a part of the NOI, but it is a part of individuals, and people bring that into the NOI, and that has to be corrected, and it is being corrected. One example that I can give you is that in our ministry class, most of the ministers are men and where are the women? . . . But the truth of the matter is we are allowed to join the ministry, and we do join, but we are not out in the forefront, and it's not that we can't be in the forefront. Our beloved sister Ava Muhammad; she is the first female in the Islamic world to be appointed as an imam so that was very good. When she was appointed as a regional minister in the Southern region, which is headquartered in Atlanta, she caught a lot of hell from brothers for that. That was not right, but it was a trial that she had to go through to expose, and for us to see, sexism, and it needs to be eliminated from the NOI and any society.

Nation women tend to accept that sexism is something they will encounter regardless of whether they are in the Nation, a *masjid*, or the church. They feel, however, that they fare better in the Nation than their counterparts in Christian and Muslim organizations partly because the NOI teaches men to value women. Sandra,[41] for example, comments, "There is sexism in every religion, class and country. It is going to take a great deal of time to bring men into the understanding of the value of the woman, but that is one of the attractive forces of the NOI, that men are being taught the value of women." Similarly, NOI member Laurie Goux comments:

> I love the NOI because women are treated in high regard. We sit to the side of the brothers, not behind or not allowed inside the mosque. We are protected by all FOI; it is their duty. The mosque in Chicago is named after a divine woman, Mosque Maryam, the mother of Jesus. The appointment of Minister Ava Muhammad was in divine order for us and for the Islamic world to see. She is brilliant and not afraid to speak the truth.

Nation women often comment that they would like to see more women become involved in the ministry classes. Opportunities for women to enter ministry remain open, yet few take advantage of the opportunity to become actively involved. The backlash against Ava's appointment as an NOI minister may well have deterred other women from joining the ministry class. However, as Khaleelah's comments indicate, many Nation women need to balance their time between work, family, and the NOI:

> What I would like to see is our concept of ministry changing. We have a lot of women who are involved in ministry but in the non-traditional sense. I wouldn't trade what I do any day for standing up and speaking at a rostrum. I feel like the most important part of ministry is in administering services. I feel like that's my role. As women we have to devote more time to study, and we don't necessarily devote the time to community that we should. I have been in ministry class since 1995 and it seems to me that there are always more women in there than men. But after leaving the class, the women have to maintain the home and work.

Competing demands on their time often result in Nation women's being unable to follow through with ministry class. Khaleelah's comments about community activism highlight her desire for more women to be active in their surrounding communities. As highlighted earlier, the majority of women interviewed are engaged in full-time employment. Thus, unlike their predecessors in Elijah Muhammad's NOI, they arguably have less time to devote to community work.

Community Activism

Nation women's work in their local communities is largely undocumented. Interviews with current Nation women reveal that they consider their efforts to reach their surrounding communities as an outgrowth of NOI teachings or the practical application of what they have learned in the organization. Community activism is not necessarily something that attracts women to the NOI. However, it does seem to take on greater importance for women once they become actively engaged with the organization. Those women who were active in Elijah Muhammad's and Minister Farrakhan's NOI tend to feel particularly passionate about community activism, as evidenced by Sudan Muhammad's narrative. Sudan was born into the NOI in 1969 in Philadelphia. Her father joined the Nation in 1953 and her mother in 1956. The death of the Hon. Elijah Muhammad proved to be upsetting for Sudan. She comments that after 1975 she began to attend public school while still wearing her NOI attire and, as a result, was teased and picked on by other students. Sudan credits her father as being instrumental in teaching her the importance of serving others. Sudan is a regular visitor at homeless shelters and hospitals in Washington, D.C. She has regularly provided food and toiletries to the homeless and those in need since 1999. For Sudan and her daughter Indigo, providing charity to others is something they feel blessed to do:

> I started in 1999—we were affiliated with the food bank at the mosque, and it was so much food, and there was case after case for 2–3 dollars, and I started taking grocery bags and making up bags of food, and I would deliver it to my neighbors, and the response I would get was just overwhelming and great. Then I would go out into the community once a week or once a month, and Allah blessed us. Actually, God is love, and you want for your brother and sister what you want for yourself. If you say having a nutritional diet is good for you, why not prepare it for somebody else? . . . The area we live in is predominantly bad so at Christmas we would go out and play music for the children, and we also taught basic piano lessons as well. We also do hair for a lot of the little

girls in the area. A lot of girls in the community are prostituting so that they can get money to get their hair done, and in the Black community hair weaves are big business . . . and a lot of these girls have sex just to get their hair done. A friend of mine had a friend who went out of business, and she gave me her supplies so we do hair. We also go to the hospitals and play the harp—Indigo actually trained her sisters to play, so we all go and play for service. My father was instrumental in teaching me how to serve our people. . . . The economy is so bad that everybody has had to come together. At the shelter there are Black, white, Asian and people from New Orleans because of [Hurricane] Katrina. We don't care about color or race—everyone deserves to have a decent meal, and a lot of the people we serve are so happy to see us because they say that what I love about you all is that you cook with such love, and you don't give us garbage.

Sudan describes the work she has been doing in the community as "underground." Other NOI members are unaware that she has been carrying out such work. In 2010 Sudan created a print magazine called *Youth Creation Community Outreach* (*YCCO*) to document her family's work in the community and to showcase the community work that young NOI members are engaged in. To date, Sudan and her daughter have published three issues of the magazine. Each issue of the magazine contains photos that document their community work and stories that highlight the importance of outworking their faith through serving others. *YCCO* magazine is essentially a way for Sudan to encourage others to serve their communities. As we can see in her narrative above, she works across racial and religious lines. The focus of *YCCO* is not necessarily propagation of NOI theology; interviews and comments within the magazine reveal a desire first and foremost to encourage others to serve their communities. In the April 2012 edition of the magazine, for example, Akilah Worthy exhorted readers to "extend your God given talents to those who need it" and to "turn business into the heart of the public."[42]

Sudan's work is not typical of Nation women's activism. Sudan's narrative illustrates that Nation women continue to make positive contributions to their communities while rarely having such work officially documented by the organization. The community activism that most

Sudan Muhammad, founder of *Youth Creation Community Outreach* magazine

Nation women engage in is irregular, on a smaller scale, or linked to their profession. JayVon Muhammad, for example, who was introduced at the outset of the chapter, developed and runs a nonprofit organization called Urban Midwifery. JayVon joined the NOI in San Francisco when she was twenty-one. Both her parents are biracial, and while she comments that the white members of her family had no problem with her involvement with the NOI, her African American family members disapproved. The primary appeal of the NOI for JayVon was its message of "Black empowerment." JayVon credits the NOI with having changed her life for the better. Her nonprofit organization provides prenatal care to young African American women and poor white women. JayVon comments that the organization serves an educational role and an outreach role also. She notes, "In the Black community, our families have fallen apart. . . . We don't have intact families so Urban Midwifery works to help young unmarried women." JayVon is aware of the fact that only a small portion of the Nation's female cohort engages in the kind of community work that she undertakes. She notes that Nation women are in no way restricted from pursuing such work but that their commitments to their families and homes often trump best intentions:

> I am pleased to say that women are represented in all areas of the NOI. Sister Ava Muhammad was even a Regional Minister in the Nation and minister of the Atlanta Mosque, which is huge. We have women doctors, attorneys, teachers, etc. . . . I would like to see more women in the Nation of Islam start organizations and get more into the communities. As women in the NOI, even though we are free to pursue our dreams, we understand that our most important role, next to being a believer/ Muslim, is wife and mother.

The foregoing narratives highlight a number of important issues. Unlike their predecessors, current Nation women's activism extends beyond the boundaries of the NOI's structures, and in this regard, they have much greater autonomy. The activism that Nation women like JayVon and Sudan engage in is largely independent of the NOI. And women's work in the community is not limited to one particular racial group. Both JayVon and Sudan reach out to and serve all sections of their communities, including whites. The activism that Nation women engage in provides further evidence of the evolution of the organization's ideas about gender and race. As we have seen, women in Elijah Muhammad's NOI were often limited to working within the NOI's structures as a result of dictates about the need to protect women. JayVon and Sudan are not chaperoned by the FOI while serving their communities, though Sudan's husband, Reamer, often helps her to distribute food parcels in the community. Thus, current Nation women no longer require the approval of men or the protection of the FOI before venturing out to embark on such work. The fact that Nation women work to serve the needs of whites also highlights the evolution of NOI teachings, especially as it relates to their early castigation of Caucasians as "white devils," a theme we will discuss further in the next chapter. Narratives from women like Sudan and JayVon serve as a corrective to popular depictions of Nation women as silent partners in the organization.

Nation Women and the Marches

The absence of Nation women from the MMM on October 16, 1995, has led to characterizations of them in popular discourse as agents of their own oppression and submissive actors within the overall movement. Missing from even the most objective assessments surrounding their absence from the March was a consideration of how they understood the ban and the various ways in which they helped organize and support the March. Nation women were instrumental in financing the MMM. Throughout 1994 Minister Farrakhan delivered a series of "Women Only" lectures to raise money for the March and to explain his reasons for excluding women. "Women Only" lectures proved popular with Nation women and indeed women on the fringes of the movement. Approximately 12,000 women attended Minister Farrakhan's "Women Only" lecture in Atlanta on June 25, 1994, and clearly not all of these women were members of the Atlanta mosque.[43] Again, here we see evidence of Farrakhan's appeal's stretching beyond the confines of the NOI. A number of factors account for Farrakhan's appeal to women outside the Nation and to those on the fringes of the organization. Perhaps most important, his lectures addressing the incarceration of African American men in numbers incongruous to their total population, the "crack epidemic," and the exponential growth of African American matrifocal families resonate with women. Farrakhan's critique of male misbehavior and irresponsibility helps to portray him as sensitive to women's concerns. His efforts to promote progressive patriarchal communities that do not infringe upon women's opportunities allow him to promote his message as both socially conservative and progressive.

Nation women were dismayed by their exclusion from the March, but nonetheless they were involved with organizing it at both the local and national levels. Indeed, as NOI member Susan notes, the NOI "can't pull anything off without the women."[44] Nation women construed the ban as a protectionary measure. Susan, for example, notes that the MMM was organized during the turmoil and racial unrest surrounding the trial of the African American sports star O. J. Simpson, who was facing charges for the murder of his white ex-wife. She comments that the MMM was organized during a time when "there was a lot of hatred for Black men," especially after Simpson was found not guilty by a jury of nine African Americans, two whites, and one Latino. Moreover, as Sarah comments, Nation women did have what she considers to be an "active role": "It wasn't that we were asked not to take part in the March. We were asked to stay home and support the men in getting there, and we had a very active role. It was a day for men, but there were ways for us to participate on that day, and we could watch."

Nation women promoted the MMM via community workshops and general grassroots organizing. NOI member Lorraine Muhammad, for example, notes that she helped to engage her community as did countless other Nation women:

> Locally, I helped participate in getting women where we lived engaged. We had local organizing committees where we tried to rally the community to support the March and help them understand the purpose and significance of the Million Man March, not only to the brothers attending, but to the sisters and families of the community and the world. I was pregnant at that time but we, as sisters, did whatever we could to help the brothers go.

Alongside women on the fringes of the movement, Nation women formed a nonprofit organization called Women in Support of the Million Man March (WISOMMM). The organization continues to work with social justice and community issues and is currently led by Frederica Bey, an irregular guest at Mosque Maryam. At the national level, NOI director of protocol Claudette Marie Muhammad served as the national deputy director of the March alongside Dr. Benjamin Chavis.[45] High-profile figures—including Malcolm X's widow, Dr. Betty Shabazz, and Winnie Mandela, the former wife of then–South African President Nelson Mandela—addressed participants at the March. However, only a handful of women were present at the event, including some Nation women who managed to sneak along. Nation women remain instrumental in archiving material from the MMM and influencing the ways

in which its legacy is documented. NOI film producer Angela Muhammad, for example, is currently working on a documentary titled *The
Million Man March: The Untold Story*. Angela joined the Nation in
1994 in Washington, D.C., after completing her undergraduate degree
in film production. After starting her own company, Vanguard Television, she set out to independently produce films and documentaries.
She describes how the idea for the documentary exploring women's
involvement in the MMM came about:

> One of the sisters came to me about three years ago about commemo-
> rating the 15th year of the MMM and one of our interviewees said the
> MMM is so much bigger than 15 years and you have to tell the untold
> stories and that's how we came up with the name. It is just to highlight
> some of the people who worked behind the scenes and to follow up with
> those people and it's also to leave a document for future generations
> because eventually those in the MMM will not be here.

The full extent of women's contributions to the MMM has yet to be
documented. Nonetheless, documentaries such as Angela's will prove
important in terms of how the NOI preserves the legacy of the March
and how women's contributions to the March will be considered.

Nation women were behind the scenes when it came to the MMM,
but their presence was more pronounced at the Million Woman March
in 1997 in Philadelphia. The Million Woman March was organized
by community activists Phile Chionesu and Asia Coney. The idea for
the MWM did not originate within the NOI, and the majority of the
women who attended were not NOI members. Nevertheless, Nation
women's presence at the March was noticeable. Farrakhan's wife, Khadijah, addressed the crowd and called for the women present to confront
family and domestic issues. During her address she commented, "A
nation can rise no higher than its women. . . . [W]e focus on women
but we cannot lose sight that we must rise as a family: men, women and
children."[46] Other speakers at the MWM included actress Jada Pinkett
Smith and R&B singer Faith Evans. Perhaps one of the most important
but understated outcomes of the MWM was the fact that it appears to
have integrated Nation women with secular women's organizations. The
event certainly inspired Nation women and encouraged them to pursue

avenues of self-empowerment and empowering others as evidenced by their narratives. Lorraine, for example, comments that it "continued to show our unity and solidarity of not only the MMM but of the women and our need to support one another and our community."

Nation women received something of a high profile in the NOI's 2005 Millions More Movement. The initiative for the 2005 March was launched by Minister Farrakhan to commemorate the tenth anniversary of the Million Man March. The 2005 MMM was noticeably more inclusive and showcased the talents of Native American and Latino members, particularly female members. As noted previously, popular studies of the NOI often depict the organization as racially exclusive. Yet, the presence of Latinos and Native Americans in Farrakhan's NOI is discernible. In his writings, Elijah Muhammad often conveyed a sense of empathy for Native Americans and Latinos. In his 1965 publication *Message to the Blackman in America*, he noted:

> The Black man produces these four colors: brown, red, yellow and white. The original people, whom the white race found here (red people), were the brothers of the Black man, they are referred to as Red Indians. The Indian part of the name must refer to the name of the country from which they came, India. The All-wise Allah said that they were exiled from India for breaking the law of Islam. All of our colors—brown, red and yellow—have ruled since the Black.[47]

Elijah Muhammad inherited his commitment to social justice issues plaguing Latinos and Native Americans from Fard Muhammad. Fard's first wife, Pearl Allen, whom he married in Oregon on May 9, 1914, is listed as Native American in the 1898 census of Klamath, Oregon.[48] Further, according to the NOI's Latino Minister Abel Muhammad, Elijah Muhammad invited a Latino family to join the NOI in the early 1930s. Abel's narrative is supported by an account that appeared in *The Final Call* newspaper:

> One early account of this is the friendship of the Honorable Elijah Muhammad with Henry Almanza Sr., a Mexican living in Detroit who had married a Black American woman, Mary Almanza. Mary Almanza, along with her 10 children, had become some of the early members of

Detroit's Temple #1 under Master Fard Muhammad. She became one of the first teachers in the University of Islam, even being arrested during the raids on the Temple. Her husband, who immigrated to the U.S. after the Mexican revolution, dined with the Honorable Elijah Muhammad frequently and was a great supporter of his cause, although never registering in the Temple himself.[49]

The presence of Latinos in Elijah Muhammad's NOI was never discernible.[50] Minister Farrakhan has attempted to recruit Native Americans and Latinos to the NOI since the 1980s. The Nation has been less successful in its recruitment of Native Americans, as the current director of the Millions More Movement Indigenous Nations director admits. She comments that "it is very rare" for a "sister in Native America" to embrace Islam.[51] Thus, when a Native American woman does join the Nation, it is celebrated and announced in *The Final Call*. On August 28, 2012, for example, the paper devoted an entire page to the testimony of a woman known as Sister Gwen/Native Angel. In her testimony, Gwen comments:

> There was once a time in my life I was so hopeless. I was married to my ex-husband and he was very abusive toward me. I was homeless with my two-year-old daughter and six months' pregnant with my son. I was drinking alcohol and lastly working in a gentlemen's club as a dancer. This however led to depression, low self-esteem and an attempted suicide. During this time I had lost sense of my outlook on life. I was so lost and I had to reflect on myself and the choices I was making. I used to have strong morals, strong values and I tried to keep on that path. However, this sickness led me to the worst stages of my life. I don't know how I could have done it without the help of Islam. What made me want to change was the fact that I was expecting my second child, Bear. I didn't want to live like this anymore; I knew deep down there had to be something better. . . . My journey in life started with hopelessness. It went back to when I was a baby at six weeks of age when my birth parents gave me up and I was raised by my grandparents so I always had a sense of loss and living in the dark. A lot of people are looking for the light and Alhamdulillah [praise due to God], I have found the light, the happiness, the truth of life . . . Islam. . . . I have a relationship with Allah (Lord of

the Worlds) Master Fard Muhammad and His Christ/Messiah, The Most Honorable Elijah Muhammad and their servant in our midst The Honorable Minister Louis Farrakhan. Long Live Muhammad![52]

Gwen is one of only a handful of Native American women to join Farrakhan's NOI. Native American women attend NOI events in very small numbers, but these women for the most part are not registered members. Indeed, it appears that they are either associated with or related to YoNasDa Lonewolf-Muhammad, who has been employed by the NOI to build bridges between the NOI and Native American communities. A number of factors account for the NOI's lack of success in recruiting Native Americans. It is only since the 2005 Millions More Movement that the NOI has publicly welcomed Native Americans into the NOI. And as *The Final Call* correspondent Askia Muhammad comments, Native Americans have proven less willing than Latinos to synchronize their spiritual and religious beliefs with NOI theology.[53] Moreover, many minority groups continue to perceive the NOI as a "Black religion" and thus consider it racially exclusive.

Latinas constitute a larger and more discernible demographic within the NOI. Yet their presence is dwarfed by the sheer number of African American women, who remain the largest female demographic within the NOI's regional mosques. According to NOI member Theresa X Torres, many of the Latinos who join the NOI are "born and raised" as Catholics. Theresa's observation helps to explain the lure of the NOI for Latinas. As mentioned earlier, not all women abandon their Christian faith upon entering the NOI. Thus, the NOI's flirtation with Christianity arguably helps Latinas connect their Catholic faith with NOI theology. Latinas are attracted to the NOI for many of the same reasons as their African American counterparts. In Theresa's narrative below we find further evidence of women finding the NOI's gender ideology empowering:

> I am a Latina of Mexican ancestry. Prior to hearing the teachings of the Honorable Elijah Muhammad I had very low self-esteem. Today, all praises due to God, I tell others that a Black man taught me how to accept my own and be myself. . . . [When I was] 22, a co-worker introduced me to the NOI and the teachings of the Honorable Elijah

Muhammad via audio tapes. When I first heard Minister Farrakhan, I was captivated by what he said and for several years I listened to Minister Farrakhan via audio cassettes. Prior to hearing the teachings of the Honorable Elijah Muhammad, I was a Catholic; I also attended Baptist and interdenominational churches and eventually left the Christian church completely. . . . Hearing the teachings of the Honorable Elijah Muhammad as taught by Minister Farrakhan got and kept my attention. I knew that there was something very special in a teaching that was penetrating the pain I had grown numb to. At times I was shocked by the things Minister Farrakhan talked about since I had never heard them talked about in any church I had ever attended. I was very surprised to hear Minister Farrakhan talk about the pain that many women and children suffered, and the problems that existed in many families including violence, incest, addictions and disunity. . . . In 1988, I became a member of the NOI. Through the teachings of the Honorable Elijah Muhammad, I learned the importance of reading and education and feel proud to say that I read my first book in its entirety as a result of what I learned in the NOI.

As noted previously, Theresa is a regular contributor to *The Final Call* newspaper and serves on the NOI's Prison Reform Ministry. Her profile in the NOI is thus relatively high in comparison to those of other Latinas. The pain and low self-esteem that Theresa mentions connects her with other minority women within the NOI who also comment that the NOI provided them with the tools they needed to overcome abusive pasts. Further evidence of this support is reflected in Sadiyah Evangelista's comments. Sadiyah found herself in an abusive relationship before joining the NOI. She describes her struggle to get out of the relationship:

About 10 years ago I found myself in a physically abusive relationship telling myself for a year I am never going back, but I did. I always said no man would ever put his hands on me, but here I was a 24-year-old new bride dealing with the very thing I said I will never tolerate. I think from the very moment the first physical altercation occurred to the very last, I planned on leaving literally about twenty-something times, but just couldn't, I thought.[54]

Sadiyah survived the violent marriage and currently resides in Texas, where she works as a lawyer. Sadiyah advertises her work in Nation women's magazines and in particular in Audrey Muhammad's *Virtue Today* magazine and Ebony Muhammad's *Hurt 2 Healing* magazine. It is noteworthy, however, that these magazines do not showcase Latinas in the same way they highlight African American women. This may be a result of numerous factors, including the ongoing problems that Latinas face within the NOI. As we have noted, workshops at annual Saviours' Day conventions address the discrimination that minority groups experience within the NOI. Some of this discrimination appears to stem from a belief that Fard Muhammad's teachings were directed solely to and exclusively for the benefit of Blacks and from disapproval of NOI Latino members who self-identify as Black. NOI schoolteacher and Latina NOI member Diamante Vega comments that those who tell her that "there is no way" she could be Black base their remarks on ignorance and a poor understanding of their history:

> As a person of Puerto Rican and Haitian descent, it is very difficult for me to call myself Black and not have others make an ignorant comment about me or even make mockery. These negative comments stem from the lack of knowledge and ignorance. It is our job to work to eliminate these stereotypes and any disunity among our people of Hispanic and Latino descent. Many people have said to me that there is no way I could be Black because of my skin color, my hair texture, the language I speak, and the birthplace of my grandparents and people. Most people don't understand that there are Black people everywhere around the planet Earth. The only thing that separates us is our geographic area and lack of knowledge that the Black man is the father of civilization.[55]

Diamante's comments highlight that the concerns minority women and African American women confront within the NOI differs. As we have seen, African American women are working toward having more women in the ministry class and working together to revise those aspects of the group they consider less appealing. Minority women, however, face multiple challenges, as evidenced by the testimonies of Theresa, Sadiyah, and Diamante. For these women, being accepted and embraced as equals in the NOI remains an ongoing concern that they are addressing via workshops at NOI conventions. As well as having more women in ministry, minority women are concerned with having their membership in the NOI recognized by the wider community. Minority women construe the teachings of Elijah Muhammad in a broad context and understand that Minister Farrakhan's teachings are aimed at an international audience. Within the NOI, however, many of Farrakhan's followers express some anxiety that broadening the appeal of the NOI may inadvertently result in the organization's becoming disconnected from African American communities. Nowhere was this seen more clearly in recent years than with the response to Minister Farrakhan's request that the NOI begin an "expanded mission" during a lecture to re-dedicate Mosque Maryam in 2008. Some members commented that the lecture had presented them with a "challenge" while others sought reassurance from Farrakhan that the NOI would remain first and foremost in the service of African American communities:

> Min. Farrakhan quieted the concerns of many who may feel that this "New Beginning" would represent the abandonment of the core principles of the mission that makes the Nation of Islam the steadfast pillar in the Black community that it has been for 78 years. "All of the mosques set up by the Hon. Elijah Muhammad are committed first and foremost to the resurrection and transformation of the Black people in America and throughout the world, for it is our condition that is worse."[56]

Concerns such as these from *The Final Call* illustrate that Farrakhan remains beholden to his followers. He may allow his followers something of an unrestricted interpretation of the group's theology, but he cannot be seen to divorce the Nation completely from its traditional base. In this way, Minister Farrakhan's own activities and theological leanings are subject to the needs and desires of his members.

Opportunities for Latinas and Native American and African American women to contribute to the NOI have grown since the formation of several ministries within the NOI in 2006. It is through these ministries that Nation women have challenged popular perceptions and effectively remade their image.

Challenging Popular Perceptions and Remaking the Image of Nation Women

The most significant development in the NOI for women in recent years has been the creation of the "Nine Ministries to Build a Nation." These ministries include the following: Health and Human Services, Agriculture, Education, Defense, Art and Culture, Trade and Commerce, Justice, Information, and Science and Technology. The "Nine Ministries" grew out of discussions held by the Commission for the Restructuring and Reorganization of the NOI. The commission was put together following Minister Farrakhan's battle with prostate cancer in 2001 and effectively oversees and implements changes within the organization.[57] Nation women have always been instrumental in carrying out traditional roles and occupations within the NOI and especially within its schools. The NOI's school system is overseen by Dr. Larry Muhammad. Currently, there are eleven Muhammad University of Islam (MUI) schools in the United States located in seven regions.[58] Nation women are instrumental in the schools. The MUI employs professional teachers and NOI members. Sudan, for example, worked as an assistant in the school while her daughter was attending the MUI. Women operate with significant agency in all of the aforementioned ministries. Khaleelah is an important figure in the Ministry of Justice and Lorraine Muhammad, introduced earlier, contributes to the Ministry of Health and Human Services. Lorraine's involvement with the Ministry of Health and Human Services stems from her own struggle with weight-related health issues. Lorraine contributes to workshops within the NOI that are run by the Ministry. This includes addressing workshop participants and preparing talks. In 2010 she published a book titled *588 Days! Balancing Act of Faith, Family & Finding Time for ME*. The book traces her weight-loss journey. The following quotation discusses how the book came about and the support Lorraine received from other Nation women:

> At the time I had six children and over the years I had gained a lot of weight to the point where during the fifth pregnancy my blood pressure became an issue. I was pretty consistently around the 200-pound weight and I realized at a certain point that I did not want to

Lorraine Muhammad, author of *558 Days! Balancing Act of Faith, Family & Finding Time for ME*

be on medication the rest of my life and I needed to be around for my children and I was just overall unhappy. On the inside I was crying and not very pleased with myself and so I decided just to start small and work my way down from 200 to 140 and as I'm going along a lot of people asked me questions about how I was doing it with all I had going on—and keep in mind I was a manager, we have six children, and we were home-schooling them at nights and on weekends. I found myself telling the same story several times and I thought there must be a need out there because people keep asking me how and I thought I would just start writing it down. It started off as a journal and ended up a book and I never intended on being an author. . . . I felt the need was out there and I wasn't the only one going through this type of situation and thought I should do my best to help someone else save their own life. . . . No one ever pressured me; most people were empathetic because I had back-to-back children and they know it's hard . . . being a working mother. . . . I never had any pressure or regulation but it was my own internal pressure and I saw other sisters going through the same thing. I would put my story on facebook; I had a page called Lorraine Muhammad's weight loss journey and people would click Like or [comment], "I have the same story," and I realized that I was not by myself.

Narratives such as Lorraine's highlight the fact that dietary laws are not rigorously enforced in the NOI. Indeed, Lorraine's comments illustrate that she drew strength from other Nation women who were struggling to overcome weight problems. Lorraine's contributions to the Ministry of Health and Human Services are based largely on her personal struggles and ability to overcome weight-related health problems. Nevertheless, the Ministry helps connect Lorraine with women beyond her local mosque study group, where she was once the director of protocol. Opportunities to engage in nonconventional ministries and leadership roles aid women's agency and facilitate their greater engagement with the Nation.

Nowhere are Nation women's agency and creativity more evidenced than in the Ministry of Arts and Culture (MAC). The Ministry was launched at the 2006 annual Saviours' Day convention in Chicago. The MAC hosts an online forum that enables both male and female songwriters, dancers, rappers, poets, and writers to connect with one another and collaborate on projects both for the Nation and other forums. Nation women use the forum to promote their artistic talents and as a launchpad for their own small-business ventures, some of which include fashion outlets, online and print magazines, and film and music production. Significantly, this enables women to carve out a livelihood from their involvement with the MAC. The activities of the MAC's female cohort empower Nation women and ultimately push the boundaries of the group's gender politics. In other words, it provides them with multiple opportunities to contest collectively those aspects of the NOI they find restrictive or less appealing. Equally important for Nation women is the fact that their activities in the MAC shatter the myth that they are passive and in the background. MAC member Connie Muhammad notes, "It can't be said anymore that women in the Nation are just quiet, in the background or have nothing to say or are subservient; those types of ideas can't be said without being disqualified."

Women like Connie would, of course, have been prohibited from engaging in such activities in Elijah Muhammad's NOI. Farrakhan, however, has often flirted with the hip-hop world and intervened in the so-called rap wars.[59] His engagement with hip-hop and rap artists is largely a result of two factors. First, Farrakhan himself has nurtured a passion for music and especially the violin from a young age. Second, hip-hop and rap artists have frequently employed the rhetoric of Black nationalist icons to advance their more socially conscious recordings. Evocative references to Marcus Garvey, Malcolm X, and Louis Farrakhan can be found emanating in the musical works of rap and hip-hop artists including Nas, The Fugees, and the late Biggie Smalls, among others. Thus, Farrakhan's efforts to reach out to the hip-hop world are a response to such references. Farrakhan has held a hip-hop summit annually since the late 1990s. The summit brings together rap artists, politicians, producers, and clergy to discuss ways in which rap lyrics and music video producers can be more socially conscious. Minister Farrakhan gave up the violin and his music career when he joined the NOI. In 1993, however, he returned to playing the violin and very gradually sanctioned his followers' engagement with the music industry.[60] In *A Torchlight for America* (1993), he noted that artistic talents were "gifts" from God to be used "responsibly":

> The artistic community has historically been in the vanguard of social change. . . . The artistic community needs to be shown its responsibilities to the overall mental and spiritual health and well-being of society and the world. Our gifts, as artists, are a blessing from God. We have a responsibility of the proper use of our gifts.[61]

The MAC's female members fuse popular culture with NOI teachings and strong socially conscious messages. Rap artists and singers form a significant proportion of the MAC's female membership. Connie Muhammad is perhaps one of the more high-profile MAC members. Connie was born into the NOI in 1974. Her love of music as a young child growing up in the Nation was discouraged, but this discouragement did not prevent her from performing as a teenager and becoming a recording artist at the age of twenty. The creation of the MAC has provided a network for Connie to promote her own genre of music, which she describes as "righteous hip-hop soul." Her music finds its primary appeal among the NOI's membership and women in particular. She regards her membership in the Nation not as a hindrance to her music career but as an alternative avenue through which she can help build independent structures for Nation members to produce and distribute their own music. She comments:

> The music industry is very much a controlled industry, and you have to take certain avenues to get to success, and if you're not able to take those avenues, then you won't make it, and that's by design, and I already understand that that's not going to be possible for me, and I'm comfortable with that. But we are building something within the already established structures of the NOI where we are self-reliant, self-sufficient, and music distribution is included.

Connie promotes her album *Shahadah* online and via the NOI's media outlets, which include *The Final Call* newspaper and women's magazines. Her artistic talents have led to her performing at the NOI's annual Saviours' Day convention, which remains the largest event on the NOI's calendar. Members of the MAC are invited to perform at the convention based on their talents. However, not all of the women who perform at the annual convention have been received as warmly as Connie.

Nadia[62] has been attending NOI meetings since she was in high school. She became familiar with the organization at the age of sixteen, when she frequented the local NOI restaurant. Nadia's husband is a registered NOI member. She has been attending NOI meetings and "following the teachings" for much of her adult life, but she has not officially joined the organization. Her reluctance stems from concern that she may have to relinquish her career as a professional dancer if she follows through with membership. She comments, "I teach dance and it is a drawback. Some people think that it is something you shouldn't do, and I love dance, and I don't want to give [it] up." Nadia admits that her husband wants her to join the NOI but that she has not experienced pressure from her local chapter in Dallas to do so. The fact that Nadia has not experienced pressure to join the Nation again suggests that dictates about endogamy are not rigorously enforced. Nadia teaches and performs belly dance, which she admits many people both inside and outside the NOI do not understand. She has, however, been actively involved with the NOI's MAC. Indeed, it was through her involvement with the MAC that she was asked to perform at the 2007 Saviours' Day convention. Her comments illustrate that dance is not embraced by all members:

> It is an extremely big event; I was very honored to be chosen. There were some people who got it and others who didn't, but I had a very good reception from the crowd. I was frightened because I normally dance in a more revealing type of costume and I was fully covered; I enjoyed it, and I tried not to have any sultry movements and that was the main thing. I made sure that when I made the costume, it wasn't form fitting.

The response to Nadia's performance was mixed. Yet in the narrative from NOI member Laurie Goux, we can see that dance has been tolerated in the NOI for some time and certainly long before the creation of the MAC. Laurie joined the NOI in Chicago in 1991. While her membership was being processed, however, she was confronted with the possibility of having to choose between the NOI and her career. The intervention of Farrakhan's daughter Donna, however, ensured that Laurie's membership was processed:

> While I was processing prior to receiving my X, I was asked what line of work was I in. I replied that I was a dancer. The sister ignorantly implied that it was night club dance. I corrected her and stated that I taught and choreographed modern, ballet, jazz, tap, Katherine Dunham Technique and African dance. Her reply was, "Well we don't dance here." I thought that was the most ridiculous thing I had ever heard. Well Donna Farrakhan got word that I was a professional dancer and thought that was wonderful. She immediately assigned me to teach exercise and dance to the MGT. The sisters loved it, and many of them took my classes outside of the NOI. Sister Donna told me that Minister Farrakhan was a student of Katherine Dunham, Calypso singer and dancer, classical violinist[;] and her mother, Honorable Mother Khadijah Farrakhan, was a great clothing designer and had a clothing design business in the Nation on 79th Street. Well she wrote a play called "Trials of a Queen" about a young college Muslim girl

faced with temptations of college life vs. belief system. I choreographed a modern solo that was her alter ego [and] as she slept in her dorm bed the dancer depicted her thoughts and inner struggle. There was a final number which we used, "Let Us Unite," a Calypso recording that Minister Farrakhan wrote and sang many years ago. The dance had vibrant costumes designed by Donna, myself and Mother Khadijah. African Bubas with pants and headpieces, colorful, Caribbean flower print circle skirts, with tops and head scarfs. It was like the wedding scene in Eddie Murphy's "Coming to America." We performed for Saviors' Day in Chicago and that was the beginning. That was the year Minister Farrakhan said, "Every civilized culture has its own music and dance and there is no reason why the Nation should not be dancing." That evening at the palace, the Minister picked up his violin again and serenaded us with his music. The Nation of Islam now dances, sings, acts, and produces all forms of art that is entertaining but has spiritual and consciousness raising messages. We have formed the Ministry of Arts and Culture. Even though this story is not readily shared with new members, I feel that I made a contribution.

Laurie's narrative reaffirms the important role that collective resistance to the early ban on dance played in bringing about the creation of the MAC. Laurie regards her struggle and Donna Farrakhan's intervention as an important turning point in the NOI. Dance is a growing subgroup of the MAC. Its recognition within the NOI highlights important changes in the organization's attitude toward arts and culture.

Music and dance are but one subgroup of the MAC. Nation women are also actively engaged in film production. The result of their creativity and collective work has been the production of documentaries and films that explore social issues and NOI history. As mentioned earlier in the chapter, Angela Muhammad has produced a documentary exploring the role that women played in the Million Man March. Angela is a stay-at-home mother, as are many Nation women. However, she is also the CEO of her own company, Vanguard Television. Angela refers to the MAC as her "career" and notes that her husband's work allows her to be at home with her children while also pursuing her talents and passion for film production. Angela's passion for film is shared by NOI member Dishonne Muhammad. Dishonne is currently working on a film titled *Faye's Story*. *Faye's Story* examines one woman's efforts to live with HIV/AIDS. Dishonne joined the NOI in 1995 in San Francisco, where she was an HIV/AIDS activist. Her work in the MAC is in many ways a continuation of the work she carried out before joining the Nation. Thus, the MAC has enabled rather than restricted women like Nadia, Laurie, and Dishonne from pursuing their talents.

The MAC has inspired women to pursue their artistic talents, but as mentioned previously, it has also challenged NOI convention and empowered women to contest aspects of the NOI collectively. Nation women's print and online magazines provide further evidence of women's agency and their efforts to negotiate and revise the organization's gender norms. Nation women have thus far launched four magazines: *Virtue Today, Hurt 2 Healing, Modesty International,* and *Youth Creation Community Outreach. Virtue Today* was created by NOI member Audrey Muhammad in late 2004. The magazine is aimed at young African American women who are either involved with Louis Farrakhan's NOI or sympathetic to its gender ideals. *Virtue Today* promotes positive images that subvert prevailing and unflattering myths associated with Black women. In promoting images of successful Black women, including Michelle Obama, the magazine's editorial board hopes to contest the U.S. media's portrayal of African American women as jezebels, mammies, and matriarchs. Audrey Muhammad became a well-known member of the NOI via her irregular articles for *The Final Call*. Her articles for the paper are titled "Get Fit to Live" and contain advice about weight loss, healthful eating, and lifestyle. Audrey's interest in women's health and fitness propelled her to write her first book, *The Sister's Guide to Fitness*, and the audio book *Get Fit to Live: Be Your Best You!* Audrey's magazine opens with an editorial note in the form of quotations from the Bible, and in particular, Proverbs 31, which outlines the qualities and requirements of a virtuous woman. At times, this is replaced by a Christian poem, like "Footprints," or a parable. It is rare to find any mention of the Qur'an in the magazine. The content of *Virtue Today* speaks to the concerns, needs, and aspirations of Nation women. Each issue contains articles that relate to family values, relationships, fashion ideas, interviews, weight loss, child rearing, and financial advice. The magazine regularly features articles that highlight the contributions or positive work of women in the NOI. Nation women are usually featured on the front cover. These women are not always high-profile figures, although Dr. Ava Muhammad and Farrakhan's granddaughter Jamillah Farrakhan have graced the cover of the magazine, the latter's appearing being in 2008. Jamillah was interviewed for the magazine following her appearance in the Rocawear "I Will Not Lose" campaign. The interview set out to address how she negotiates her faith with the demands of modeling. In the magazine she comments:

> Everyone loves it. It wasn't anything that compromised me. Even my friends thought it was great, but I did lose a few friends in the process because of envy or jealousy or whatever. I did some research on the internet about myself and read some rude and mean comments. Some people said, "What kind of thing is this, she's not dressed like a Muslim." Or who is this girl and what does she think she is doing?[63]

Jamillah's modeling career has, as noted, played some role in revising Farrakhan's rhetoric on the industry. Nation women are not involved in the modeling industry in large numbers, but they are very much involved in the fashion industry. *Virtue Today* advertises a selection of fashions by and for Nation women. Collectively these fashions have helped Nation women to cultivate an image of themselves as feminine and trendy yet modest.

Audrey's magazine strikes a balance between promoting a new image of Nation women and maintaining some sense of NOI gender norms. In recent years, a new column titled "Brothers We Admire" has been added to the magazine. This column tends to include NOI ministers such as Nuri Muhammad. *Virtue Today* provides women with a great deal of advice about issues related to marriage and domestic science. The fall 2011 issue of the magazine carried an article by the NOI's Detroit and Miami representative, Rasul Muhammad, titled "Why Should You Get Married?" While outlining the benefits of marriage, Rasul noted:

> The human being is designed in need of companionship . . . . [P]rolonged periods of the human being alone has an adverse effect on your nature. All human beings need intimate companionship to further our maturation into God.[64]

We can see marriage being promoted here as not only ideal but essential for one's well-being. Comments such as these are found in numerous editions of the magazine. In the spring 2012 edition, for example, NOI New York minister and marriage counselor Abdul Hafeez Muhammad reinforced Farrakhan's directive that unmarried MGT women should remain "patient" and "trust in Allah until the right brother (FOI)" comes along.[65] The annual singles retreats hosted by Hafeezah Muhammad and the NOI highlight the emphasis the organization continues to place on pairing up NOI members. This strategy, however, has not always worked for the NOI. As NOI member Mary[66] comments:

> To be honest, in the NOI at the minute we have a very high divorce rate and the Hon. Minister Louis Farrakhan is, of course, not pleased with that because we are taught that Allah hates divorce and our beloved brother does not do weddings because we are not making our word bond when we say to death do us part, so at this point in time, it's like a disease that has to be treated. We have [singles] retreats every year where Muslims are taught how to interact with each other. We also have an annual event for married couples. Workshops and events now cater to married couples because the Hon. Minister Louis Farrakhan teaches us that family is the cornerstone and there is no NOI without family.

Nation women tend to embrace traditional gender roles on the basis that such roles do not hinder their freedom. The women interviewed embrace the concept that their first commitment is to their home and family, as evidenced by JayVon's comments earlier and Mary's comments above. Thus, the articles in the magazine that concern marriage can be read as either reinforcing traditional dictates that pressured women into marriage or indeed as speaking to the concerns of women who long to marry within the organization.

Audrey's success with the magazine has inspired other Nation women to create online, digital, and print magazines. These include *Modesty International*, *Hurt 2 Healing* (digital magazine), and *Youth Creation Community Outreach* (print magazine). *Modesty International* is an online magazine that is connected with a blog talk radio website called Modest Models. The magazine was founded by NOI member Tamorah Muhammad. Tamorah joined the NOI in the central region mosque in 1997 at the age of twenty-one. Tamorah grew up in the Pentecostal Church. However, she comments that she did not really "get anything" from being a Christian: "[The NOI] was very different from Christianity. They were so humble and they greeted me with a smile and they invited me out again and the sisters called to check up on me and see how I was." Tamorah felt embraced by the Nation and settled quickly into the group. After her first year in the Nation, she began courting and married an FOI. She explains how Modest Models came about and its ethos:

> Modest Models was created because I was asking one day, "Allah, is it that you want me to bring a change to the NOI in a positive way?" And I saw models on the TV and then the word modesty popped into my head and so I said I could create an organization called Modest Models, Inc., based around purity, being chaste and teaching women how to go about their everyday life being modest. Modesty is not just about dress code, it's about modesty of the heart and brain and so we are going to teach women that no this is not the proper way to go about getting men. Instead of thinking between your legs, think with your mind, and that's what we are teaching the women in Modest Models, Inc. We also have Facebook; we have 1,100 members—it's a combination of Muslims and Christians.

In Tamorah's narrative we find further evidence of Nation women embracing NOI dictates about modesty and their efforts to reach out to their Christian counterparts. *Modesty International* advocates and reinforces the NOI's conservative gender ideology much more aggressively than *Virtue Today, Hurt 2 Healing*, or indeed *YCCO*. In a recent online edition of the magazine, NOI member Nojma Muhammad wrote an article titled "Badges of Dishonor." Among the labels she included as dishonorable to Black women were "Wifey" and "Miss Independent":

> Miss Independent- "I-N-D-E-P-E-N-D-E-N-T, Do you know what that means? I know Destiny's Child [has] us PROUDLY declaring our Independence from men, specifically BLACK MEN. You have "your own

car," your "own house," you have an abundance of degrees, right? There is nothing wrong with being proud of your accomplishments, and if you are on your own, then you should be able to pay your OWN bills, since you are an adult. I mean, that makes sense, right? So why get upset when we see Brothers with women that don't look like us? Or those [who] say they have NO desire to be with Black women? We are looking at the "effect" but not the "cause." Haven't we been telling them we don't NEED them? I can do this WITHOUT you? Who would go/stay where they are not needed? We talk about the Brothers, posting how they hate or dislike Black women, but could it be BECAUSE we exuded hatred towards them FIRST? . . . If you are proudly claiming independence, then you have lost the right to talk about the caliber of Black men and why you don't have one, because a synonym for Independence is alone, and that is exactly where you will end up, ALONE![67]

Nojma's attack on Black women who "proudly" claim their independence from Black men signals that she regards the uplift of Black men as a priority that far exceeds concerns about gender equality. Indeed, Nojma's comments appear to be scolding women who have achieved success and economic independence. Nojma construes Black women's earning power not as a positive indication of their success but as a liability to building and sustaining relationships with Black men. Her comments about Black women's successes in terms of educational achievements and earning power tend to mirror Farrakhan's critique of the ways in which women's successes can in fact emasculate Black men and drive them from the home, as shown earlier in the chapter.

Modesty International has grown exponentially since its formation in early 2010. According to Tamorah, she now has a staff of more than twenty volunteers who contribute to the magazine and online forum. The online magazine is, however, almost a replica of *Virtue Today* in that it covers the same stories, often highlights the same women, and offers the same dietary and lifestyle advice.

Hurt 2 Healing is a monthly magazine produced by NOI member Ebony Muhammad. Ebony utilizes online networking to market the magazine. She notes, "Online social networking allows me to build relationships with people all over the world. There are no boundaries or limitations."[68] The magazine is much more daring than its counterparts;

it offers women similar advice about relationships and lifestyle, but it has the feel of being much more uncensored and aimed more exclusively at women. The October/November 2012 issue, for example, carried an article titled "Do's and Don'ts: 7 Tips to Find Your 'Mr. Right,'" in which one woman noted, "Don't allow your desire to be married to cause you to settle for less than the man God has already predestined you for" and "when looking for Mr. Right, let go of Mr. Wrong first."[69] At first, such comments may not appear particularly daring. However, they signal that Nation women are encouraged to take charge of their own personal lives and no longer rely on the NOI to partner them with men in the FOI. Similarly, the magazine covers such topics as managing "sexual urges" and overcoming "painful relationships." It is noteworthy, however, that *H2H* is also aimed at Christian women and women on the fringes of the NOI. In the February 2011 edition of the magazine, for example, Mavis Jackson extended her thanks to the NOI for embracing her in spite of her Christianity during the annual Saviours' Day convention: "It was an unforgettable spiritual encounter that I will always have beautiful memories of. . . . I thank all the brothers and sisters in the Nation of Islam for welcoming me with open arms in spite of my professing Christianity."[70] *Hurt 2 Healing* has the feel of a glossy magazine, packed with interviews with Nation and non-Nation members. Its link to the NOI is always clear, but this does not always dominate the magazine.

Youth Creation Community Outreach is the latest installment of Nation women's magazines. Its audience is small, and unlike *Virtue Today, H2H,* and *Modesty International,* it does not evince a disproportionate emphasis on the NOI. The content of the magazine is driven by Sudan Muhammad's desire to put into practice Elijah Muhammad's teachings on community uplift. Thus far Sudan has published three editions of the magazine. The magazine contains interviews with young community activists, parenting tips, recipes, and photographs illustrating Sudan and her family's work in the community. Like its counterparts, however, it is aimed at Christian women also as evidenced by the fact that the April 2012 issue carried a full back page notice advertising "Prophet Valentine Williams" healing ministries.[71] Sudan's magazine contains socially conscious messages that reflect but do not always reference NOI teachings. Her daughter's musical gifts are, however, referenced in the magazine, and music as therapy is something that is encouraged in each issue.

The Ministry of Arts and Culture provides women with greater agency than ever before in the NOI. Indeed, many of the activities of the MAC's current female cohort would shock if not surprise outside observers who regard Nation women as agents of their own oppression. Equally, however, Nation women's involvement in music, modeling, and dancing would have certainly horrified Elijah Muhammad. Not only does the MAC provide opportunities for women to network and highlight their work, but it also enables them to revise the boundaries of the NOI's gender norms, thus giving those norms greater agency. The magazines that Nation women have created illustrate their efforts to negotiate the NOI's traditional teachings with broader culture and in particular with trends in fashion and music. The magazines differ slightly, but all have a focus on family and thus tend to demonstrate that Nation women embrace the concept that their first responsibility is to their home and family although, it is important to note, they do not see this as their exclusive role.

Leading Women and the Council of Laborers

Today's Nation women hold some of the most high-profile positions the group has to offer. As mentioned earlier, both Ava Muhammad and Donna Farrakhan Muhammad have served as ministers in the NOI. Claudette Marie Muhammad has served as the NOI's director of protocol and public relations, and Native American member YoNasDa Lonewolf-Muhammad directs the Indigenous Nations Alliance. Yet other women who are neither ministers nor directors also hold a prominent role in the NOI. Elijah Muhammad's former secretary Tynetta Muhammad has a reasonably high profile in the Nation and delivers lectures on an irregular basis at Mosque Maryam. Tynetta is referred to affectionately within the NOI as the "wife" of the Honorable Elijah Muhammad, as is Evelyn Williams, also a former secretary. Tynetta and Evelyn were introduced to the wider NOI family at the 1992 Saviours' Day convention as the "wives" of Elijah Muhammad. They both provided testimony in support of Elijah Muhammad's moral character at the convention. The testimonies from both women were prompted by fresh questions about Elijah Muhammad's moral character following the release of Spike Lee's film *X*.[72] Nation women tend to accept that Elijah Muhammad did in fact have sexual relations with the secretaries. However, they explain the encounters as having taken place in the context of marriage and as a result of divine providence, or, as one woman notes, "These wives were permitted for him by God. Not to play with, not in a lustful manner. However, in order for him to teach and know the nature of the women that he was going to be teaching and leading up for God. . . . [t]hese wives were divinely permitted. He did not go plucking for wives. This is a divine family and it was known to be that. God permitted these things to happen."[73] Tynetta Muhammad appears regularly in *The Final Call* newspaper, and her son Ishmael Muhammad has served as Minister Farrakhan's national assistant for more than a decade. Indeed, it is possible, if not likely, that Ishmael will succeed Minister Farrakhan.[74] Though the former secretaries do not operate in the NOI as ministers, they are important figures. Their testimonies provide the NOI and its female cohort in particular with evidence that counters negative charges relating to Elijah Muhammad's domestic life. Women such as Dr. Ava Muhammad play an important role in the NOI's council of laborers, or executive board, entrusted with managing the NOI following Minister Farrakhan's health problems in 2006.[75] The executive board is composed of an upper and lower tier of NOI ministers who have been instrumental in the NOI for some time. As noted, women such as Ava and Claudette have a place on the board and will prove instrumental in any decisions taken about its future leadership or theological trajectory. The elevation of women to such positions in the Nation is no small feat. It not only signals their own achievements in breaking down barriers of exclusion within the Nation but also evidences the important changes that have taken place within the organization under Minister Farrakhan's direction.

According to the women interviewed, Nation women are not oppressed in the NOI, nor are they agents of their own oppression. Their agency and influence are evinced through their contributions to the Nation and their reflections on the opportunities it provides them. Women continue to find the NOI to be a place where their concerns and ideals are addressed. They embrace the organization's gender ideology and actively contest and revise those aspects of the Nation they find restrictive. Nation women conscientiously choose to attach themselves to the Nation rather than to Sunni Islam because they feel that they generally fare much better in the NOI than their counterparts in Sunni Islam. Their observation, however, is based on limited interaction with their Sunni Muslim counterparts. Nation women fuse their Christian or indeed Sunni beliefs with aspects of NOI theology while never fully divorcing themselves from either. Their unrestricted interpretation and presentation of NOI theology present them with the freedom to express their respective faiths as they see fit.

The patriarchy that the NOI subscribes to is one that emphasizes the necessity of male leadership and male-headed households. Women embrace the NOI because of and not in spite of this. Nation women feel empowered by NOI teachings that relieve them of the burden of balancing competing demands with meeting bills. Yet they recognize that sexism is inevitable, though not something that is rooted in Minister Farrakhan's teachings or the NOI's structures. Nation women's concerns vary considerably. Latinas and Native American women struggle to be accepted on an equal footing with their African American sisters. African American women, on the other hand, are largely concerned with furthering and extending their opportunities in the NOI and eradicating male chauvinism from within the organization. Nation women are remaking their own image in the popular imagination. In doing so, they are contesting the boundaries of the NOI's gender politics, modernizing the organization's dress code, negotiating gender norms, and effectively shattering the myth that they are silent bystanders in the organization.

4

Women in the Nation of Islam and the Warith Deen Mohammed Community

Crafting a Dialogue

It was a "historic meeting," Robert Franklin, then-president of the Interdenominational Theological Center (ITC), averred in describing the panel featuring Imam Mohammed and Minister Ava Muhammad. Titled "The Spiritual State of Black America," the meeting occurred in 2000 in Atlanta at the ITC, a historically Black consortium of seminaries. The audience consisted of members of the ITC community, as well as of members of both the NOI and the WDM community. Holding *The Final Call*, the moderator, Reverend Gerald Durley, further attested to the significance of the occasion:

> *The Final Call*, only a few days ago . . . [states], "We Are a Family, Minister Farrakhan and Imam Mohammed Unite. Twenty-five years after the departure of the Most Honorable Elijah Muhammad and the separation in the family of the Nation of Islam, the Honorable Minister Louis Farrakhan and Imam W. D. Mohammed stood together February 27th in a sold out United Center declaring their unity, speaking of the universal nature of Islam, the need for changing lives abroad, and the need to transform lives at home."

In the spirit of unity and transformation, Minister Ava Muhammad and Imam Mohammed were brought together at the ITC to present Islamic perspectives on the condition of Black communities; however, gender roles in Islam took prominence in the discussion from the very beginning when Reverend Durley introduced the two speakers as "two imams." His comment foreshadowed an exchange between the two leaders that revealed their differences of opinion on gender and religious leadership in Islam.

Imam Mohammed's opening comments on the panel's primary topic, the spiritual condition of African Americans, were brief. "Our spirituality as a people is different from the spirituality of other ethnic groups," he began, "because we lost our continuity as a people in terms of our cultural life and religion, or human spirit, when we were brought from our motherland and sold into slavery." African Americans' saving grace, however, was that "we never forgot in the depths of our souls that we once had a connection with humanity and with our Creator that was inherent in us." Imam Mohammed proposed that we now live in a time in which we allow the world and its evils to guide our souls instead of being guided by our innate humanity. He ended by posing a question: How many of us are taking "the responsibility to respect our humanity"?

Minister Ava Muhammad began her talk with a standard Islamic opening, praising God and praying blessings on the prophets, including "Moses, Jesus Christ, and Muhammad ibn Abdullah." After thanking Allah for the Honorable Elijah Muhammad, she humbly recognized the men in her presence, "Imam Warith Deen Mohammed, Dr. Gerald Durley, and Dr. Robert Franklin; I am the peer of none of them." Minister Ava focused on one aspect "of our problem," stating, "We strongly believe in Islam that at the root of our problem is the absence of marriage. . . . Virtually all of our overwhelming social, economic, and health problems are the result of the breakup of the divine institution of marriage and the corresponding breakdown of the family structure." Minister Ava deferred to the imam: "Imam W. D. Mohammed gave us a strong and eloquent predicate and reminded us of how we went astray." She contended that the first step to changing the tide is turning to God for direction. Further, Minister Ava discussed the need for a whole, sound self in order for one to have a healthy marriage and used a Qur'anic reference: "We don't go into a marriage as a fraction looking for somebody to make us a whole. The Holy Qur'an teaches that Allah created everything in pairs, and so we seek our mate so that we can enhance one another and help one another meet the ultimate goal, which is oneness with God." She ended her remarks by listing actions that the Nation of Islam planned to take in the cause of marriage, including the Million Family March.[1]

Bringing together Minister Ava and Imam Mohammed, the organizers of this program recognized the important connection between
the two groups, as branches of the original "Nation of Islam family." Despite this connection, the two groups have remained disconnected. A decade after Minister Farrakhan announced unity and
reconciliation in 2000, he has remained loyal to Elijah Muhammad's teachings. Nation women today show greater consciousness
and connection to Sunni Muslims than was experienced in Elijah
Muhammad's organization because of the growth of Sunni Islam
since the 1970s and contemporary Nation women's freedom to
interact in society. As demonstrated by Minister Ava's comments,
Nation women are in touch with the language of the Qur'an and
the Prophet Muhammad. Yet Nation women and women in the
WDM community demonstrate very minimal, if any, interest in
relations with one another. As a result of their minimal encounters, women from both groups express misunderstandings of the
other, these misunderstandings often having to do with perceptions
of gender practices. It is enticing to consider the types of conversations that would likely occur if unity had taken on any real meaning for women of the two groups. The themes that emerged from
the exchange between Imam Mohammed and Minister Ava resonate
strongly with the themes that emerged from interviews with women
in the two groups. The most prominent themes are the two groups'
levels of engagement with mainstream Islam, engagement with concerns in the Black community, and conceptions of gender equality,
especially as it relates to women's leadership in mosques.

Harmony and difference between Minister Ava and Imam Mohammed regarding these themes arose when Lawrence Mamiya was introduced to pose questions. He asked Imam Mohammed to explain if the
reconciliation between him and Minister Farrakhan meant that the two
groups would merge. To Minister Ava, Mamiya stated, "I was a part
of the audience . . . when Minister Jamil Muhammad . . . introduced
you as, quote, 'The first female imam in the United States and in the
world.'" Mamiya noted "that as Minister Farrakhan moves the Nation
of Islam closer to orthodox Sunni Islam, the pressures on him will grow
and intensify to conform to Islamic tradition." Given that Sunni Islam
does not permit women to function as imams within *masjids*, where

mixed-gender prayers occur regularly, "Do you think Minister Farrakhan will give in to these pressures for conformity," Mamiya posed, "or
will he stand firm and attempt to lead the whole Muslim world in the
new direction and new Islamic tradition of women as imams?"[2]

Imam Mohammed answered the question about the groups' possible
merging by stating that the Islamic tradition encourages "independent
thinking" and that "we don't want one leadership type for all Muslims.
The whole population of Muslims will benefit greatly if we have different personalities, different thinkers leading the effort to carry Islam to
more and more people." Imam Mohammed said that prior to the reconciliation, he had already embraced Minister Farrakhan as "a Muslim
with all the Muslims in the world" because in the previous year he had
established *jum'ah*, or the Friday congregational prayer. Imam Mohammed made very clear, "We don't want to merge into one group. That will
deprive us of something that I've already mentioned."

Minister Ava began her response to Mamiya by stating, "The secular
posture that the Nation of Islam takes on certain issues is often confused with our theology. . . . We have always believed in the universality
of Islam, that Allah is one God . . . but as the imam pointed out, we are
a peculiar people, and Islam in its universality has the power and the
adaptability to respond to prevailing conditions."

Minister Ava then moved on to the question of pressure to conform
to the Islamic tradition on the issue of female imams, starting with
an analogy of evidence presented in the court, noting that evidence is
assessed based on two important characteristics—its admissibility and
its weight:

> The only thing that has weight with Minister Farrakhan is the word
> of God. The tradition of Islam, the Sunnah or practice, is not divine
> law. . . . I have never seen in the Holy Qur'an anywhere, anything that
> justifies exclusion of the female. In fact, what I have seen is a world
> that . . . has been crippled by the absence of the manifestation of the
> feminine attributes of God through the female in deliberative pro-
> cesses. . . . We would probably have [fewer] wars than we do have if
> women were present in the deliberating process. And so I do not foresee
> Minister Farrakhan being affected at all by the opinions of anyone in the
> Muslim world who is averse [to female imams]. Certainly, their opinion

184 << WOMEN IN THE NOI AND THE W. D. MOHAMMED COMMUNITY

is admissible because we respect opinion, but does it have any weight? I think not.

Although Imam Mohammed did "not want to turn this into a debate," he made it a point to respond:

> I have no problem with a woman being a minister. But I do have a problem with a woman saying she is an imam. That title is just not for females. Now, my mother had me taking care of the chicken yard. I never saw a female chicken crow as beautifully as a male. It just can't crow like that male rooster.

Minister Ava responded, "This is why I prefaced my remarks and closed them with opinions are admissible but they carry no weight."[3]

Perhaps Imam Mohammed did not intend to start a debate, but from the response of the audience, Minister Ava had won it. If this meeting had occurred in a majority Sunni context, however, the admissibility of Minister Ava's evidence may have been questioned for her basing a legal opinion solely on the Qur'an. Indeed, it took a Sunni Muslim woman in the audience to compel Imam Mohammed to expound further on the Sunni tradition, her request suggesting her sentiment that Imam Mohammed had not best represented the opportunities for women in his community. When the moderator opened the session for Q&A, this woman in the WDM community was the first to speak:

> Sister Ava has been so beautiful to witness . . . and she responded to so many things that we as sisters are happy to hear her talk about. But I do want to ask our imam, Warith Deen Mohammed, to explain to us what sisters did in the early leadership under the Prophet Muhammad: Khadijah . . . and Aisha, a person who assisted and taught religion. And we feel as sisters in this community, we have done some of the same things.

Imam Mohammed began his response by discussing the increased rights for women and regard for female children as a central component of the Prophet Muhammad's mission. He then clarified his previous statement regarding female imams:

What I said about the rooster crowing more beautifully than the hen—I hope I wasn't saying to you that the rooster is the highest figure in the society. He is not. An imam preaching the Qur'an, teaching the people the Qur'an, leading the people in prayer, is not the highest figure in the society. The highest figure in the society is the most rounded person in their knowledge of society. And if a woman [fits this description] . . . , the Muslim society supports that woman. . . . In the time of Muhammad the Prophet, women scholars were recognized, and many of the women scholars were the teachers of the imams. Aisha [a wife of the Prophet] was one of them, as the sister who asked me to respond knows. She wants me to tell you that women were respected for their education, for their knowledge, for their character, for their spirituality, for their moral excellence, etc. And the most pious religious leaders of the men respected Aisha so much that when she spoke, they would all remain quiet and they would listen for wisdom from her mouth.[4]

In the spirit of the woman in the audience who wanted others in her company, including Nation women, to know about women's leadership in the Sunni tradition, it is intriguing to pose the question, What would one group of women want the other to know about them? Pondering this question can shed light on the divergent and convergent ways in which the two groups pursue the advancement of African Americans and the ways in which women pursue voice and leadership in their communities currently. How do Sunni women with a Nation legacy currently assess and work for women's leadership in their communities? Exploring this question addresses current Nation women's impressions of their Sunni sisters.

A Few Close Encounters, a Few More Distant Impressions

Women in the NOI have encountered women in the WDM community and other Sunni communities in various contexts. One Nation woman interviewed interacts with these women through her homeschooling group, another through a Muslim sorority, and another through her midwifery work. One Nation woman has a sister who is Sunni. In most of these relationships, women have not discussed the theological differences between their communities, preferring to keep the conversation "light" or only to aspects of the religion in which they have commonalities. The preference to avoid deep discussion sometimes stems from Nation women's awareness of the tension between them and Sunni Muslims, readily demonstrated in casual encounters between the two in public spaces. The majority of the Nation women interviewed shared stories about greeting Sunni Muslims—African American and immigrant—with the standard Islamic greeting and being ignored or treated with offensive remarks or unfriendly looks.

Tiffany[5] was one of the few women to describe a real friendship with a woman in the WDM community. She offers us some idea of the type of dialogue that might occur between women in the two groups. Tiffany has been following the teachings of the Nation of Islam for more than twenty-five years. She never thought much about Imam Mohammed or the history of the split between him and Minister Farrakhan until ten years ago, when she met on the job a friend who was a part of the WDM community. Tiffany was curious to know why her friend had joined Imam Mohammed instead of Minister Farrakhan. The friend, who was never a part of the Nation of Islam, states that her choice had mostly to do with a greater comfort she felt in the WDM *masjid* compared with the NOI mosque in that particular city. Tiffany was also curious to learn from her friend how the teachings of Sunni Islam differed from those of the Nation. Only on occasion have the two women had deep discussions about the differences in their communities. More often they keep their conversation to "girl talk," which includes dress, gender roles, and marriage. Their views on these topics tend to be aligned, and both have "this pet peeve when you get into it about guys that want to take on a second wife." But their conversation does "get higher here and there," Tiffany notes. "She is more scripturally knowledgeable than I am. I probably don't read the Qur'an nearly as much as I should." When Tiffany does read the Qur'an, she sometimes calls her Sunni friend to get her thoughts on a particular verse. Tiffany has been invited by her friend to attend her *masjid*, but Tiffany has not "had the chance." Also, her husband did not want her to go. "So I left it at that."

Cassandra[6] has never attended a WDM *masjid* either, though the nature of her relationship to the WDM community made this surprising. In 2006 Cassandra "married an FOI" whose mother had joined the

Nation in 1972. Cassandra describes the transition as "upsetting" for her husband, then age twelve, but he, along with his mother, remained in the WDM community for twenty years. Having "very loving memories" of the Nation of Islam from his childhood, he felt that the "sense of community" in the Nation of Islam was lost in the WDM community. The Million Man March was the impetus that inspired him to finally return to the Nation. "Minister Farrakhan's talking about community, strengthening the family, and taking responsibility for their children was very powerful for him, and so he wanted to be a part of that movement." He rejoined but has still held on to certain Sunni beliefs and practices.

Cassandra recognizes the benefits of marrying an FOI who spent twenty years in the WDM community. His Arabic surpasses that of most in the Nation of Islam, which assists in her own desire to study the language. Also, "he had a very rich and deep understanding of *hadith* which I didn't have being in the Nation, and he had a deep understanding of Islamic history in general. This marked difference [in my husband compared with other FOI] has really helped me evolve spiritually, to really study the religion of Islam." But while Cassandra has positive impressions of the WDM community in terms of its knowledge of the religion, she has had negative experiences with her husband's family members who have remained with Imam Mohammed, one in particular whom she describes as "arrogant" toward members of the Nation. Therefore, when asked if she feels any connection with women formerly in the Nation of Islam, Cassandra responds, "I don't feel any type of connection. . . . Not that I wouldn't pursue a friendship with that sister; however, my interaction with persons from that community hasn't been generally welcoming or positive—it's kind of been adversarial."

Cassandra's general impression of Sunni Islam is such that, as she plainly states, "It's not attractive for me to leave the Nation of Islam; it doesn't make sense." Much of her aversion has to do with negative experiences at *masjids*. She first visited *masjids* during a "searching period" in which she visited various religious communities. She found the Nation of Islam to be "the only Muslim community that was open and receptive. When I encountered other sisters from other communities, it was almost like [you've] got to know the secret handshake or the password before they'll even start talking. . . . And within the Nation of Islam, it wasn't like that." Since joining the Nation, Cassandra has occasionally attended *jum'ah* or Ramadan dinners at Sunni *masjids* at the request of her husband but has stopped this practice because the gender separation leaves her alone with women who "usually are not welcoming."

Cassandra's multiple references to strict gender separation in Sunni *masjids* suggested that she had never attended a WDM *masjid*, where gender separation occurs but is not as pronounced as the gender barriers in most immigrant *masjids*. Despite Cassandra's husband's long time in the WDM community and the couple's visits to Sunni *masjids*, never once has she visited a WDM *masjid*, or any Sunni African American *masjid* for that matter, not even during her period of spiritual exploration before joining the Nation. She has attended immigrant *masjids* only. In particular, the gender barriers separating men and women in worship have given Nation women, like Cassandra, a negative impression of women's treatment in Sunni Islam:

> I feel in some ways that in the Nation . . . different rights that I have as a woman haven't been tampered with. I've gotten my education, I can work outside the home if I choose to, or stay in the home if I choose to. I don't have to do *jum'ah* behind the curtain and different things of that nature. There's a feeling that if I join another community, I would be subjugated to chauvinism or misogyny. As an African American Muslim woman, I already have to deal with chauvinism [in the Nation of Islam]. Because of men's lack of understanding—their interpretation of Islam— we get so subjugated to these sort of things. But I feel like it would be worse in another community.

Many Nation women tend to feel that they fare better than Sunni women, but their point of comparison usually is not women in the WDM community but women in immigrant *masjids* or abroad. In the ITC panel session, when Minister Ava described flawed interpretations of the Qur'an, she referred to women in Saudi Arabia being forced to wear black. "I was the only sister at *jum'ah* prayer that had on white," she said, describing a visit there. Yasmin Otway, a woman in her twenties born and raised in the NOI, when asked about her impression of women in the WDM community, describes a group of women she observed in a particular neighborhood in Atlanta known for its *masjid* with Saudi leanings. It became clear that these were in fact not women in the WDM community, and Yasmin acknowledged that she might be mistaken. "I don't really make a big distinction." Nonetheless, this is her description of them: "To me they seemed unhappy, and a lot of them seemed to be subject to some kind of—with the way that a lot of them seemed to act almost kind of muted and angry and unhappy—like almost some kind of abuse." Nation women who have attended a WDM *masjid*—and only a quarter of the women interviewed have done so— describe women's position in the WDM community as progressive, but they too refer to women abroad or immigrants when giving their general impression of how the Nation has a more progressive stance on women compared with Sunni Islam.

Only two of the women interviewed, Nisa Muhammad and Nicole Muhammad, have attended a WDM *masjid* on a frequent basis. Nisa, the founder of Wedded Bliss Foundation, sometimes attends *jum'ah* at a WDM *masjid* in Washington, D.C. She easily stands out in her MGT garments but feels well received. "We interact wonderfully," she says about the women there. Nisa has enjoyed hearing the stories of women now in their eighties who joined the Nation of Islam in the 1950s. She describes these women as courageous for wearing their garments during that time, taking their children out of the "white man's school," and being visited by the FBI. When she talks to these women, "they are so happy to see me in my MGT garment, and they say they miss those days."

Nicole Muhammad also wears her MGT garment when she attends a WDM *masjid* in Philadelphia and describes receiving "a warm cur- rent" from the sisters. "They still love to see that [Nation] spirit. They just give a big ole smile, a big ole hug." She contrasts her experience at the WDM *masjid* with that at Salafi *masjids*. Salafis, a group of Muslims with conservative interpretations and practices influenced by Islam in Saudi Arabia, have a strong influence and presence among African American Muslims in Philadelphia. Salafi women vividly mark African American Muslim space in Philadelphia with their black garments and face covering, or *niqab*. At the Salafi *masjid*, Nicole describes an atti- tude wherein "if you don't have *niqab* on, it's like to them you're not living Islam." As a result, she attends the Salafi *masjid* less often, but she does on occasion respond to the haughty attitudes of these women by reminding them that Nation women were the first to publicly identify as Muslim in a hostile environment. "I strive to let sisters in the Salafi community know that if it wasn't for the sisters prior to me in '75, I wouldn't be able to wear a *khimar*, headpiece, veil or whatever; none of us would. I wouldn't be able to carry the name Muhammad."

Nisa, Nicole, and Cassandra have had enough contact with members of the WDM community to make assessments based on a clear understanding of distinctions between the WDM community and other Sunni communities. Nicole describes women in the WDM community as having the same opportunities and liberties as women in the Nation of Islam. She does, however, note that because there are women ministers in the Nation of Islam, it appears that the Nation has more structures in place to grant women greater leadership roles. Nation women regularly comment on the ordination of women ministers as an indication of women's favorable status in the NOI. Similarly, Nisa feels that the MGT captain position places Nation women at an advantage because the captain is a leader representing women on the governing board. Cassandra says that while she has great respect for the WDM community, certain interpretations and practices make joining that community undesirable, and a major one is the practice of polygyny. Although she understands that it is accepted in the Qur'an, she states, "I don't think we as a people are mature enough to handle that sort of life- style with our history in this country." If Cassandra had more interac- tions with women in the WDM community, she would find that many share her resistance to polygyny.

As is the case for women in the Nation, women in the WDM com- munity give hardly any thought to women in the other group. The chance that former Nation women would visit an NOI mosque is rare, as most have a "been there, done that" attitude. As a result, sev- eral Sunni women state that they have no impression of women in the Nation. But there are a few exceptions. Jessica Muhammad introduced herself to a Nation woman in her step class but has never had any "in depth conversation" with her. A few thoughts about the woman have run across Jessica's mind:

> I'm thinking, "Oh that's good. She's out; she's taking advantage of the freedom that she has as a Muslim woman. And she's learning to dance,

and she's enjoying herself without having her husband right there." I'm also thinking about her dress. She dresses conservatively, a little more so than me, and I'm wondering if it's due to the influence of the Nation of Islam, or is it her personal preference.

Jessica's comments indicate that her sentiments about the old Nation of Islam, in which women had greater restrictions, influence how she views this woman. She is pleasantly surprised about the woman's freedom but at the same time notices her strict dress, which Jessica attributes to the Nation. After the change with Imam Mohammed, Jessica relaxed dress standards for herself, choosing not to always wear the *hijab*. Nonetheless, Jessica's statement is ironic given that many Sunni women also dress conservatively. Jessica agrees that the *hijab* is important to Sunni women, but "sometimes they'll have the *khimar* on but with a tight skirt." This Nation woman, however, made sure "that her top was coming down under her butt, and that her slacks were generally loose." Jessica notes that she "still associate[s]" this degree of modesty "more with the Nation."

Other women in the WDM community suggest a type of oppression that Nation women are experiencing, but of a spiritual nature. Mary Hamidullah,[7] for example, notes, "I have problems with Farrakhan because I think he does know, but his community does not [know that Nation teachings are false]. He is holding his community back." Amatullah Sharif, of The Mosque Cares (also known as the Ministry of W. Deen Mohammed), suggests a divine plan that before Minister Farrakhan's death, "our people will be teaching his people, helping his people come into Islam."

Su'ad Sabree describes in very gendered terms a form of religious oppression experienced by Nation women and presents herself as a teacher to them. An award-winning fashion show coordinator from Atlanta, Su'ad was invited to spend two months in Chicago to coordinate a fashion show for the Nation. The fashion show's theme was women's empowerment across faith communities. Women from the two groups interacted during practice, and the Sunni women felt arrogance from the Nation women who were very disciplined in their modeling. For them, "Everything was straight drilling [like the orchestrated steps of the MGT drill team], so when they looked at us as we modeled, it was almost like we weren't disciplined or we weren't the right Muslim women. I guess we were just so out of the box for them," Su'ad says, referring to the Sunni women's more mainstream American modeling choreography.

Su'ad feels that everything has remained stagnant in the Nation. "It was like they're doing the same thing. It's like a copy." Imitating the women, she continues, "'All praises due to Allah for the Honorable Elijah Muhammad,' 'As-salaam 'alaykum, my sister.' All of that outwardly mannerism." Like Jessica, Su'ad judges the women based on the old Nation of Islam. The women personify "the structure of it, but they don't have the soul of it, whereas in the Nation of Islam how we grew up, we believed in the structure of it, but we had another thing going with our soul." What Su'ad means by the "soul of it," is, as discussed earlier, the belief held by many old Nation women in an unseen God. "My mother was in the church, so she already had it in her. . . . My mom's concept was you can't see Allah so she couldn't connect Master Fard as God."

Su'ad tried to impart the concept of Allah as an unseen power to the women and found many of them humble and open. "They have a light that was not turned on because they keep them in the dark with [the attitude of] 'Minister Louis Farrakhan as the man, Minister Louis Farrakhan as the way of life, Minister Louis Farrakhan can do anything.'" The people keeping the women in the dark, Su'ad describes in gender-specific terms: the male "ministers and secretaries under Minister Louis Farrakhan." Su'ad got the impression that most of the women were not reading the Qur'an. "I kept telling them read your Qur'an, read your Qur'an for yourselves, so you can understand what Allah is trying to tell you. See, this is how we speak from Imam Mohammed who's teaching us to learn the religion for yourself." According to Su'ad, the response of the women was, "Sister, you need to be a minister because we never heard any talk like this, like do for yourself, read *your* Qur'an." Su'ad further describes her impression of the condition of these women:

They were like, "Sister, we're sort of hungry." They were sort of like looking for something different because they have to listen to the brothers, and the brothers are the soldiers of the community. So the women don't really question the man because that's how we were taught in the Nation, that the man is the maintainer and the provider and [men] tell us what we need to do in this life, and we just go along with it. So it's sort of still on that level in the Nation.

It is not surprising that Sunni women measure contemporary Nation women's freedom in terms of access to religious knowledge. As we saw earlier, the ultimate form of liberation that Sunni women experienced in the transition was not women's rights but the Sunni understanding of God and the freedom to study their religion for themselves. Upon asking Lynice Muhammad to imagine a conversation with a Nation woman, she says, "The main thing that I would encourage her to do is research for herself and not just listen to what your minister is saying. Imam Mohammed always taught us, 'Don't just take my word for it; you go back and study the Qur'an, and you go back and study what others have written about Islam.'" At the same time that this idea of liberation is associated with a religious awakening, it also takes on a meaning specific to women's liberation as Sunni women encourage Nation women to challenge male leadership. Among Sunni women, the contrasting perspective to "teaching" Nation women is also present. In an imagined conversation with a Nation woman, Safiyyah Shahid says, "I would be sure to be very sensitive to their sensitivities. . . . I would not be trying to prove them wrong or say your rituals are not caught up with [those of] mainstream Islam."

Based on these encounters and impressions, and the misconceptions revealed through them, an in-depth dialogue between Sunni and Nation women is likely to take the following form. Nation women would want Sunni women to understand that Nation women consider themselves part of the larger *ummah* (Muslim community), they have been exposed to Sunni Islam yet have no interest in leaving the Nation, and they are diverse in their religious beliefs. Women in the WDM community would want Nation women to understand that WDM *masjids* are not immigrant *masjids* and that the culture and the Islamic message of WDM *masjids* continue to resonate with the concerns of African Americans. They would also want Nation women to know that their *masjids* are very different from immigrant *masjids* in terms of gender practices. The gender attitudes within WDM *masjids* that Sunni women find troubling, they attribute to remnants of the old Nation's leadership structure that have survived in their communities, not to Sunni Islam. Regarding gender practices in Sunni Islam that appear to keep women subjugated, such as the prohibition on women imams or the allowance of men to have multiple wives, Sunni women have produced pro-woman interpretations.

"We're Still One *Ummah*": Universality, Evolution, and Diversity in the Nation of Islam

"I don't have any ill feelings when it comes to that community at all because we're taught not to. . . . We're still one *ummah* at the end of the day," states Nicole, who attends *jum'ah* at various *masjids* in Philadelphia. Minister Farrakhan's decision to establish and encourage *jum'ah* as a practice for his community has greatly increased this sense of belonging in the *ummah*. Additionally, there are not Nation mosques in every area or not every Nation mosque holds *jum'ah* service, which increases opportunities for Nation members to attend Sunni *masjids*. In 2012 Minister Farrakhan appointed the first imam to Mosque Maryam in Chicago, Sultan Rahman Muhammad, the great-grandson of Elijah Muhammad, raised Sunni. *The Final Call* covered a Unity prayer service in Charlotte in October 2012 and featured pictures of Imam Sultan leading the prayer. He comments in the article, "This is a sign, through this Jumu'ah . . . that . . . members of the Nation of Islam are uniting with the Islamic world. This is our goal and this has been the work of the Honorable Minister Louis Farrakhan for many, many years."[8] Even with the changes that appear to bring the Nation closer to Sunni Islam, most Sunni Muslims will not embrace Nation members until its theology changes.

Nation women do not regard their theology as taking them outside the fold of Islam or the *ummah*. They emphasize the universality and diversity of Islam, a tradition that accommodates diverse cultures, circumstances, and human needs and, therefore, diverse interpretations of the Qur'an and Sunnah. "I think that whenever you're on a spiritual path, whatever it is that illuminates you or strikes you, then that's what you should follow," states Saaudiah Muhammad. "I'm a member of the Nation of Islam, and this is where I want to be by choice. I have no plans to be anyplace else. . . . Now, to say one [Muslim community] is better than the other, I don't do that. . . . There may be some theological differences, but the essence of Islam remains the same." JayVon Muhammad also emphasizes her clear choice in the midst of other understandings of Islam:

> I go to *jum'ah* prayer, I read the Qur'an; but even in doing that, even in all of the different sisters that I meet, . . . even in all the people I love, I still believe in the core teachings of the Nation. And I don't believe it has to be divisive. . . . I believe as long as we both believe that Allah is God and we both practice our religion, then we shouldn't have a problem with each other.

The offense that many Nation women take to the comments of "divisive" Muslims is heard in Saaudiah's comments:

> When I was introduced to the teachings of the Honorable Elijah Muhammad, I knew beyond the shadow of a doubt the teachings were true and correct so I'm not intimidated by quote-unquote orthodox Islam, which I really don't like to use that term because it sets up a sense of classism. . . . I don't distinguish; a Muslim is a Muslim to me, and it's not my place to judge, and it's not my place to ask asinine questions such as, "Do you pray?" I mean that's so offensive, to have another Muslim ask me, "Do I pray?" "Excuse me, do *you* pray?" That's my response to anyone that asks me that because they're thinking that Muslims in the Nation of Islam, we don't pray. *Really?* No, we pray. I mean, give me a break.

Nisa would want Sunni women to know that in no way are Nation women held back by Minister Farrakhan from engaging Sunni Muslims. Nisa was introduced to Islam by her sister, a Sunni Muslim, but made the choice to join the Nation. As previously described, she attends a WDM *masjid* and others in Washington, D.C. Although she is not sure whether she is in the majority or minority, she says, "I know a lot of sisters who do this." When her two youngest sons were killed in a car accident in 2010, she held the funeral at an immigrant *masjid*. She is the organizer of the national Ramadan Prayer Line held every day at 5:00 a.m. during the sacred month. "We have speakers from the entire Muslim community: Louis Farrakhan, Imam Suhaib Webb, Imam Zaid

Shakir, Imam Siraj, Dr. Aminah McCloud . . . so I don't see divisions."
She was interviewed by the Islamic Society of North America's magazine *Horizon* for an article on her Wedded Bliss Foundation and has
conducted marriage workshops at WDM *masjids.*

Nation women are well aware that the Nation, since the passing of the
Honorable Elijah Muhammad, has introduced new practices—for example, fasting with other Muslims in Ramadan—but they clearly distinguish
between abandoning Elijah Muhammad's teachings, which they see
Imam Mohammed having done, and interpreting those teachings in ways
that fit their current context, which they see Minister Farrakhan doing.
In this way, they believe neither that everything has remained the same
for the group nor that they are going against what Elijah Muhammad
desired. Rather, they describe Islam as a religion that evolves and adapts,
as presented by their teacher Minister Farrakhan. He once remarked:

> I thank Allah so much for the man that came to try to put us on the road
> to Islam. The starting point is not the finishing point. The starting point
> is letting us know that we have a journey. . . . Fard Muhammad devel-
> oped a methodology . . . unorthodox as it may seem . . . yet [through
> it] we would evolve from a nationalist, Black thinking people into the
> universal message of Islam.[9]

To say that Islam is evolving versus changing allows Nation women
to adapt the teachings of Elijah Muhammad to their current context
without rejecting the old teachings. As Khaleelah Muhammad states,
"The concept of the universality of Islam I think is broader [in today's
Nation], but it's not because the teachings have changed, it's just that the
understanding of the teachings have been opened up."

To grasp what Khaleelah means by this, it is helpful to consider how
she and others respond to the question of whether the Nation continues
to teach that the white man is the devil. Most Sunni Muslims are unclear
on what exactly the Nation teaches today. Su'ad reports about the Nation
women with whom she interacted, "They were trying to say that the
white man was the devil, and I was trying to let them know that that's
out, because you have to deal with the white man every day." According
to Khaleelah, however, "The minister tells us that the Honorable Elijah
Muhammad said for them to stop calling the white man the devil and to

use the term the enemy or the slave master's children, because while that may be true and is true, it's just that [calling the white man the devil] could be incendiary, and you lose potential audience members."

Yasmin Otway responds this way to the question, Does the Nation still teach that white people are the devil?

> Not like that. . . . Maybe for that time when people were just coming in . . . , [but] you evolve. Islam and the Nation are definitely about evolution. At that time, maybe people needed to hear that stuff. . . . It's not necessary [to proclaim that now], but you know what is going on, you know what you see and you know what is. . . . Those teachings are still there, but that's not what anyone's focus is. . . . What matters now is getting ourselves together . . . and bringing out the God in us.

JayVon previously described holding fast to the "core teachings" despite encounters with various types of Muslims. When asked if she continues to believe in this particular core teaching about whites, she responds, "Yes, I believe that. . . . I do believe that the white man is the newest member of the human family. Like I believe that whites were created 6,000 years ago through a scientific process and that they've been acting up ever since." JayVon refers to a lecture she viewed on YouTube that quoted former Nation women stating that they never really believed that whites were the devil. JayVon continues:

> I was like, hmmm, I don't know how that couldn't make total sense because it makes total sense to me . . . in terms of the one group in the human family who has traveled the world and caused war and wickedness. . . . I also believe that the Black man has the devil inside him. The devil part is based on *behavior*, not on race, but when you look at the . . . one that went around spreading disease, started war, killed people, crashed economies, [it's the white man]. . . . But I do not believe that the white man [has the market cornered] on being the devil. . . . Whoever is doing wickedness is being devils.

In none of the women's responses is the original teaching about whites repudiated. Instead, new understandings of the teaching are presented.

The belief that God came down in the person of Fard Muhammad is the original Nation teaching upon which Sunnis primarily base their opinion that Nation Muslims are not real Muslims. Nation women explain why this original teaching remains compelling to them today. JayVon states, "That makes total sense to me, and sometimes I wonder how other people couldn't believe that if God wanted to talk to them, He would come and talk to them. To me that's so real and so practical." Similarly, Khaleelah remarks, "[The belief that God is a man] is completely liberating for me. It heightens the prospect of what we call God potential for me." She explains:

> I have unlimited potential to be like Him, because He is a man. And so to me that makes sense. . . . As I'm walking around in the community, I look and I say, "Oh my God, imagine if that person knew that she had God potential, imagine if he knew he had God potential, imagine if he knew God was a man?" And not only a man, but a man like him, a Black man, wow! It's not racist, it's empowering. It's true, and it's empowering.

Nisa explains the teaching about Fard Muhammad quite differently. "Minister Farrakhan has stated to Islamic scholars that we worship Allah. We don't worship a man born of a woman. We worship Allah, and . . . Master Fard Muhammad came . . . with designs specifically to bring Islam to the Black men and women in America." Her comments echo well those of Minister Farrakhan:

> We know that [Master Fard Muhammad], a human being born February 26, 1877, is not the originator of the heavens and the earth, but the good that we gained from [him] . . . was that he raised from among us a man that would get us started in a process that, even though the Islamic world would have liked to have helped, . . . they [immigrant Muslims] didn't have the right methodology and approach for the condition that we were in.[10]

Nisa continues, noting that people often refer to point number twelve on the back of *The Final Call*—the declaration that Allah appeared in the person of Master W. Fard Muhammad—"but if you look at point number one, *we believe that there's no God but Allah*. That's it!" Nisa continues:

And so the methodology in which Islam was presented to the Black man or woman was unique because it was a prescription for a sick people. . . . The Honorable Elijah Muhammad [was] mirroring the teaching of the Prophet Muhammad, peace be upon him. When he went to teach, he didn't give everybody everything all at once. There was Islam in Mecca and then there was Islam when they got to Medina.

Earlier, we saw that Nation women have different religious beliefs because of the way in which Minister Farrakhan adapts his message to his varying audiences, from church congregations to Islamic scholars. Cassandra, whose husband was in the WDM community for twenty years, provides another reason why some Nation women demonstrate understandings closer to Sunni Islam. "Many of my sister friends are married to believers who were around during that time [of the transition], that were either in Imam Warith Deen Mohammed's community for a while," like Minister Farrakhan, "or left the Nation completely and came back." The family members of such old time members are forced to think about these theological differences as well, which influences their interpretation and increases the diversity of thought and practice in the Nation community. A relative of Cassandra's husband, for example, returned to the Nation after fifteen years in the WDM community, but she does not believe that Elijah Muhammad is still alive, one of the new Nation's teachings, because she was around during the time of his death. She also has doubts about the "God in the Person" teaching.

In Cassandra's view, "There are a lot of people who are within the Nation who don't agree with every philosophy, . . . but they want themselves . . . [and] their children to be in this positive, productive environment." Further, she states, "People will stay within the Nation for their love of Minister Farrakhan, and also a love of the tradition and the reputation that the Nation has generated over the past eighty years now." She likens this tendency to non-Catholics' sending their children to Catholic school for its "reputation of quality education and discipline."

Black Consciousness and Activism in the WDM *Masjid*

Downplaying theological differences, Nation women are more likely to say that the difference between the Nation and Sunni Islam is the

Nation's "focus on improving the condition of African Americans." In Nisa's words:

> We believe that we have *the* best religion, and we have a responsibility to raise those up who are on the bottom. . . . I think that is the main difference, is that we look at the condition of our people, and we take that very seriously, and we have an understanding and a presentation of Islam that ignites in them . . . to say, "You know what? *Allah is God.*"

JayVon had been in conversation with Pakistani men who attempted to discredit the Nation. In her response to them, she also notes the Nation's unique aim to bring Islam to African Americans:

> I grew up in the ghetto, and there were many liquor stores owned by people who told me they were Muslims, yet they never said *as-salam 'alaykum* to me or tried to save me, so I don't want to hear the drama; save it. . . . Don't be critical of the Nation of Islam when that's how many Black people learn about Islam although they interact with people [immigrants] who say they're Muslim all the time in their community.

Nisa also speaks out about immigrants when she describes why Elijah Muhammad's "specific prescription of Islam" continues to be relevant. She presents how a newcomer to Islam who is Black feels when attending an immigrant *masjid*:

> Nobody's gonna speak to me. Nobody's gonna say, "How are you doing? *As-salam 'alaykum.*" Nobody's going to connect with me at all. And the kind of subtle racism, *I see that.* But I am trying to come into Islam, and I don't want to feel like I'm less than anybody else, but with the teachings of the Honorable Elijah Muhammad, you're not going to feel like you're less than anything.

As we saw earlier, Khaleelah left Sunni Islam for the Nation because of ill treatment at an immigrant *masjid*. Women in the WDM community would want Nation women to know that they can certainly relate to Nation women's bad experiences in immigrant *masjids*, but that the WDM *masjid* experience is not the immigrant *masjid* experience, and that is due to the legacy of the Nation of Islam within the WDM *masjid*. It is also attributed to Imam Mohammed's approach to lead his community with limited influence of immigrant Muslims.

Islah Umar joined the Nation in 1973 in Queens, New York, but is now a Sunni Muslim and lives in upstate New York, where she attends an immigrant *masjid*. The WDM *masjid* she attended when she first moved there thirty years ago has since closed. "The sadness that I speak to my daughter about is not having more African American Muslims who have made the transition and who have enough money to help the community keep going." She continues, describing the plight of Black Muslims in immigrant *masjids*: "They don't want anything from us except mere contact or maybe cleaning the bathroom, or watching the kids. They are not interested in the person and their background. If you are a lawyer, they seem to have some use for you, or a doctor or a teacher, but if not, they don't regard us."

Although she attends an immigrant *masjid*, she carries herself with a level of confidence and independence that she considers absent among some of the other Black Muslims at the *masjid*. She attributes this to her Nation legacy:

> People who came through the Nation of Islam primarily do not beg foreigners for anything. People who came through Sunni Islam or whatever else, [having never been in the Nation], they will go to foreigners and ask them for money, cars, a place to stay, and it almost looks like [doing so] doesn't bother them. We would rather do it ourselves or be without it. It's a pride; it's a sense of I can do it myself; I do not need you to accept me; I do not need you to run my school because we did that too. I do not need you to open a business for me because we did that too. There's a definite difference to how we relate to everybody. . . . We have a different posture. . . . If we don't have it, we won't ask you for it. That's the way we feel. And the motto of the Nation of Islam was do for self. And that's why we feel that way. Do for self: "Up you mighty Nation, you can accomplish what you will."

As well as teaching her to do for self, the Nation legacy has left her with the understanding that "I have a personal relationship with Allah that I have to maintain." Islah's explanation of how the Nation legacy deepens her connection with God would resonate with any Nation woman. "We felt like we were not like anybody else in the world, like the best kept secret, like a covered jewel, that one day they are going to turn around and look up and all these 'lost–found' Black people are going to be Muslims, and they are not going to know how it happened, who helped us or who did it." Here Islah is speaking a language shared between old and new Nation women, testifying that the immigrant Muslim community or the *ummah* abroad did not bring them to Islam, but God did:

> So being able to worship without the affirmation or without the support from other people came from that as well. You don't need a whole lot of other people to say you are a good Muslim. You are a good Muslim because Allah called you. There was an independence that was learned from the Nation of Islam: that we are unique, that we are valuable, that we are not beholden or needing anybody else to come and get us, because none of them did, none of them came and got us. This man who came, Fard Muhammad came, then Elijah Muhammad was appointed, so we don't feel any sense of obligation to these foreigners or to white people or to anybody else for Allah finding us because somebody else came to get us. So . . . [the ability] to worship without a community or worship with a community that's not ours, and not feel that we are lost in it, that's from the Nation of Islam.

Islah's remarks demonstrate a type of transformed Black consciousness. Her confidence does not emanate from a pride in Blackness but rather a pride that God chose and elevated her despite the belief that still prevails in some contexts that Blacks are not worthy. Her faith is informed by a consciousness of what African Americans have suffered and an understanding that God—not any race: Black, white, or immigrant—elevated a group of people from their suffering to a new human condition. Similarly, Imam Mohammed never abandoned Black consciousness, or awareness of the unique plight of African Americans in this country, when he took on the task of introducing his community to the Sunni understanding of God.[11] Rather, he continued to address the particular yearning that brought his followers to a Black nationalist version of Islam in the first place. His strategy was to connect the two—the inherent nature to connect with a God who does not prefer one race over another and the African American soul's demand for a beautiful, dignified human identity:

> I am trying to get African Americans who still have the burden on them of [finding their] identity . . . to go back to your better identity. The better identity that God gave us is not our racial identity . . . or our national identity. The better identity for Muslims in Islam according to our Holy Book—[the identity that] God gave us—is our human identity, which is to be understood as the aim for excellence in the human nature. . . . God created us for human excellence, and this is our common heritage.

Focusing on this inherent, God-given potential, Imam Mohammed accomplished two goals. First, he empowered his followers to reclaim the nobility that was taken away from them. Second, he instilled a motivation that, instead of reflecting a desire to achieve parity with another race, resonated with an inherent yearning to meet the standards that the Creator designed for all humanity. "Black Nationalism . . . [or] Black Muslimism is just a strategy to accomplish the real thing." The real thing is "answer[ing] the demands in my soul for respect to come for me and my people!"[12] In Sunni women's expressions of their reformed race consciousness, they often echo Imam Mohammed's emphasis on the drive for excellence shared among all human souls. Bayyinah Abdul-Aleem, of Philadelphia, states, "I believe that our efforts within our [WDM] communities have . . . [been] to incorporate a deeper understanding of what it means to be our best self—away from being our best African American self to the exclusion of all others, to being our best self period."

Unlike Islah, most Muslims in the WDM community attend WDM *masjids*. As Islah's comments might suggest, these *masjids* are strikingly independent of immigrant influence. Also, they are distinct from other Sunni Black *masjids* in that WDM *masjids* carry the Nation legacy. Having transitioned from Nation temples, WDM *masjids* can be found in most major cities, including new *masjids* established in the 1980s and '90s. They are known for their Black culture, Muslim preaching that reminds of Black Christian ministers, and pioneers, or old folk from the Nation of Islam, seated in chairs instead of on a carpet, a few of whom persist in performing the occasional solo rendition of call and response, shouting to the imam, "That's right! Teach!" The young adults in WDM *masjids*—the overwhelming majority of them were babies, toddlers, or yet to be born during the transition—never lived the Nation of Islam experience, except vicariously through the occasional reminisces of Nation days over imam rostrums, what members of the community call the pulpit from which the imam speaks, or in the mini-*khutbahs* (sermons, allusion to *jum'ah* sermon) of former Nation members in *masjid* lobbies or Muslim restaurants. Many of them attended Sister Clara Muhammad School, but not above a few years, as most barely stayed open beyond the 1980s or '90s. A total of ten schools remain today in cities including Atlanta, Brooklyn, Baltimore, and Stockton, California.[13]

WDM *masjids*, and particularly their forming part of a national community still tied to the leadership of Imam Mohammed, represent the primary heritage of the Nation of Islam for Sunni women. Women continue to patronize the community newspaper available in their *masjids*, now named the *Muslim Journal*. Imam Mohammed abandoned the term "Bilalian" in the early 1980s because of concerns from other Muslims that his community would be seen as a sect that identified with Bilal above the Prophet Muhammad.[14] Thereafter, the community identified itself as African American and, more important, Muslim. The *Muslim Journal* continues to feature a lecture by Imam Mohammed in its centerfold and to report on activities or individuals affiliated with various WDM *masjids* around the country. Before Imam Mohammed's death, women attended the community's annual national convention, usually held on Labor Day in Chicago, or Imam Mohammed's annual Ramadan session, or any local events sponsoring a lecture by Imam Mohammed. In a lecture on establishing model community life or a lecture on the symbolic significance of the various prayer positions—the imam's topics were varied and far-reaching—it was not uncommon for Imam Mohammed to begin or interrupt with reflections on his father's work or the mission of Fard. As he decided to do in the very beginning, Imam Mohammed continued to honor the legacy while moving far beyond it.

Cultivating "community life" is a concept that marks the language and vision of Imam Mohammed and brings continuity between the past and present. "The responsibility we have to accept is responsibility of our life in *community*."[15] Imam Mohammed continued to encourage his community to establish and produce for themselves, in every area imaginable, from business to education to social services. But unlike in the case of the old Nation, where much was built upon debt, corruption, and coercion, he encouraged his community to take responsibility for their families by also acquiring education and skills, working mainstream jobs, and collaborating with like-minded people who had common goals across racial and religious lines. This approach led to *masjid* communities that are fairly mainstream in identifying as American and African American. They are not cut off from the culture and concerns of their non-Muslim neighbors. At the same time, they aspire to fashion individuals and families with strong Muslim values and practice. This means that much of their activism revolves around maintaining and growing *masjid* communities that have a positive influence in their immediate surroundings, almost always Black neighborhoods.

The first generation of women in the WDM community, those who made the transition with Imam Mohammed, have laid the cultural foundation of WDM *masjids*. They have lived the lives of American women, most working outside the home while raising families. Raising Muslim children in a Muslim home was a primary concern. They have continued certain dietary traditions from the Nation: bean soup, bean pie, and wheat bread instead of white. They have brought their personal strivings into the WDM *masjid*, the main location for cultivating community life for themselves and their families. They have had a range of committees and groups to choose from to do their work, local and national, and so they have had many roles from which to contribute: teachers, directors, fundraisers, consultants, lecturers, event planners, cooks, writers, and artists. The types of activities in which women have carried out these roles include founding and running full-time Muslim schools and Sunday school programs, organizing Muslim fashion shows, organizing community workshops on a range of topics from health to domestic violence, establishing shelters for Muslim women and children, planning national WDM community conventions, participating in interfaith outreach, sponsoring Muslim youth organizations, producing Muslim television shows, leading Girl and Boy Scouts troops, feeding the homeless, and protesting the establishment of liquor stores in the areas surrounding the *masjid*.

The Atlanta Masjid of Al-Islam is one of the most prominent *masjids* in the WDM community, and much of this is attributed to the Mohammed Schools, which includes an elementary school and high school. Its first five graduating classes, between 1992 and 1997, included students who matriculated at top universities, including Harvard, Duke, and Stanford. The vision for the Mohammed Schools is rooted in the MUI. The MUI affiliated with the Atlanta temple closed in 1977 because of financial struggles. The *masjid* community reopened its school as a Sister Clara Muhammad School in 1980, and the first principal was Theresa Muwwakkil, who held a Doctor of Education. A high school program was added in 1989 and named W. D. Mohammed High School.

Sandra El-Amin, a graduate of Smith College, joined the Mohammed Schools in 1984 as a fourth-grade teacher. She served the high school as an English teacher in the 1990s and was promoted to principal of the elementary school. In 2001 she was appointed director of the Mohammed Schools, where she contributed much until her resignation in 2005. Sandra continues to feel passionately about the Nation's vision to educate African American Muslim children in the community's own schools:

> I'm still for that. . . . I still think that as African Americans, we need an educational program and a philosophy that addresses some of our special needs, because I still feel we are a special needs community, and we've had a unique experience. And I think that the self-esteem and cultural identity of our people can be best served by schools that address that need. . . . Once children have a strong sense of identity and purpose, and they know who they are, you can put them in a variety of different environments where they can flourish. . . . It goes so well with our unity principle, that one God created all humanity . . . and that there is value in *all* cultures. [With this understanding of one humanity], then you understand that the well from which you spring is not a polluted well. It has crisp, clear, clean, refreshing water just like everybody else. And sometimes you can't get that from just drinking out of somebody else's well, and having somebody else tell you about yours.

Sandra's remarks again indicate a transformed race consciousness. It can be described as an awareness that the need for human excellence is shared by all ethnic groups as part of a common human makeup, with attention to the ways in which African Americans have been historically denied this dignity and require at times a unique focus and approach to acquiring this common human excellence. Sunni women would want Nation women to know that this last point is not lost on the WDM community and that it reflects in the culture and aspirations of WDM *masjid* communities.

Shafeeqah Abdullah attends a second WDM *masjid* in Atlanta, and she provides another glimpse of how women are inspired by Imam Mohammed to elevate African Americans in the pursuit to emerge as a model Muslim community: "Following the example of Imam W. D. Mohammed, and certainly continuing what we have learned from the Honorable Elijah Muhammad, we have to form this model moral community in our lifetime." Shafeeqah's "particular interest" is building a "cultural center," which she proposed to the *masjid* board on which she serves:

> The cultural center is important because we don't have a place where we can gather and express ourselves. We go to the masjid, of course, for prayer . . . , but culturally speaking, we need a place where we can express ourselves, express our culture, where we can have events and fundraisers and activities for the whole family and community. And this building will be an ongoing income profit for the community because we could rent it out and present it to other individuals or groups who might need it. Every community needs to have an avenue of expression.

With plans to rent out the cultural center to other groups, Shafeeqah's do-for-self Nation mentality is expanded by Imam Mohammed's concept to work with others.

Like women in the Nation, women in the WDM community have also founded organizations through which they carry out activism beyond the *masjid*. Sandra and Lynice Muhammad started organizations that focus on women specifically, and while African American women make up the majority of those served, services are not limited to any particular racial group. After resigning from her position as director of the Mohammed Schools, Sandra founded Sacred Diva, "a community-based organization addressing the spiritual wellness of women and girls in all walks of life. Sacred Diva is concerned with cultivating respect and appreciation for feminine energies, attributes, and gifts." Sacred Diva partners with other organizations to serve women who have experienced different types of life trauma, including homeless women and abused and neglected teenage girls. In addition to African American women, Caucasian, Hispanic, Pakistani, and Indian women have been among her clients.

Lynice's organization, the Coweta Teen Mothers and Babe Service Center, is especially noteworthy because it came about as a result of the close connection and love shared between two women, one in the Nation and the other in the WDM community. Lynice was raised in the Nation in Detroit and made the transition without her mother, who remained active in the Nation until her death. Lynice's mother owned ten acres of land in Coweta County, Georgia, where Lynice planned to open a home for teenage mothers. The vision of Lynice and her mother was to provide the young women "therapeutic counseling and overall character building with emphasis on self-esteem building and instilling a sense of independence." Circumstances did not allow her to use her mother's property, but the dream of the women came true when Lynice opened the home in 2007 closer to Atlanta. Lynice gives tribute to her mother on the organization's website. "The Coweta Teen Mothers and Babe Service Center (CTMBS) is the original idea of Mrs. Muhsinah Bilal, the mother of 11 children." The program assists teen mothers in developing "skills associated with academic achievement; newborn child care; the basics of household management (housekeeping, cooking, time management, caring for a child, and budgeting); the elements of nutrition, health, and emotionally intelligent parenting; and good communication." African American women, African women, and Latinas have participated in the program.[16]

As in the case with Nation women described earlier, women in the WDM community are generally not associated with traditional grassroots organizing. However, regular forms of activism in poor communities are initiated by women and carried out through the *masjids* or Muslim women's organizations such as Sisters United in Human

Service (SUIHS), led by a group of women affiliated with the Atlanta Masjid. SUIHS has established a weekly feeding program in the historic African American neighborhood of Sweet Auburn. Alongside feeding the homeless, another popular area of activism for African American *masjids* is prison-related programs. Black *masjids* have traditionally surpassed immigrant *masjids* in "community involvement," with WDM *masjids* reporting the highest level of community work of all *masjids*.[17]

Women's Leadership and Exegesis in WDM *Masjids*

WDM *masjids* are the least likely of all Sunni *masjids* in the United States to place a barrier—for example, a curtain, screen, railing, or wall—between the men's and women's prayer sections. The 2011 American mosque study showed that roughly 75 percent of immigrant *masjids* use a gender barrier, compared with 39 percent of African American *masjids*. Most of the Black *masjids* using a barrier are not affiliated with Imam Mohammed. Only 10 percent of WDM *masjids* use a gender barrier, whereas 68 percent of Black mosques unaffiliated with Imam Mohammed use one.[18] Women and men do worship in separate sections in WDM *masjids*, with the women behind the men, but in a common prayer hall in which women can view and hear the imam easily.[19] This is also the arrangement adopted by Nation mosques that offer *jum'ah* services.

Zakiyyah Muhammad, a Sunni woman who occasionally attends Mosque Maryam to hear Minister Farrakhan lecture, passionately speaks on why a gender barrier is absolutely unacceptable in a Black *masjid*:

> I don't go to mosques where they got these rags dividing the men from the women. How dare an African American imam divide his woman from a man by putting a partition or rag up. They got a mosque here in Chicago where the sisters have to go 'round the backdoor. I wouldn't set foot in a mosque like that. I have a problem with brothers' setting sisters up in demeaning positions. I don't allow it. I don't dare go to a mosque where I got to sit behind a rag like I'm some inferior being, and here I have come through slavery. I've come across the Atlantic with you on the

slave ship, picked cotton with you in the field, saved you from massa's whipping and hanging you, and you gonna put me behind a rag because a foreigner comes across the water and tells you that's the set up? Oh no, not me. I ain't havin' it.

With strong voices like Zakiyyah's, women in the WDM community see their *masjids* as generally gender progressive. Rarely do they express any concern about the fact that the women sit behind the men in their own mosques. They commonly offer the argument that the Muslim prayer ritual, or *salat*, requires bowing and prostrating, and the focus should be on God. Men sit up front, they argue, because they are more likely to be distracted by women's rear body parts bending in front of them. Women's sitting in the back does not signify inferiority but rather practical logistics in a worship context in which men and women need separation, otherwise women would be forced, as part of *salat*, to touch bodies with male strangers. Imam Mohammed held this view that women and men should feel comfortable in the prayer line, and therefore not mix, but at the same time, he challenged the idea of women's having to sit behind men. At the 1994 Chicago Sisters' Meeting, he stated:

> I'm always challenging these so-called authorities who say they know everything about the *hadith*. They haven't produced for me any evidence that the Prophet said women have to be in the back. . . . [Women can] pray to the side. You can be as close to the speaker as the men are. [It's] going to change, eventually. . . . The world has been dominated by men and your justice is just coming. [You just] have to . . . put pressure on us.[20]

Women in the WDM community generally feel that they have influence on the vision and culture of their *masjid* communities. As Jeanette Nu'Man states, "We have a voice; women are heard. Women are listened to."

Women in the WDM community would want Nation women to understand that they associate Sunni Islam with greater gender freedom because their MGT experience was quite different from current Nation women's. Zakiyyah compares the two experiences:

They wear false nails and fingernail polish. We couldn't wear our nails long, and the only nail polish we could wear was clear. We could only wear two styles of uniform at that time, but now the sisters can be more versatile in their dress, and the uniforms are beautiful. . . . Some sisters wear scarves halfway down their head. They'd put us out of the mosque if we tried to walk in there with a scarf like that under the Messenger [Elijah Muhammad]. . . . I heard that there are Muslims staying together now, fornicating, and there are no investigations and there's no [punishment]. So you answer to Allah more so now than you did to the brother investigators who would investigate these things.

Many Sunni women miss MGT more than any other aspect of the Nation, but they do not miss the restrictions, the scrutiny, and the policing. While present-day Nation women who experienced the transition express frustrations about the fact that people went back to the streets when Imam Mohammed relaxed NOI laws, Sunni women find greater liberation in choosing righteous behavior for themselves, as described previously. Interestingly, Zakiyyah views this to be the case for Nation Muslims today as she describes them as answering to Allah now.

Nisa describes a benefit to MGT as having a woman leader represent the concerns of women. "I don't have to talk to the imam. I can talk to another sister about my concern." As seen earlier, Sunni women liked that with the transition they could speak to and address their concerns directly to Imam Mohammed. However, women found that in their local communities this strategy was not always effective because imams did not necessarily have the egalitarian outlook of Imam Mohammed, or they were not willing to relinquish the hierarchical governing structure of the Nation for a more democratic one, a situation that has continued to affect these communities today. Women in two different cities suggest this impact. "We still have a lot of obstacles to overcome to be fully appreciated." This woman states that imams in her *masjid* are not following the prophetic model of *shura*, or consultation, in which women were included. A woman in a different *masjid* community states, "There are opportunities now, but we had to grow to this; I think it was very chauvinistic for a very long time." Women note that the challenges they have faced with imams probably have less to do with attitudes about women's inferiority or any desire to keep them back than with "egos," opposition to ideas or people whom the imam does not agree with or like, and a mentality that the imam has the final word in the decision-making process. Several women attribute this to the old Nation leadership structure. Mary Hamidullah states, "I think that the leadership from the Nation of Islam just kind of moved into the transition. There has been a camaraderie, I would say, among the leadership that has continued, and I don't think that was easy to break through."

The leadership role of the imam varies in American *masjids*. Literally, the word "imam" means "prayer leader." Historically, the meaning of "imam" extended to a spiritual or religious authority. Imam Mohammed referred to the imam in both of these capacities, as a prayer leader and as a religious authority, when he commented during the ITC panel that he accepts women as ministers, which can encompass a variety of functions including teaching, but not as imams leading men and women in *salat*. Those who have described Minister Ava as the first woman imam in the world do not make this distinction, although it is an important one. Like Imam Mohammed, most American Muslims are not opposed to women as religious authorities or scholars. Leading the *salat*, the most fundamental aspect of the term "imam," is where questions and debate arise. In this sense, Minister Ava is not the first woman imam in Islamic history, or perhaps not an imam at all. There are isolated cases of women leading men in *salat* prior to Minister Ava's appointment.[21] According to a woman who has been a member of Muhammad Mosque No. 15 in Atlanta, Georgia, for eighteen years, Minister Ava's stint there was only a year, in which the member did not recall the minister's ever leading the *salat*.

In the movement for women imams in the United States, popularized by Amina Wadud's woman-led prayer, the Islamic sanction for women to lead men in *salat* is a component of a broader project to expand Muslim women's leadership in all realms. Resisting the imam role as male-exclusive is symbolic of resisting men's dominance in various leadership capacities in Muslim communities.[22] Indeed, the imam is more than a prayer leader in American *masjids*. In 54 percent of *masjids*, the function of the imam is extended to include the role of the organizational leader of the *masjid*. The imam serves this dual role in 47 percent of immigrant *masjids* and in 89 percent of African American *masjids*. When the imam functions as the prayer and religious leader only, the organizational leader is a president or director elected by the community. Almost all *masjids* have an executive committee or board of directors. The board of directors has the final decision-making power in most immigrant *masjids*. In African American *masjids*, however, the majority (65 percent) grants imams the final decision-making power.[23] Because of the imam's overarching influence as prayer leader, teacher, and power broker, the legal sanction against female imams locks women out of a critical leadership position in their communities.

Although the imam has the final decision-making power in most Black *masjids*, the board does collectively make decisions for the community and shares duties with the imam in many imam-dominated *masjids*.[24] Thus, the *masjid* board is an important avenue for women to influence their communities. In 2000, more WDM *masjids* (92.5 percent) allowed women to serve than did other Black *masjids* (60 percent) and immigrant *masjids* (66 percent).[25] But allowing women to serve did not mean that they necessarily served in a given period. Barbara[26] was the first woman elected to serve on her WDM *masjid* board in 2002. According to her, it really did not make a difference whether a woman was on the board or not. "I think that this is some of the influence of the first experience of the Nation of Islam, and that is, that the imam is the one who had the influence, who had the power. Regardless of what the recommendations were, it all boiled down to what the imam ultimately wanted."

Ten years later, the board of Barbara's *masjid* has been restructured such that the imam no longer has final decision-making power, and at least two women must serve. Three women currently serve, and there is male and female representation from the second generation who were never in the Nation. One of the old Nation women currently serving states, "I have not experienced a problem with the respect and implementation of input made by any of the women on the [board] during the time that I have served." She believes that less representation from men of the first generation and more from the second have greatly affected respect for women's contributions.

Nisa describes the governing board in the NOI when she explains the advantage of having the MGT captain speak on behalf of the women. Nisa, formerly an MGT captain, explains, "The MGT captain is a member of the 'Board of Laborers' in her mosque, or at the regional or national level, if applicable. The Board [comprises] the Minister, FOI Captain, Secretary (Treasurer), Director of Protocol, and the Sister Captain of the MGT-GCC herself." The final decision-making power lies with the board, not the minister. Again, this demonstrates evolution in the Nation that Sunni women do not account for.

With or without boards, men exert the greater religious authority and power in American *masjids* as a result of the imam's role to lead the weekly *jum'ah* prayer and the traditional prohibition on women leading men in this prayer. *Jum'ah* begins with a religious sermon (*khutbah*) and ends with the *salat*. Most Sunni women express agreement with women's exclusion from this role, or indifference to it. Even women who protested imams for their chauvinism appeared unbothered by the restriction on women imams. Jeanette states, "I'm not concerned that only men can be imams. I've never cared enough to investigate why." Similarly, Muhsinah states, "I am not of that—I don't want to use the word feminist because it's used in the wrong way—but I am not of that ilk where I want to protest because the female is not included in that position at this point. It doesn't concern me, it really doesn't."[27]

When women discuss their views about women imams, they assume the meaning of imam as the role is carried out in most WDM *masjids*, as both a prayer and organizational leader. Many view the restriction on women imams through the frame that they interpret Imam Mohammed's gender ideology, that men and women hold equal but complementary roles. Daa'Iyah Muhammad states, "I think [the restriction is there] because that load . . . is too much for a woman. . . . I don't think God created us that way." The idea that God has given men and women distinct roles comes across in Safiyyah Shahid's comments, but in a slightly different manner. Safiyyah builds upon Imam Mohammed's teaching that both men and women have the capacity to carry out any given role socially defined as male or female:

> In a sense, I do think that you're able to better navigate the waters as a male in certain aspects of society in terms of bringing the whole community along. . . . Even in our society, women reach a ceiling where they cannot go any further, and so the man I think has been given that role by God where they can be the leader, but that doesn't mean that the woman can't be a leader in her own right because at the [Mohammed

Schools], I'm the leader though I'm female and there are males work-ing under me. But in terms of the leadership of males and females in the community, I think that right now in our development and from what I can understand of the Qur'an, that leadership is in the hands of the male, but it may be called another thing for a woman. She may not necessarily get up and lead prayers. At times she can't even lead the prayers, but men are not constricted in that way; the menstrual cycle doesn't stop him from praying [an allusion to the prohibition on wom-en's performing *salat* when menstruating]. So there are certain aspects that God gave to the woman and to the man, but at the same time, it is the woman who produces the male. . . . She nurtures that imam up, so she has her role too, and she has a very significant role because we know how Imam Mohammed talked about the influences of Sister Clara Muhammad. Now we have these schools, and we have this great movement in our community because of a woman. Maybe we didn't call her the imam, but remember when the Honorable Elijah Muham-mad was imprisoned, she led the community. So we're just talking in a sense technical terms, but the reality of it is that women exercise lead-ership. . . . Their influence is strong even in the *masjid*. . . . So look at that influence as opposed to [just leading the prayer]. But when you're home, you lead your own prayers if your husband is not there. You don't stop praying, so then you become the imam. It's just not in the public sphere.

The idea that the imam role is innate to women but expressed in a different fashion is similarly presented by Bayyinah, who believes that "Muslim women already are imams, but not in terms of leading Islamic congregations in a physical sense, but . . . within our home." Safiyyah's and Bayyinah's comments highlight the fact that leadership in public is valued over leadership in private. They resist this notion by highlight-ing that women are imams in a different sphere. Bayyinah states, "In terms of the guidance and leadership that we can give our children, we already have that position."

It should be noted that Safiyyah's reference to society as patriarchal (that is, the "glass ceiling" comment) as a possible reason that God has intended for men to be imams—that men can better guide and elevate an entire community in a world dominated by other men—is strikingly similar to one of the explanations that Amina Wadud offers as to why men dominate in leadership roles in the Qur'an:

> As with other matters in society, the Qur'anic solutions to social problems reflect the prevailing attitudes in ancient Arabia. . . . Certainly where males had public privileges, experiences, and other advantages, they were best suited to operate in the political and financial arena. It was erroneously concluded that men would always have the advantages that would make them most suitable for leadership. Yet these advantages were not restricted to men in the Qur'an. Provided the woman has the motivation, opportunities should be made available. . . . Despite this difference in opportunities between men and women, even at the time of revelation, there is nothing implied or stated in the Qur'an which supports the opinion that males are natural leaders. . . . However, there is the implication that the Qur'an inclines towards seeing necessary tasks fulfilled in society in the most efficient manner. . . . To force even modern patriarchal societies to submit before a female ruler would be detrimental to the harmonious welfare of that society. However, choosing the one best suited for the tasks at hand is a dynamic process. . . . A more independent and insightful woman might better lead a people into their future endeavors.[28]

Wadud emphasizes that a change in times requires a change in gendered leadership. Although Safiyyah does not present this concept, she alludes to it when she states, "But in terms of the leadership of males and females in the community, I think that right now in our *development* [italics added] and from what I can understand of the Qur'an, that leadership is in the hands of the male."

Imam Mohammed also offered commentary on why men dominate as leaders of communities, or prophets, in the Qur'an and, like Wadud, did not suggest that men are naturally better leaders or teachers than women. He used the Qur'anic examples of women receiving revelation to show that women have the same innate makeup as men to receive and teach God's word, but God has designed for men to carry out this role as prophets for certain reasons. Imam Mohammed offered the distinct physiological nature of men as a reason:

So the Qur'an is not then going to give us women prophets like men prophets. . . . The man has been dominant [in the role of prophet] because of the differences in the . . . physiology of the male and the female sex. Because of the differences, you then have this great, pronounced image or presence of men in these roles. But it doesn't mean that women don't have exactly what men have. The Qur'an says, "And God revealed to the mother of Moses, and God revealed to the mother of Jesus." Peace be upon all of them. So that tells us that, yes, women can get revelation from God. He does communicate with women too. So even that unique kind of nature, phenomena [sic], or whatever it is that is in males that we look at and say, "Man gets Revelation," Allah is saying in the Qur'an, "Yes, women get it too!" But man, because of his nature again, he has a predominance, or a pronounced image in that particular nature, and he dominates.[29]

Therefore, while women and men both carry the capacity for diverse roles, one gender may dominate in certain roles. Again, it does not mean necessarily that a specific gender is incapable of a specific role, with the exception of women's exclusive capacity to bear children.

Other Sunni women embrace the restriction on women imams in light of their specific circumstances as Black women. Through this lens, they recognize women's capacity to carry out the gender roles that have been traditionally prescribed for men, but that this extended capacity has been to the detriment of African American women, who have been left to provide for the family and raise children.[30] We saw women accepting the gender ideology of the old Nation for this reason, and Shafeeqah similarly embraces men as imams as a way to ensure that they take the responsibility to lead:

A woman naturally wants to be led, and especially in this way of life. We got a lot of problems with husbands who have difficulty taking on the role that we feel that they should take on. So I feel very comfortable [with the idea of male leadership]. Like on the board of trustees [of the masjid], there are two women right now. There are seven altogether, so five of them are brothers. The convener and the co-convener are men, and I just love the leadership because this is a natural role that they are supposed to take. We as women, we have experienced having to be the head of the household and having to make all the decisions and work and distribute the money, doing all that, and men are supposed to have that kind of leadership in the community. And it's natural. So I love it.

Although Shafeeqah presents a very essentialist view of men's role as leaders, it is based on the understanding of a particular context's making this role for men essential, indicated in her words "especially in this way of life," in which women have historically taken on every responsibility. In other words, they want African American men to stand up.

A handful of Sunni women interviewed do not agree with the restriction on women imams. One is Sandra El-Amin, who was the director of the Mohammed Schools. She was also the wife of the imam at the Atlanta Masjid until they divorced in the months before she left her position at the school. Sandra began reading the work of Muslim feminists, including Fatima Mernissi. She was quite inspired but kept her sentiments private. Sandra explains, "For many years I preached outwardly whatever I thought was appropriate for my position either as the imam's wife or the director of the school." Sandra believes that was the right approach at that time but says, "I don't think the person who I am now could have carried that out as well now as I did then." She now feels "freer" to voice her perspectives because she does not carry the title of imam's wife or of director of the school. She playfully refers to this new place as her "coming out."

As part of coming out, Sandra has begun to carve out her philosophical position as a Muslim woman. "I've discovered that there are things about Islam in the way it's interpreted and preached by men that take away from its pure concept." She believes that the woman imam prohibition is one of those things. "I don't agree with that at all. I think it's a very old, antiquated idea, and as many times as I've read the Qur'an, I've never seen it expressly stated there. . . . I'm going to go ahead and tell you this; one of my favorite scholars is Amina Wadud." Sandra presents her regard for Amina Wadud in this confession-like manner because she understands that Wadud has become a controversial figure in the American *ummah* since her 2005 woman-led *jum'ah* prayer. Sandra further elaborates on her marginal position:

I think that a woman is equipped and knowledgeable enough to lead the prayer and, in many instances, know and understand the religion better than many men. And if we go with the idea that the most learned or knowledgeable person who has the highest character and is accepted by the community can lead, then that person can be male or female. And I don't see that there is anything inherent about being a man that renders him more suited for that position.

Jessica shares with Sandra an unpopular perspective on women imams and tells a story that involved an exceptional encounter with a Nation woman. Jessica had been in agreement with the exclusion of women from the imam position based on the argument that men might be distracted by women praying in front of them. However, she came to realize that "when it came down to the actual *khutbah*, the world needs a feminine perspective, to hear the softer side of God." Like Sandra, Jessica also states that she was "happy" about Amina Wadud and Saleemah Abdul-Ghafur, one of the organizers of the woman-led prayer. "If I had to credit somebody, it probably would be them for me officiating the wedding ceremony that I did last month. They were forerunners." Jessica was inspired by Amina Wadud's and Saleemah's courage, but she too had a history in her *masjid* of exhibiting the type of courage that Imam Mohammed encouraged when he stated to a group of women, "Do what women did in the day of the Prophet. They had the courage, no matter how big the male was, if he said something that they didn't think was rational or acceptable, they would call attention to it right out in the public. . . . That's the way you should do these brothers! Make them answer."[31] In this spirit, Jessica has always had a good relationship with the imams in her community and felt free to tell them what was on her mind. Therefore, when the opportunity arose for her to officiate a wedding, she shared the news first with the former imam, Sandra's ex-husband, and then with the current imam from the second generation:

I felt like I needed to—not to get a sanction, but just as a courtesy—let Imam Mansoor know. But before I could get a chance, Imam Plemon walked in and I found myself telling him. When I told him I was getting ready to officiate a wedding, he said [in jest], "I ain't surprised; I heard my ex-wife just did a eulogy." Then I said something like, "I'm not gonna say anything about equality right now, but what I will say is that I believe in spiritual expression." He said, "Naw, here's the real reason why you can do it; if you can have babies, you can do anything you wanna do." I saw that as, "OK, you got my blessing sister 'cause y'all can do something we can't do." And then when I told Imam Mansoor, it was even better. Imam Mansoor said that . . . a lot has been lost in the general history of how influential the women were in the propagation of this *din* [religion] and how we have a lot of wiggle room that we haven't taken. He said, "No, it's not radical what you're doing." So I went in there [the wedding ceremony] with much confidence, and they welcomed me. And this particular family by the way, they're mostly influenced by the Nation of Islam. So for them it was really no big deal because they have the example of Ava Muhammad.

Yasmin Otway, the woman who asked Jessica to officiate her wedding, was almost a teenager at the time that Minister Ava was appointed to head her mosque, but ironically, Yasmin has no recollection of a woman minister, which might be explained by her family's irregular attendance there. Other influences, including her parents' progressive outlook, are what made her determined to have a woman officiate her wedding:

I just don't think spiritual authority belongs to just a man, and I don't see why a woman who can bear all the prophets [cannot exercise this authority]. . . . I'm the type of person who is going to try and support these things [women's leadership] in every way I can, and this was an opportunity for me to do so.

Although Jessica did not know that Yasmin was a Muslim when she agreed to officiate her wedding, Yasmin had figured out that Jessica was. Jessica caught Yasmin's eye from the very beginning of their yoga class. "She fascinated me when I saw her. She looks almost regal to me, and she reminds me of my mom. She's very stylish and so put together." Jessica's "energy" and "modest, stylish" dress indicated to Yasmin that Jessica was not your everyday woman, and she sensed that she might be Muslim. Her hunch was confirmed when she heard Jessica state her last name, Muhammad.

The two women may have met once, Yasmin tried to recall, but they certainly did not talk on any regular basis, so the idea to approach Jessica about the wedding came "out of nowhere. It kind of forced its way in my mind, 'Ask Jessica. Ask her if she officiates.'" When she asked and Jessica agreed, Yasmin recalls, "I could tell that she felt really good, and I definitely felt great." Yasmin had figured that Jessica was not in the Nation, but that did not matter. "If you're a Muslim woman, you're a Black woman, that's what really mattered to me, and you're great." Yasmin and Jessica's relationship is interesting in light of the fact that the Nation has facilitated the position of women ministers whereas the WDM community has not, yet Yasmin found the woman to officiate her wedding not inside her community but in the Sunni community. Their story indicates that Sunni women do function as leaders and religious authorities even without the formal office of woman imam.

Outside of the restriction on women imams, polygyny is the other controversial topic that comes up when Nation women describe why they preferred their community to the WDM community. Minister Farrakhan strongly discourages the practice for members of his organization. Cassandra goes further to say that it is not allowed for the "general believers" in the Nation:

> Polygyny is an acceptable practice within the Qur'an; however, there are certain conditions that need to be met which I don't think are able to be met in these times. I don't think we as a people are mature enough to handle that sort of life. And I think that men have often taken on this practice not for the spiritual purposes, or that they received the divine call from Allah, but for sexual reasons, which I don't agree with necessarily, which can lead to abuse of women. So in that aspect, I don't believe in that practice.

The practice was justified for Elijah Muhammad, according to Cassandra, because "the Honorable Elijah Muhammad received divine revelation that he needed to do that because at the time, he was building the Nation and his wife was now barren. He needed to have more children to further his message and further his seed." But otherwise, for the "general believers" it is discouraged because Black families have a hard enough time staying together without this extra burden. In the

American context, polygyny is known to break rather than build marriage. Minister Farrakhan's firm stance against polygyny for his followers likely means that it does occur less in the Nation than in the WDM community. Imam Mohammed made very clear that men have the right to carry out the practice but that "the qualifications are not easy. You've got to be careful there. It's very difficult."[32] Because of the hardship and the caution that imams in the community exercise in discussing the topic, incidents of polygyny in the WDM community are few and far between but have occurred enough to have shaped a highly nuanced discourse around the issue. Although they acknowledge that God has allowed it, and they accept it theoretically, women in the community have tended to resist it as a personal choice. Outside of emotions such as jealousy, women's resistance is based on real cases in which men have attempted the practice but have failed to care for both women in a just manner, a condition that the Qur'an states must be met in order for it to be approved in God's eyes. Women have also protested the manner in which men have gone about it, sometimes secretly in the beginning. Like Cassandra, some women in the WDM community despise that men do it for sexual reasons and believe that the Prophet Muhammad did it and did not discourage it in his community for specific reasons— for example, the loss of men in war, the growth and development of Islam—that do not apply to our time or culture.

The vast majority of the Sunni women interviewed speak favorably about the practice but also refer to having "evolved" or "grown" in their understanding, indicating their initial resistance. Safiyyah recalls when the practice was first introduced during the transition. There was an "uproar" when a few cases actually occurred. "It threatened our security, in our minds, that it was something that could be a man's choice, that this person is gonna get more than me, and I got to share with you and so forth, and so it was an unsettling time, but I think that now we have matured as a community." Safiyyah no longer sees polygyny as a threat and even teases her husband, "I just want my weekends free. Let her have you so I can have my Saturday and Sunday by myself." Having "developed and grown," she even sees it as a "solution" in some cases. "There are many good women in our community who may not even have a chance of marriage. And a lot of women say, 'Oh, all the good men are already taken.'" She believes that resistance has also subsided because men have begun to do it "properly," especially in terms of having the economic stability to afford two wives. With less emotional resistance from women and a proper approach from men, in terms of thinking it through to make sure that they are qualified to take on this enormous responsibility, Safiyyah believes that it can help women rather than break up marriages, which it had done in most of the early cases that she witnessed.

Aware of the harm that polygyny has caused in the past, Jessica begins her thoughts on the practice with concern about how it is carried out:

> I view polygyny as something that we could use if we could figure out a standard where the man would meet the woman after he and his wife talked about it. . . . I think that the reason polygyny has not caught on with our community is because the trust has been broken between the original wife and husband. Generally what has happened in our community has been that the wife finds out at the same time everyone else in the community finds out that this man has had a relationship with this woman enough to the degree that he asked her to marry, and they went ahead and got married in some instances before the wife found out.

Jessica's idea of a standard demonstrates that while women have had a terribly difficult time embracing this practice that God has allowed, they are willing to meet their men halfway and have imagined ways to make it favorable and positive for women as opposed to the way men have carried it out to make it appear and feel that it benefits only them. Jessica's comments further demonstrate that women have rendered a female-empowering interpretation of polygyny as an opportunity to give charity to another woman, the reward for which—God's pleasure and favor—is the ultimate benefit for women:

> [Given] what's happened in our community, and I'm talking about [the] general community [African Americans at large], regarding the ratio of men to women, if ideally done, this would be a wonderful way of giving charity to someone else who is in need. Allah said that He created us, men and *jinn* [creatures in the unseen world], for worship and we translate that into service. And if we see a woman who is lonely and in

need, don't we want the same for our sisters? Don't we want for our sisters what we want for ourselves? And so if I could share my resources, which would also include sharing him, that would give me even more. And Allah would provide me with even more, and it would also give me some free time to go to dance class and yoga while he's with her this week.

Both Jessica and Safiyyah see polygyny as a solution in light of the high rate of women, Muslim and non-Muslim, without husbands. Given the known plight of Black women disproportionately managing as heads of households, often in poverty, Sunni women's interpretations of polygyny demonstrate that they, like their Nation sisters, continue to see Islam as a means to bettering the lives of African American women, men, and children.

In light of Minister Farrakhan's talk of unity with Sunni Muslims, this chapter presented a dialogue between Nation and Sunni women. The dialogue was crafted because of the very limited interaction between the two groups of women. Because their encounters are few, each group of women holds misconceptions about the other. Sunni women tend to imagine Nation women as stuck in time, living the same experience in the Nation as they did more than forty years ago. As a result, Sunni women overlook the Nation's evolution, particularly their new interpretations of the original NOI doctrine. Also, some Sunni women view Nation women as experiencing oppression because Minister Farrakhan refuses to lead them to Sunni Islam. However, when Nation women are given the opportunity to confront these assumptions, they make very clear that they understand the distinctions between the Nation and Sunni communities and that they have chosen the Nation because it appeals to them spiritually and intellectually. Nation women have also concluded that the Nation offers them more rights and opportunities as women. Not only have women chosen the Nation of Islam above Sunni Islam, but also some have left Sunni Islam for the Nation. The case we have highlighted, in which Khaleelah left Sunni Islam, came about because of the racism experienced at an immigrant mosque. In general, Nation women tend to form their opinions on women's treatment in Sunni Islam based on encounters at immigrant *masjids*. But WDM *masjids*, unlike many immigrant ones, tend not to have the strict gender separation and attitudes that Nation women associate with Sunni Islam. At the same time, WDM *masjids* tend to be imam-dominated communities. Sunni women, however, view this as a remnant of the old Nation and therefore believe that movement away from the Nation experience toward the ideals of Sunni Islam positions women for greater leadership.

To the contrary, Nation women view their organization as more gender progressive than Sunni communities because of the Nation's ordination of female ministers. Women in the WDM community do not have the opportunity to head a mosque because during the transition, "ministers" became "imams," and the essential duty of the imam is to lead the *salat*, which traditionally only men are allowed to do. In most WDM *masjids*, leading the *salat*, ministering, and managing the mosque have been conflated into one position, that of imam, thus restricting women's leadership potential. Indeed, by appointing women as ministers, and not imams, the Nation of Islam offers a way for women to lead as spiritual and organizational guides for men and women within the mosque community.

However, we discovered that many women in the WDM community do not see the male-exclusive imam position as a problem in light of their being a "special needs community." The crafted dialogue allowed Sunni women to address misconceptions that Sunni Islam overlooks the unique needs of African Americans. Sunni women understand how Nation women come to this conclusion based on their attendance at immigrant mosques. However, within WDM *masjids*, elevating African American families and neighborhoods remains an important goal. Sunni women's sustained, though reformed, Black consciousness is apparent in the way that many women think about the role of imam. Many welcome an exclusively male leadership role because for too long, African American women have had to function as leaders in their private and public lives as men have not always been present and accountable. Certainly, Black Christian women who visit Black *masjids* are amazed that men outnumber women in mosque attendance, compared with men's minority presence in Black churches.[33] Sunni women embrace gender norms in Sunni Islam that might otherwise seem to privilege men—for example, that only men are obligated to attend Friday prayer and permitted to lead the Friday prayer. They embrace these gender rules in light of their hopes for Black men to assume greater responsibility for themselves and their families.

Fascinating about the dialogue was discovering the common ground that women of both groups have, as is apparent in the story of Jessica and Yasmin. Both groups of women value marriage and their role as mothers. While they hold varying views on the idea of women imams and ministers, they take their obligation to build Black families most seriously. Although Nation women do not state that the role of imam is not intended for women, as some women in the WDM community suggest, Nation women acknowledge the difficulty of both carrying "the duties of being at the rostrum every Sunday" and caring for their families, which Khaleelah notes is "our first responsibility." Indeed, in an interview with Ebony Muhammad for *Hurt 2 Healing* magazine, Minister Ava alludes to the challenge of "day-to-day mosque administration" when she describes her decision to adopt two girls *after* leaving her position at the mosque.[34] For both groups of women, the needs of African American communities influence their gender perspectives. For example, the majority of women in both groups do not like the idea of polygyny for themselves; however, hypothetically some women in the WDM community make a case for the practice in light of the substantial number of single women in their *masjid* communities. At the same time, a Black-conscious interpretation of polygyny is also used to protest the practice, as a Nation woman demonstrates. "It's not that it's not done in Islam, but it is totally discouraged in the Nation of Islam, and that is because the Black man has been destroyed, and he's hardly in a position to take care of one wife." But after this statement, she shared off the record (though she later granted the authors permission to use her additional comments without her name) that she was in fact the second wife of a Sunni Muslim man. "I had no idea that I would marry somebody other than an FOI." However, a series of events and emotions led her to marry the man as a second wife. This surprising story again demonstrates that Nation and Sunni women share more common ground than what might ordinarily appear.

Conclusion

Feminist and womanist scholars have described Nation women as guilty of reproducing their own oppression because they accept traditional gender roles, including men as providers and women as homemakers. Yet Nation women have strategically embraced these gender roles in the context of the broader struggle for racial equality. As we have seen, women joined Elijah Muhammad's NOI for its racial uplift message and its community-building activities. When former members describe what attracted them to the Nation, the gender ideology is often secondary or not mentioned at all. Rarely did Muslim Girls Training attract them in the first place. Nonetheless, it became one of the most endearing experiences for old Nation women, particularly because of the sisterhood and affirmations of Black womanhood it engendered. Early Nation women, even those college-educated, embraced the Nation's complementary roles as part of their Nation-building project, which included empowering African American men to reclaim their invaluable roles in their families and communities.

Throughout this book, we have seen examples of Nation women's interpreting Nation ideologies for themselves and navigating gender practices in their favor. This was certainly the case in how women handled MGT's function of scrutinizing and policing women. Early Nation women conceptualized their role in the home not as a restriction but as a tool for liberation and advancement of their entire community. It was when they felt men and women restricting them to this role that they resisted. Even MGT captains, who were obligated to follow the dictates of Elijah Muhammad, encouraged women to educate and elevate themselves in ways that at times went against Nation norms. Elijah Muhammad himself encouraged women's work and education when they benefited the organization. Former Nation women make it very clear that the emphasis on women's contribution to the home did not mean that women thought themselves inadequate to do the work of men. Rather, they were making a choice to commit to the strengthening of their marriages and the raising of their children first. When former member Terri Ali expresses her love for MGT, it is representative of the way in which women of the Nation of Islam understand how outsiders perceive their embrace of traditional gender roles as a step backward whereas Nation women see it as a step forward, back then and now:

> We were the Muslim Girls Training and General Civilization Class, and we considered ourselves as soldiers in Islam. We were nation building, and so I don't think the women in the Nation of Islam saw themselves as, you know, "Oh, we're just women" or "Oh, women don't do this and women don't do that." We were prepared to do whatever we needed to do for nation building, but clearly we expected our men to be in front. But if our men fell short, we wouldn't fall backwards. So just this whole idea of staying at home and having babies and nursing our children, it was a beautiful understanding that only women can do this. But we didn't see it as a default. And let me just add this: I think the things that we were told not to do as women were more or less the things that kept Black women out of the streets: no drinking, no gambling, no sexual solicitation, no being with men who are not your husband, don't listen to music, don't watch a lot of television, just things that would keep you from being derailed and forgetting your mission and forgetting who you are. I mean, I knew sisters who were still working, but it was encouraging them towards marriage and home life. . . . When you look around the world and how the reference to Muslim women is almost like, it's almost like chattel. Now that's not how Allah has it in the Qur'an but how people are living it. I just never want people to misconstrue our home-focus activities. To me, it was allowing us to recapture what we had lost through the slavery experience.

Terri states that it was in the context of Nation-building that women accepted the rules and regulations of the NOI, again bringing our attention to the context of racial discrimination in the United States in which women used Nation dictates and tools—not for oppression, but for liberation. Dress is another prominent example. Women liked the fact that their modest garments set them apart as women not to be viewed as sexual objects, especially by white men who had historically treated them that way during slavery and during their employment in white homes.

Diet was another tool of liberation. The Nation of Islam viewed diet as a critical component of transformation, evident in the way that giving up pork has become a hallmark of becoming a Black Muslim. Thus, women as cooks in the home and the temple saw themselves as making a major contribution to the Nation's goals. Not only were they nourishing healthy Black bodies, but they were also bringing in revenue for their families and temples. Nothing illustrates this role more than the creation of the famous bean pie. Nation women and their food creations became the trademark of Muslim restaurants and meals that have survived in the Resurrected Nation of Islam and the WDM community.

Nation women's ownership over dress and diet allowed them to contribute greatly to the self-help programs that characterize the Nation of Islam. As we have seen, women established their own businesses in the Nation. They also contributed to the Muhammad University of Islam as directors, teachers, counselors, and nurses. Nation women found various avenues in their organization, from MGT to MUI, to serve as leaders and workers in the Nation-building project. In some cases, when the civil rights movement seemed to have failed women, they found greater hope in the Nation of Islam. The narratives provided by Ana Karim and Amidah Salahuddin, for example, suggest that they welcomed the opportunity to work in gender- and race-segregated settings within the Nation.

As the Nation of Islam moved beyond the civil rights era and brought forth two new leaders, Imam Mohammed and Minister Farrakhan, Nation women found greater opportunities for themselves. The women who followed Imam W. D. Mohammed into Sunni Islam describe the Nation's transition period as "freeing." Foremost, it was freeing because many women either never believed in the old Nation's theological doctrine or found it hard to reconcile with their personal beliefs about white people or the nature of God. Many found it easy to follow the imam because they understood his succession as the hope and desire of Elijah Muhammad. Imam Mohammed was sensitive to the need among Muhammad's followers to maintain continuity between the old and the new. Thus, he thoughtfully introduced Sunni Islam through an approach that presented both Fard Muhammad and Elijah Muhammad as the architects of the community's evolution to Sunni Islam.

Women describe Imam Mohammed's leadership as freeing also because of his new gender ideology, which was based primarily on his understanding of the Qur'an and the Sunnah, wherein women are viewed as equal spiritual and intellectual counterparts to men. At the same time, Imam Mohammed's gender ideology maintained some continuity with the Nation of Islam. His attention to women's liberation was certainly influenced by his great esteem for his mother, who contributed tremendously to the organization while also dedicating herself to her husband and children. The Nation's goal to elevate African American families and communities also influenced Imam Mohammed's gender ideology. This influence is seen in the way in which Imam Mohammed always talked about women's rights and women's leadership in the context of the condition and needs of African Americans as a whole. Through this lens, he introduced concepts such as "mothers to society," "man means mind," and "woman means womb of mind." Using these concepts, he imparted the ideas that women were the nurturers of intellect, and therefore society; that they were intended to participate in and influence society; and that their unique capacity as mothers offered forms of leadership and insight to society that men did not ordinarily provide. Imam Mohammed's gender ideology supported the idea of complementary roles promoted in the Nation; he continued to emphasize women's role as mothers as important to strengthening Black communities. The difference, as Sunni women explain, was that neither men nor their role as provider was seen as superior to women or their role as mother. Most important, Imam Mohammed used the Qur'anic concept of *nafs wahidah* to demonstrate that women were indeed capable of achieving and producing that which men achieve. He showed that although men and women dominated in separate roles for the functioning of society, both have the innate capacity to carry out all forms of gendered roles because they come from a common soul that is both male and female in quality. One major way in which Sunni women interpreted Imam Mohammed's gender ideology was that they were meant to extend their contribution beyond the home in every aspect of society.

The transition was freeing for women also because Imam Moham-med actually removed the structures and dictates that limited women's movement and individuality and established new structures for wom-en's mobilization. He gradually ended MGT and established CERWIS (Committee to Enhance the Role of Women in Society) to support the expansion of women's roles. Not only were women happy to be free of dictates such as wearing a uniform and not going out for a movie, but also they cherished the freedom and independence to make deci-sions for themselves. They were now motivated to act a certain way or to dress a certain way based on what God wanted of them based on their understanding of the Qur'an, not fear of Nation officials. Most outstanding, Imam Mohammed appointed the Nation's first female minister, Amatullah Um'rani, and the first female editor of the *Muham-mad Speaks* newspaper, Ana Karim. The appointment of a female min-ister signaled the importance of women to study Islam and teach it to others. Although Um'rani did not function as a minister in the tradi-tional sense—that is, leading a temple or mosque—she was a minister of men as well as of women. She lectured in front of men during temple meetings, and she wrote a regular column for the Muslim newspaper. The granting of this title alone was a symbol of resistance to the way women had been excluded from certain leadership roles. Eventually Imam Mohammed changed the title of "minister" to "imam." Because women could not be considered as imams in Sunni Islam, female reli-gious authorities in the community became known as "instructresses." Moreover, mosques offering "imam classes" opened these up to women.

The first female editor of *Muhammad Speaks*, Ana Karim, reports that one of the most difficult aspects of her job was resistance from imams who were not accustomed to women leaders. Other women also report resistance from their local *masjid* imams to the new initia-tives broadening women's roles in the community. Nonetheless, women found ways to continue to make their impact on the new *masjid* com-munities. One of the most apparent ways in which women contrib-uted to the culture of WDM *masjids* was through dress. Encouraged to decide for themselves how to dress modestly as African American Muslim women, Sunni women produced fashions that came to dis-tinguish the WDM community from other Sunni *masjid* communi-ties. The legacy of the Nation of Islam in which women were already dressing modestly, abstaining from extramarital sex, and fasting, along-side Imam Mohammed's encouragement for women to be independent thinkers and leaders, made the transition into Sunni Islam smooth for many women.

The second leader to emerge from the Nation of Islam, Minister Louis Farrakhan, is most responsible for popularizing Black Muslims in contemporary America. As this book has highlighted, current Nation women's narratives are influenced by how they perceive public attitudes pertaining to Minister Farrakhan and the NOI more generally. Contemporary Nation women are eager for their critiques of the organization not to be co-opted into a broader narrative that portrays Minister Farrakhan and the Nation as misogynistic. Nation women are acutely aware of the fact that public perceptions of both Minister Farrakhan and the NOI have been shaped by the media and edited sound bytes of NOI lectures. In recent years, the NOI has taken steps to make the organization and the content of its teachings more accessible in the hope that this will allow individuals to make their own judgments about the Nation. All of the NOI's Sunday lectures are available to view on webcasts, the transcripts of Minister Farrakhan's lectures are published in *The Final Call*, and both Minister Farrakhan and his ministers engage in online forums. These efforts have effectively transformed what was once a very secretive group into an organization that today is just as accessible as, if not more so than, its Christian and Sunni counterparts. Lorraine Muhammad comments that these initiatives within the NOI allow "people to do their own research":

> I guess one of the main things is that I would hope your readers do judgment for themselves and not take what's in the media as gospel as well as the things that are in the media about the Muslim world and Muslim communities. To look at things with an open mind and not be judgmental based on a two- or three-second [sound byte]. The minister is doing a lot, and I think that one of the things that [are] changing is that people have access to books, webcasts; we archive our webcasts and people can do their own research.[1]

Women's awareness of negative portrayals of the organization and their desire to present Minister Farrakhan in a positive light certainly influenced how women responded to interview questions, generally careful not to critique. However, they were forthright in their discussions of what attracted them to the Nation, the contributions that women make to the group, and the reasons why they embrace the Nation's traditional gender roles.

The present-day NOI's female membership is diverse. Nation women's backgrounds, educational and career paths, faith, and community service distinguish them from one another. Nation women share a commitment to the organization and to Minister Farrakhan. However, their experiences, faith, and level of involvement with the organization differ. As we have seen, Nation women tend to synchronize either their Sunni or Christian beliefs with aspects of the NOI's theology. This in itself provides them with greater freedom of religious belief and expression of faith within the organization. Not all Nation women engage in community service. Yet, significantly, it is the NOI's history of community service and current efforts to be more involved in their surrounding communities that evoke feelings of pride in Nation women. Susan,[2] for example, comments:

> Hopefully what I see is growth, more service to the community and a legacy that we hand down to our children to make sure that the NOI is always here and will be here for generations to come. I instill in my children that the NOI is their community and family. I want to see the NOI at the forefront and a service to the community at large.[3]

Nation women often comment that they have witnessed an evolution in Minister Farrakhan's NOI. This evolution relates mostly to issues of theology, women's leadership, and dress. Nation women regard the evolution of the NOI as a natural process but one that should not come at the expense of the organization's central ethos of racial uplift and community advancement.

Opportunities for women to exercise leadership in Minister Farrakhan's NOI have grown significantly. Current Nation women hold both ministerial and managerial positions that enable them to exercise authority over their male and female counterparts at both a local and national level. Minister Farrakhan's decision to install Ava Muhammad as a minister in the southern region in Atlanta illustrates that the gender ideology of the NOI has evolved. More important, Ava's appointment set a precedent in the Nation and was followed by the emergence of other female ministers.

More than early Nation women, contemporary Nation women highlight the appeal of MGT in their deciding to join the group. Like their Sunni counterparts, they embrace traditional gender roles. They also believe that performing these roles helps to elevate and restore their families and communities. Significantly, Nation women are not confined to the home or coerced from the workplace as a result of their involvement with the Nation. Many women in fact welcome the Nation's efforts to return the burden of provision to men. As was the case during the time of the old NOI, structural racism manifests itself in ways that directly and adversely affect Black women. They continue to encounter racialized stereotypes and a pervasive culture that portrays them as jezebels, mammies, and matriarchs.[4] Nation women liberate themselves from these pervasive stereotypes by embracing the organization's feminine but modest dress code and by returning the burden of provision to their husbands while at the same time pursuing education and professional careers. Nation women construe their choices about gender roles to be based very much on the realities of their experiences. In JayVon's comments below, we can see that her desire to perform traditional gender roles stems from both how she understands the history of Black women in America and her belief that the feminist movement in the United States is irrelevant when it comes to her concerns:

> In response to our men being broken, women had to become the heads of households and strong enough to raise families on their own. Today, the world would make one think that it is "old-fashioned" or oppressive to go back to our traditional roles as women. The thing is, many Black women in America have *never* had the opportunity to function in their natural roles. When I think of the [feminist] movement, I think of the white woman's fight . . . fighting her man to vote, or work, or for equality. That was never our fight, but somehow we have embraced it. . . . Women in the Nation of Islam are not in competition with men, but rather we recognize our part.

JayVon's belief that the "feminist movement" in the United States does not speak to or for Black women is shared by other Nation women. Their critique of the feminist movement is the result of a conviction that the natures of white and Black women's burdens are fundamentally different. Within feminist circles, Nation women are accused of sacrificing or suppressing their concerns about gender discrimination for the benefit of Black men. This charge is one that Nation women encounter regularly and something they consider to be based on misinformation. Nation women are permitted to hold every available position of power that the group has to offer. Thus, nothing in the structure of the NOI or in its constitution actually oppresses women or limits their opportunities. Nation women consider the organization to be actively engaged in the promotion of gender equality as shown in Shernett Muhammad's comments:

> The Nation of Islam is an equal opportunity entity that believes in freedom, justice and equality for all its citizens. There are nine ministries in the Nation. Women may join and chair any one of these ministries. . . . Therefore, there are no aspects of the Nation that I can see that [do] not appeal to the woman.

Nation women are active in all of the ministries that Shernett outlines above. Practical considerations that involve balancing work and family commitments, however, often prevent Nation women from being more active or influential in these ministries. However, this limitation is one that Nation women feel they would experience in both the church or in Sunni Islam. Thus, as far as they are concerned, nothing in the Nation's structures prevents them from pursuing their talents and interests.

The ways in which Nation women relate to the organization have been effectively transformed as a result of technology. Online forums and webcasts allow women to engage with the NOI in the absence of a local NOI mosque. Some of the women we have met, including Nadia, watch NOI webcasts weekly and travel to nearby mosques for special NOI events. This kind of interaction with the NOI allows women to remain actively involved even if they cannot physically be present at the local mosque. Technology has, of course, also diversified the ways in which women contribute to and propagate NOI teachings. Nation women's magazines reflect the positive ways in which they have embraced technology to both propagate NOI teachings and connect Nation women across the United States. Indeed, in the absence of a local mosque, the magazines help build bridges and connections with other Nation women.

This book has also explored the way in which Nation women connect with Sunni women, especially in light of Minister Farrakhan's movement back and forth between his version of Islam and Sunni Islam. The two groups of women rarely interact, which has led to significant misconceptions about one another. Some Sunni women are very critical of Minister Farrakhan for not leading his community to embrace Sunni Islam fully. Others, like Bayyinah, are more hopeful that Minister Farrakhan will eventually lead the community toward mainstream Islam:

> I embrace all Muslims, even the sisters of the NOI as fellow Muslims. . . . I also embrace [Louis Farrakhan] for his effort toward directing the NOI toward orthodox Islam. . . . I wish he would be a little bit more forceful but with patience and time, I'm sure they will be able to make more direct inroads in their understanding and become more understanding of orthodox Islam.

As we have seen, however, many Nation women are familiar with Sunni Islam, but they choose the NOI because they see it addressing their needs more than do Sunni communities. Nation women believe that the NOI, unlike other mosque communities, addresses the unique conditions of Black Americans. However, we found that Nation women and their sisters in the WDM community share similar concerns about their families, communities, and social ills, and both see their mosque communities doing much work to address these concerns. Both groups of women are active in their surrounding communities. Their activism is in part inspired by the legacy of the original Nation. Women in the WDM community aspire to build model *masjid* communities, including Muslim schools, to have positive impacts on their families and neighboring communities. Some do social outreach beyond the *masjid*. Nation women contribute to their communities by providing relief and education to families and young women. Their work, like that of their

counterparts in the WDM community, is not confined to one particu-
lar racial group. We see examples of this with Sandra El-Amin's Sacred
Diva and Sudan Muhammad's *Youth Creation Community Outreach*
(YCCO). Significantly, this service reveals that current Nation women
have embraced Minister Farrakhan's revised interpretation of Fard
Muhammad and Elijah Muhammad's mission as aimed to help both
African Americans and whites.[5]

The Nation of Islam's evolution to embracing whites is representative
of the community's general understanding that the original founder
and leader, Fard Muhammad and Elijah Muhammad, respectively,
were presenting a particular version of Islam that would eventually lead
to new insights. This understanding is no different from what Sunni
women believe is taught by their teacher Imam Mohammed. And
although Sunni women made the transition to a universal understanding of Islam, the realities of racism continue to affect them and how
they view whites. The harsh realities of racism brought Jessica Muhammad, whom we met earlier, to the Nation of Islam. Twenty-five years
later she was confronted with an unexpected test that made her face
her unresolved issues with whites and truly embody the teachings of a
universal Islam. Jessica's eldest son chose to marry a white, non-Muslim
woman. When asked to describe her feelings about his interracial marriage, she answered:

> I've lived under the *terror* of Jim Crow and the Ku Klux Klan era and
> the white man's *reign*. I had a hatred in me for white people, and it was
> as a collective, not individually, but collectively. And that was one of
> the things that appealed to me regarding the Nation of Islam's doctrine.
> I felt like [white people] were the devils. But when Imam Mohammed
> came in, I kind of broke . . . [away from] that pain from growing up,
> and [came to] an understanding too that all . . . had a purpose in it, a
> divine purpose. I started really buying into the fact that we're all [broth-
> ers and sisters]—and of course reading Malcolm X's autobiography, I
> started appreciating diversity. Thinking that I was appreciating diversity,
> I bought into [the idea] in Islam that there is no difference and we're
> all one. And so I didn't teach my children any differently. I taught them
> that we can love everybody. . . . So my boy grew up with that. It's not
> like we took him outside of his [African American Muslim] community

to practice that love. Basically he grew up just like you did. . . . But of course he also had the interactions with "the other" when we'd go to swim meets. So I guess that was one reason why he didn't see [white people] as being different either because he was competing against them. And he went out to Stanford [University], and he had roommates who were Caucasian and Indian. . . . So he ended up marrying this white woman. She came to my door, before they got married, she came for a visit, and I thought that I had my stuff checked in terms of my racism. Girl, that stuff bubbled up that I had suppressed and I got deathly ill. I went to the *masjid* and cried all day after I visited a couple of sisters; my stomach ached, you name it, that's what I experienced that day. And so I cried. I asked him why did he choose a white woman when we have all these beautiful Muslim girls who deserve his attention. And you know I saw him as one day having some money, and it would be a Black girl who best deserved to come up out of poverty. I pulled out all those history books and family [histories] and showed him how my great-great-granddaddy had done this and this. And so he looked at me and said, "Mama, you know you never told me not to like white people." And I had to shut up. And I had to let it go and learn to trust Allah again in every situation.

Jessica laughed at herself as she narrated her response, which demonstrated that she has further healed and embraced the idea that whites can indeed be her sisters and brothers—quite literally, they can be family.

In other ways, outside the need for Islam to address their experiences of racism, we discovered that Nation and Sunni women were more alike than different. Most interesting is that the aspect of the Nation of Islam legacy that most connects women is that which goes against dominant cultural assumptions of women's advancement in the larger society— that is, women's training as homemakers in MGT. When Sunni women describe what they miss about the Nation of Islam, many of them mention MGT above anything else, and often it is the only thing they miss. Janet Saboor states:

I would have liked to see a lot of that maintained, and when I look around today, we need it because the sisters, the youngsters, they don't

know how to do anything. They can't cook a meal from scratch, seriously. They are not taking care of their kids. They are not feeding their
families. . . . [In the Nation], we were seeking out that knowledge [of a
healthy diet] always and we were passing that knowledge on always.

As Janet's comments show, the Nation's diet is another aspect commonly noted as missed, which is very much connected to MGT.

Safiyyah Shahid, formerly the sister captain in Atlanta and director
of the Mohammed Schools, reports that people tell her all the time that
she "[needs] to get some classes going," referring to MGT. She "wouldn't
want to revive it," but she can understand why people feel the need for
it today. We see less frequently among today's mothers "the high standards and high expectations" taught in MGT. Back then, "the children
were well behaved because that's where the focus was—on how to raise
them—and you had a community standard." She saw this standard prevailing even among African American women outside the Nation who
kept their homes "orderly" and "beautiful." "But now," states Safiyyah:

The value system has changed and everybody's trying to get that dollar,
and we women sometimes feel like, "Hey, I'm more than just a homemaker; I want to use my intellect, and I want to satisfy myself through
involvement in the community, and through founding a group or whatever." And so what happens is more and more the focus is taken off of the
children because then somebody else begins to take care of the children.
The daycare takes care of the children whereas, during that time, the
women themselves were taking care of children or their friends [were].
It was never that you went to a daycare, that was only later, a later development that you begin to pay for someone to take care of your kid. You
don't know what was going on while they were in the daycare center for
eight hours while you were on the job. So it changed, and so even now,
because of the convenience, it's so convenient to go to McDonald's and
get your child a burger because you're tired, you're busy; always takeout
because, "I'm so tired, I've been working all day." That's what women tell
their husbands. "I work just like you. And so why don't you do it? Why
don't you sweep?" [But now there is a new trend]; it seems to me that a
lot of Caucasian women are refocusing on the home. Many of them are
leaving these corporate jobs so they can raise their children, so that they

can take them to the park. I see it all the time. I see them in the park. I see them in the grocery store.

It is interesting that these comments come from a working woman with a significant leadership role in her WDM community. Yet the comments are not surprising given Imam Mohammed's concept of mother leadership. Sunni women were encouraged to utilize their talents and skills for work in the larger society, but the concept of mother was still prioritized, theoretically if not always practically or seamlessly, for many women.

Another striking example of this commitment to the mother role comes from Sandra El-Amin, who also served as director of the Mohammed Schools. Sandra did not express the fondest memories of MGT and protested its "rules and regulations that were unfair to women," controlling their movements. We saw earlier that Sandra has quite radical views on prayer leadership, not representative of most women in her community. However, her view on gender roles has not changed much from what she describes as Imam Mohammed's view:

> A woman can pursue any career she likes, but if you have a family, the society can't afford for her to neglect that kind of primary responsibility. So, I feel like if you are blessed to be a mother, you need to be a mother, and that takes precedence over anything else. At the same time, I don't think there is anything that a woman cannot do.

Bayyinah Abdul-Aleem, like Safiyyah and Sandra, is a professional woman. She does not remember her Nation temple discouraging women from working, though she concedes the possibility that if the message was to stay at home, she "didn't choose to hear" it "as an educated female." Yet she too wishes that aspects of MGT lessons were still imparted to women in the community:

> I feel that if there were more emphasis on the need for men and women to develop their skills as men and women and get more definitive advice or guidance on how to work within those rules to develop a good, strong Muslim family, I believe that would be good. . . . Unfortunately, a lot of Muslim families and individuals just threw out all of the information

and the guidance and direction that they learned in the Nation of Islam, believing that none of it had a real merit for living in society today, and that's unfortunate.

That Sunni women continue to embrace the aspects of MGT which made women conscious of their unique roles as women, particularly in terms of mothering, demonstrates that African American women continue to have the same concerns about restoring strong families in their communities as they had in the 1960s. They continue to desire the elevation of their families first.

Presenting the narratives of educated, professional Nation and Sunni women who embrace traditional gender roles challenges feminist critiques of the Nation of Islam. JayVon, in particular, brought our attention to the ways in which white feminist aspirations do not resonate with Nation women and the everyday realities of Black women. Feminist and womanist scholars are conversant with this criticism. Womanist scholars work to highlight the voices of Black women, like JayVon, who define gender liberation in the context of the realities of racism in women's lives. Womanist scholars have begun to broaden their analysis of Black women's experiences to include Muslim women.[6] Certainly, Nation and Sunni women's belief that gender liberation must be defined in terms of elevating the entire family and community resonates with womanist thought and its focus on elevating women, men, and children. Womanist scholar Debra Majeed has introduced the term "Muslim womanism" and anthropologist Carolyn Rouse has noted that while Black Muslim women and womanists both seek to better the lives of women and men, "what feminists and womanists can do that Muslim feminists cannot is innovate beyond the perimeters established by the Muslim community (local and/or international)."[7] This book provides much material to advance theory on the ways in which African American Muslim women contribute to womanist perspectives.

This book also contributes to discussion among scholars of the Nation of Islam and scholars of Islam in Black America, including Edward Curtis and Sherman Jackson, who have paid attention to the way in which leaders of the old Nation used Islam to respond to the particular needs of Black Americans. NOI scholar Edward Curtis notes that "the history of the NOI invites American Muslims of all sorts to confront and debate the issue of diversity in Islam and the extent to which Islamic practice should respond to the local circumstances and exigencies in which Muslims find themselves."[8] From this book we are reminded that it is not only the past Nation of Islam that exemplifies the historical tendency for new Muslim communities to imagine into Islam ways to address their particular needs; the present-day Nation of Islam also shows new Muslims continuing in this creative process, and in more dynamic and complex ways today given Nation Muslims' engagement with mainstream Islam. An interesting example is the innovation in the NOI of Muslim women ministers. Both Imam Mohammed and Minister Farrakhan introduced this leadership role for women in their respective groups. However, as we have seen, this position did not persist for women in the WDM community because of Imam Mohammed's Islamization process in which he changed the title of minister to imam. The Sunni prohibition on women imams, or prayer leaders, prevented women from aspiring to the position of imam, even though it incorporated more than leading the prayer. Knowingly or not, Minister Farrakhan avoided this dilemma by maintaining the title minister—a title that resonates with Black Christians. The title allowed the organization to take on a progressive gender stance on the terms of the broader Black religious landscape. At the same time, it allowed the organization to engage and compete with Sunni Muslims on their terms, at times substituting the term "imam" for "minister" to make the claim that Ava Muhammad was the first woman imam in Islamic history. More studies on the present-day Nation of Islam, the WDM community, and how they compare with each other or with other American Muslim communities will be important to identifying the competing ways in which American Muslim groups make Islam relevant in their particular contexts.

NOTES

NOTES TO THE INTRODUCTION

1. Thomas Hauser, *Muhammad Ali: His Life and Times* (London: Anova Books, 1991), 131.

2. Jamillah Karim, "Through Sunni Women's Eyes: Black Feminism and the Nation of Islam," in *Black Routes to Islam*, ed. Manning Marable and Hishaam Aidi (New York: Palgrave Macmillan, 2009), 163.

3. Karl Evanzz, *The Messenger: The Rise and Fall of Elijah Muhammad* (New York: Random House, 1999), 409; Fatima Fanusie, "Fard Muhammad in Historical Context: An Islamic Thread in the American Religious and Cultural Quilt" (Ph.D. diss., Howard University, 2008).

4. Robert L. Boyd, "The Storefront Church Ministry in African American Communities of the Urban North during the Great Migration: The Making of an Ethnic Niche," *The Social Science Journal* 35: 3 (1998): 322.

5. Edward E. Curtis, *Islam in Black America: Identity, Liberation and Difference in African American Islamic Thought* (Albany: State University of New York Press, 2002), 46.

6. E. U. Essien-Udom, *Black Nationalism: A Search for an Identity in America* (New York: Dell, 1964), 55; and Dawn-Marie Gibson, *A History of the Nation of Islam: Race, Islam, and the Quest for Freedom* (Santa Barbara, Calif.: Praeger, 2012), 23.

7. Allan D. Austin, *African Muslims in Antebellum America: Transatlantic Stories and Spiritual Struggles* (New York and London: Routledge, 1997), 22.

8. Michael Gomez, *Black Crescent: The Experience and Legacy of African Muslims in the Americas* (New York: Cambridge University Press, 2005), 143.

9. Aminah B. McCloud, *African-American Islam* (New York and London: Routledge, 1995), 19.

10. C. Eric Lincoln, *The Black Muslims in America* (Boston: Beacon Press, 1961), 110.

11. Hatim Sahib, "The Nation of Islam," *Contributions in Black Studies* 13, art. 3 (1995): 67.

12. Claude Clegg, *An Original Man: The Life and Times of Elijah Muhammad* (New York: St. Martin's Press, 1997), 17.

13. Clara Muhammad, "An Invitation to 22 Million Black Americans," *Muhammad Speaks*, January 13, 1967, 19.

14. William A. Sundstrom, "Last Hired, First Fired? Unemployment and Urban Black Workers during the Great Depression," *The Journal of Economic History* Vol. 52, No. 2 (June 1992): 417.

15. Rebecca Sharpless, *Cooking in Other Women's Kitchens: Domestic Workers in the South, 1860–1960* (Chapel Hill: University of North Carolina Press, 2010), 138.

16. Sahib, "The Nation of Islam," 68.

17. Debra M. Majeed, "Clara Evans Muhammad: Pioneering Social Activism in the Original Nation of Islam," in *The Encyclopedia of Women and Religion in North America*, ed. Rosemary S. Keller and Rosemary R. Ruether (Bloomington: Indiana University Press, 2006), 746–53.

18. Clegg, *An Original Man*, 12.

19. Majeed, "Clara Evans Muhammad."

20. Rosetta E. Ross, *Witnessing and Testifying: Black Women, Religion, and Civil Rights* (Minneapolis: Fortress Press, 2003), 145.

21. Ajile Rahman, "She Stood by His Side and at Times in His Stead: The Life and Legacy of Sister Clara Muhammad, First Lady of the Nation of Islam (Ph.D. diss., Clark Atlanta University, 2000), 101.

22. Erdmann Beynon, "The Voodoo Cult among Negro Migrants in Detroit," *American Journal of Sociology* (May 1938): 900.

23. Clegg, *An Original Man*, 79.

24. Essien-Udom, *Black Nationalism*, 67.

25. Rahman, "She Stood by His Side," 66.

26. Manning Marable, *Malcolm X: A Life of Reinvention* (New York: Viking, 2011), 90.

27. "Aims, Purpose, and Teachings of the MCI": Reference Number: 25-20607. Date: September 20, 1942 (FBI File: Fard, Wallace D.).

28. Beatrice X, "What Islam Has Done for Me," *Muhammad Speaks*, June 19, 1964, 7.

29. There are many versions and spellings of Imam Mohammed's name. The imam was originally given the name Wallace Delaney Muhammad, which he later changed to Warith Deen Muhammad after embracing Sunni Islam. Sometime in the 1990s, he changed the spelling from Muhammad to Mohammed because this was the original spelling of the family name given by W. D. Fard Muhammad. The spelling Mohammed is used in one of the earliest studies done on the Nation of Islam, Sahib, "The Nation of Islam." Throughout the book, we refer to the imam as Imam Mohammed. Quotations from other sources may use one of the other spellings.

30. Warith Deen Muhammad, *As the Light Shineth from the East* (Chicago: WDM Publishing Co., 1980), 20.

31. Sahib, "The Nation of Islam," 70–71.

32. Bayyinah S. Jeffries, "A Nation Can Rise No Higher Than Its Women": The Critical Role of Black Muslim Women in the Development and Purveyance of Black Consciousness, 1945–1975 (Milton Keynes, UK: Lightning Source Ltd., 2007), 207.

33. Essien-Udom, *Black Nationalism*, 146.

34. Elijah Muhammad, *Message to the Blackman in America* (Chicago: MEMPS Press, 1965), 55.

35. Elijah Muhammad, *The Messenger Magazine*, Vol. 1, No. 1, 1959.
36. Herbert Berg, *Elijah Muhammad and Islam* (New York: New York University Press, 2009), 83.
37. Muhammad, *Message to the Blackman in America*, 60.
38. Berg, *Elijah Muhammad and Islam*, 83.
39. Anna Karriem, *The Divine Sayings of the Honorable Elijah Muhammad: Messenger of Allah, Volumes 1,2 & 3* (Phoenix: Secretarius Memps Publications, 2002), 7.
40. Lincoln, *The Black Muslims in America*, 22–23.
41. Marable, *Malcolm X*, 123.
42. Malcolm X, *The Autobiography of Malcolm X* (New York: Penguin, 1965), 85.
43. Ibid., 118.
44. Ibid., 138.
45. Section V: Publicity and Recruitment of Members. Part A: Publicity. p. 29 (FBI File: Nation of Islam).
46. To Director, FBI, (25-330971) From: SAC, New York (105-7809) (412). Subject: Nation of Islam (Chicago). Date: 7/16/59, p. 4. (Verbatim account of series in FBI File: Nation of Islam.)
47. Ibid.
48. Mattias Gardell, *Countdown to Armageddon: Louis Farrakhan and the Nation of Islam* (London: Duke University Press, 1996), 64.
49. X, *The Autobiography of Malcolm X*, 402.
50. Minister Louis X, "Malcolm-Hypocrite," *Muhammad Speaks*, November 4, 1964, 15.
51. Jabril Muhammad, *Closing the Gap: InnerViews of the Heart, Mind and Soul of the Honorable Minister Louis Farrakhan* (Chicago: FCN Publishing, 2006), 116.
52. Gardell, *Countdown to Armageddon*, 101.
53. Curtis, *Islam in Black America*, 109.
54. Essien-Udom, *Black Nationalism*, 93.
55. Annual Muslim Convention, 1975. Chicago, Illinois. (E. Muhammad FBI, Section 16.)
56. Muhammad, *As the Light Shineth from the East*, 110.
57. Author interview with Khayriyyah Faiz, June 8, 2010.
58. David Gates and Tracy L. Robinson, "The Black Muslims: A Divided Flock," *Newsweek*, April 9, 1984, 15.
59. Michael Marriott, "Black Women Are Split over All-Male March on Washington," *The New York Times*, October 14, 1995, 8.
60. In 1983 Minister Farrakhan changed the name of the NOI's annual convention from "Saviour's Day" to "Saviours' Day." "Min. Farrakhan announced that Black men and women must be the 'saviours' of themselves and their communities. He also announced that the spelling of the commemoration would change to 'saviours,' in the plural form to represent that responsibility." Ashahed M. Muhammad, "Saviours' Day: A Timeline and Brief History," accessed November 1, 2013, http://www.finalcall.com/artman/publish/article_4423.shtml.

61. Ashahed M. Muhammad, "Common Origins, Struggle Unite Blacks and Latinos," *The Final Call*, March 18, 2009, 17.

62. Nisa Islam Muhammad, "Project Modesty Contest Comes to Saviours' Day," *The Final Call*, February 12, 2009, 36.

63. Jerry Thomas and Byron P. White, "Farrakhan Returns Facing New Scrutiny," *Chicago Tribune*, February 26, 1996, 11.

64. Louis Farrakhan, "A Celebration of Family: The Honorable Minister Louis Farrakhan Delivers the Saviours' Day 2000 Keynote Address" (DVD: Final Call, 2000); Steve Kloehn, "Farrakhan Points to New Path," *Chicago Tribune*, February 28, 2000, 1.

65. The transcript of Louis Farrakhan's address is available in the 4 November 2008 edition of *The Final Call*, 20–21.

66. Author interview with Nisa Islam Muhammad, July 11, 2009.

67. Author interview with Jeremiah Wright, March 23, 2010.

68. Evelyn Brooks Higginbotham, *Righteous Discontent: The Women's Movement in the Black Baptist Church, 1880–1920* (Cambridge, Mass.: Harvard University Press, 1994), 3.

69. Belinda Robnett, "African American Women in the Civil Rights Movement, 1945–65: Gender, Leadership, and Micromobilization" in *Martin Luther King, Jr. and the Civil Rights Movement: Controversies and Debates*, ed. John Kirk (New York: Palgrave Macmillan, 2007), 151.

70. Ibid., 149.

71. Belinda Robnett, *How Long? How Long? African-American Women in the Struggle for Civil Rights* (New York: Oxford University Press, 1997), 42.

72. Lily D. McClair and Helen A. Neville, "African American Women Survivors of Sexual Assault: The Intersection of Race and Class," in *Classism and Feminist Therapy: Counting Costs*, ed. Maria Hill and Ester D. Rothlam (New York: Haworth Press, 1996), 110.

73. Author interview with Sonsyrea Tate, August 2, 2009.

74. Author interview with W. Muhsinah Abdullah, June 8, 2010.

75. Beverly Guy-Sheftall, "Introduction: The Evolution of Feminist Consciousness among African American Women," in *Words of Fire: An Anthology of African-American Feminist Thought*, ed. Beverly Guy-Sheftall (New York: The New Press, 1995), 17.

76. Elijah Muhammad, "Be Yourself and Do Something for Self," *Muhammad Speaks*, July 4, 1969, 20.

77. Lee Baker, *From Savage to Negro: Anthropology and the Construction of Race, 1896–1954* (Los Angeles and London: University of California Press, 1998), 36.

78. "The Woman in Islam," *Muhammad Speaks*, January 17, 1962.

79. Barbara Welter, "The Cult of True Womanhood: 1820–1860," *American Quarterly* XVIII (2): 151–52.

80. Hazel V. Carby, *Reconstructing Womanhood: The Emergence of the Afro-American Woman Novelist* (New York and Oxford: Oxford University Press, 1987), 25, 35.

81. Deborah Gray White, *Ar'n't I a Woman? Female Slaves in the Plantation South* (New York: Norton, 1999), 29.
82. Dorothy Roberts, *Killing the Black Body: Race, Reproduction, and the Meaning of Liberty* (New York: Pantheon, 1997), 25, 36.
83. Patricia Hill Collins, *Black Feminist Thought: Knowledge, Consciousness, and the Politics of Empowerment* (New York: Routledge, 1990), 67.
84. Ibid., 71, 73.
85. Ibid., 77.
86. Wallace D. Muhammad, "Impact of Islam on the Muslim Woman," *Muhammad Speaks*, Special Edition 1961, 7.
87. Edward E. Curtis, *Black Muslim Religion in the Nation of Islam* (Chapel Hill: University of North Carolina Press, 2006).
88. Higginbotham, *Righteous Discontent*.
89. Before his passing, Imam W. D. Mohammed referred to his ministry as the W. D. M. Ministry.
90. Alessandro Portelli, "The Peculiarities of Oral History," *History Workshop Journal* 12 (1981): 100, 99–100.
91. Ibid.
92. Author interview with Yasmin Otway, January 7, 2013.

NOTES TO CHAPTER 1

1. Report made at Washington Field Office. Subject: Nation of Islam. Date: August 24, 1973 (FBI File: E. Muhammad, Section 15).
2. Jeffries, *"A Nation Can Rise No Higher Than Its Women,"* 154.
3. Ula Taylor, "As-Salaam Alaikum, My Sister, Peace Be unto You: The Honorable Elijah Muhammad and the Women Who Followed Him," *Race and Society* 1:2 (1998): 183.
4. Sister Shirley Morton, "What Teachings of the Messenger Mean to Women," *Muhammad Speaks*, June 3, 1966, 25.
5. The MGT & GCC Handbook on Femininity, Muhammad Temple of Islam.
6. "Application," Appendices: Nation of Islam FBI File, Part 1.
7. "What *Courier* Readers Think: Muhammad Articles Called Undesirable," *Pittsburgh Courier*, August 31, 1957, section 2, 15.
8. Lincoln, *The Black Muslims in America*, 202.
9. Rahman, "She Stood by His Side," 88.
10. Pseudonym.
11. The MGT & GCC Handbook on Femininity, Muhammad Temple of Islam.
12. Rahman, "She Stood by His Side," 85.
13. Tynetta Deanar, "Dress Should Identify Black Woman," *Muhammad Speaks*, July 19, 1962, 27.
14. Tynetta Deanar, "Why No Make-up? Cosmetics Procedure Two People in One: Not for Our Women," *Muhammad Speaks*, February 1962, 24.
15. Elijah Muhammad, "How to Eat to Live," *MS*, November 25, 1966, 11.

16. Berg, *Elijah Muhammad and Islam*, 93.
17. Ibid.
18. Taylor, "As-Salaam Alaikum, My Sister, Peace Be unto You," 188.
19. Harriett Muhammad, "For and About You: How Will Power Will Pull Weight Down," *MS*, September 11, 1964, 29.
20. Berg, *Elijah Muhammad and Islam*, 83.
21. X, *The Autobiography of Malcolm X*, 186.
22. Sister Loylyn X, "Marriage," *MS*, November, 28, 1969.
23. Ibid.
24. Harriett Muhammad, "For and About You," *MS*, December 14, 1964, 14; December 18, 1964, 16; February 14, 1964, 17.
25. Pseudonym.
26. Pseudonym.
27. Robnett, *How Long? How Long?* 8.
28. Also see Curtis, *Black Muslim Religion in the Nation of Islam*, 73. Curtis quotes Ana Karim from the *MS* paper where her name is spelled differently from its current version. After learning about Karim from Curtis, the authors found her contact information through a source at the *Muslim Journal* newspaper.
29. Jeffries, "A Nation Can Rise No Higher Than Its Women," 212.
30. Rahman, "She Stood by His Side," 48.
31. Jeffries, "A Nation Can Rise No Higher Than Its Women," 207.
32. Michael J. Klarman, "How *Brown* Changed Race Relations: The Backlash Thesis," *Journal of American History* 81, no. 1 (June 1994): 81–118.
33. Adam Fairclough, *A Class of Their Own: Black Teachers in the Segregated South* (Cambridge, Mass.: The Belknap Press of Harvard University Press, 2007).
34. Rosalind X, "What Islam Has Done for Me," *MS*, February 12, 1971, 18.
35. "Portrait of Top Educator Reveals Messenger's Inspiring Teachings," *MS*, October 28, 1966, 16.
36. Muhammad, *Message to the Blackman in America*, 73.
37. Section V11. Part A: Foreign Contact. Reference Number: CG157-5366 (FBI File: E. Muhammad, Section 14).
38. Pseudonym.
39. "Elijah's Legacy," *The Chicago Defender* (Daily Edition), March 3, 1975, 9.
40. Gibson, *A History of the Nation of Islam*, 42.
41. *The Messenger Magazine*, Vol. 1, No. 1, 7–12, 1959.
42. Sister Tynetta X, "The Woman in Islam," *MS*, May 1960, 3.
43. FBI Nation of Islam File, Part 3.
44. Karriem, *The Divine Sayings of the Honorable Elijah Muhammad*, 5.
45. Margary Hassain, "The Woman in Islam," *MS*, November, 28, 1969.
46. Pseudonym.
47. X, *The Autobiography of Malcolm X*, 404.
48. Pseudonym.
49. Rahman, "She Stood by His Side," 75.

50. From SAC, Chicago (100-35635) To: Director, FBI (25-330971) Subject: Nation of Islam. Date: April 26, 1962, 1–2 (FBI File: E. Muhammad, Section 7).

51. Security Matter: Nation of Islam. 199-3166 Chicago, Illinois, April 30, 1962 (Clara Muhammad FBI File).

52. Leon Forrest, "A Majestic Lady of Courage, Gentleness," *MS*, August 25, 1972, 3.

53. Robert Davis, "Muhammad Says: Thank the Whites," *Chicago Tribune*, February 27, 1974.

NOTES TO CHAPTER 2

1. For further explanation of why Imam Mohammed selected this name, see Muhammad, *As the Light Shineth from the East*, 93, 100–1. For examples of the ways in which community members interpreted the label Bilalian, see Curtis, *Black Muslim Religion in the Nation of Islam*, 180–84.

2. Mattias Gardell, *In the Name of Elijah Muhammad: Louis Farrakhan and the Nation of Islam* (Durham, N.C.: Duke University Press, 1996), 108–12.

3. "Royal family" refers to the family of Elijah Muhammad. Gibson, *A History of the Nation of Islam*, 72; Clifton E. Marsh, *From Black Muslims to Muslims: The Transition from Separatism to Islam, 1930–1980* (Metuchen, N.J.: The Scarecrow Press, 1984), 91; Lawrence H. Mamiya, "From Black Muslim to Bilalian: The Evolution of a Movement," *Journal for the Scientific Study of Religion* 21, No. 2 (1982): 144–45.

4. According to Essien-Udom, during the period of his field research in 1960, several followers told him that "Allah has chosen Minister Wallace to succeed him [Elijah]." Essien-Udom, *Black Nationalism*, 81.

5. Gardell, *In the Name of Elijah Muhammad*, 101; Michael Saahir, *The Honorable Elijah Muhammad: The Man Behind the Men* (Indianapolis: Words Make People Publishing, 2011), 171.

6. Essien-Udom, *Black Nationalism*, 81–82; W. D. Mohammed, "Sacred Activism and Power of Inclusion," Wisdom University Conference, Tulsa, OK, May 9, 2007, a lecture of which parts were printed as W. D. Mohammed, *Return to Innocence: The Transitioning of the Nation of Islam* (Homewood, Ill.: The Sense Maker, c/o Muslim Journal, n.d.), 10; Sahib, "The Nation of Islam," 56, 74; Elijah Muhammad, *The Supreme Wisdom* (1957; repr., Newport News, Va.: National Newport News and Commentator, n.d.), 51; for further discussion on the study of Arabic among NOI members, see Curtis, *Black Muslim Religion in the Nation of Islam*, 44–46.

7. Zafar Ishaq Ansari, "W. D. Muhammad: The Making of a 'Black Muslim' Leader (1933–1961)," *American Journal of Islamic Social Sciences* 2, no. 2 (1985): 255–56.

8. Saahir, *The Honorable Elijah Muhammad*, 175; Ansari, "W. D. Muhammad," 256; Steven Barboza, *American Jihad: Islam After Malcolm X* (New York: Doubleday, 1993), 100; Mohammed, *Return to Innocence*, 3.

9. These words are Wallace's when he described in a 1959 lecture that he would teach on "the religious side of the Honorable Elijah Muhammad's teachings." His religious propensity was even evidenced in the list of general orders for the Fruit of Islam. Duties included keeping the "Prayer Formula of W. D.

Muhammad." "Minister Wallace—1959, Introduced by Malcolm X," Ummah-stream on Vimeo, accessed February 27, 2013, http://vimeo.com/19587952; Essien-Udom, *Black Nationalism*, 156, 145.

10. In a 1959 lecture in Harlem where he was introduced by Malcolm X, Wallace defined a Muslim in Qur'anic terms, "one who willfully submits their will to one divine supreme being," and called him "*rabbil-'alamin* [Lord of the worlds]." But Wallace also commented that "the Honorable Elijah Muhammad met God." "Minister Wallace—1959, Introduced by Malcolm X," Ummahstream on Vimeo; Wallace Muhammad Interview with the Bureau. Date: 8/4/64 (FBI File: E. Muhammad, Section 8).

11. Mohammed, *Return to Innocence*, 5, 3.

12. Marsh, *From Black Muslims to Muslims*, 79; Section IV: Dissidents/Leadership, pp. 24–25 (FBI File: Nation of Islam).

13. Curtis, *Black Muslim Religion in the Nation of Islam*, 111; "Inheritors of the Faith," PBS *This Far by Faith*, accessed February 27, 2013, http://www.pbs.org/thisfarby-faith/transcript/episode_5.pdf; Clegg, *An Original Man*, 222–24; Rahman, "She Stood by His Side," 105.

14. "Inheritors of the Faith."

15. Marsh, *From Black Muslims to Muslims*, 112–14; Saahir, *The Honorable Elijah Muhammad*, 182.

16. Saahir, *The Honorable Elijah Muhammad*, 190–92.

17. Muhammad, *As the Light Shineth from the East*, 11.

18. Sahib, "The Nation of Islam," 74; W. D. Muhammad, "Blessings on Our Community," Los Angeles, February 25, 1979, unpublished transcript.

19. Saahir, *The Honorable Elijah Muhammad*, 190; Muhammad, *As the Light Shineth from the East*, 32.

20. Mamiya, "From Black Muslim to Bilalian," 145–49; Muhammad, *As the Light Shineth from the East*, 29, 200–1, 14–15.

21. Gardell, *In the Name of Elijah Muhammad*, 104; W. D. Muhammad, *The Man and the WoMan in Islam* (Chicago: The Honorable Elijah Muhammad Mosque No. 2, 1976), 7.

22. Abdul Aleem Seifullah, "Women: Equals? Inferiors? Superiors?" *Bilalian News*, August, 26, 1977, 5.

23. Mamiya, "From Black Muslim to Bilalian," 145–49.

24. Saahir, *The Honorable Elijah Muhammad*, 183.

25. Mohammed, *Return to Innocence*, 7–8.

26. Malikah Omar, "Believer Reflects on the Wisdom of the Hon. W. D. Muhammad," *Bilalian News*, January 23, 1976, 18.

27. Ansari, "W. D. Muhammad," 251.

28. "Discussion—Our Leader Imam W. Deen Mohammed 1," interview with Benjamin Bilal, July 3, 2002, accessed November 22, 2012, http://www.youtube.com/watch?v=moczjeZTD2o&feature=relmfu.

29. Muhammad, *The Man and the WoMan in Islam*, 49.

30. Monica A. Coleman, *Making a Way Out of No Way: A Womanist Theology* (Minneapolis: Fortress Press, 2008).

31. Marsh, *From Black Muslims to Muslims*, 116–17.

32. "Researching Our Faith May 7, 2006—Our Leader Imam W. Deen Mohammed 1," accessed March 1, 2013, https://www.youtube.com/watch?v=Jmabcp8GUjY.

33. Seifullah, "Women: Equals? Inferiors? Superiors?" 5.

34. Muhammad, *The Man and the WoMan in Islam*, 12–13.

35. Seifullah, "Women: Equals? Inferiors? Superiors?" 3, 5.

36. Hafeezah N. Kashif, "Woman: Her Identity and Her Role," *Bilalian News*, August 26, 1977, 2; Muhammad, *As the Light Shineth from the East*, 214.

37. Also Imam Mohammed said, "Man should mean humanity and humanity includes both male and female." Muhammad, *The Man and the WoMan in Islam*, 8; Muhammad, *As the Light Shineth from the East*, 47.

38. Muhammad, *The Man and the WoMan in Islam*, 1–2, 11.

39. Ibid., 6–7; W. D. Muhammad, "The Deep Sleep," *Bilalian News*, January 23, 1976, 19.

40. Muhammad, *As the Light Shineth from the East*, 45–46.

41. Muhammad, *The Man and the WoMan in Islam*, 20–21; for further discussion on Qur'anic statements about the roles of women and men, see Amina Wadud, *Qur'an and Woman: Rereading the Sacred Text from a Woman's Perspective* (New York and Oxford: Oxford University Press, 1999), 22, 70–74.

42. "Sonia Sanchez on the Teachings of the Nation of Islam," OpenVault, WGBH Media Library and Archives, accessed March 2, 2013, http://openvault.wgbh. org/catalog/sbro-mla001033-sonia-sanchez-on-the-teachings-of-the-nation-of-islam; "Social Justice Movements—The Nation of Islam," Columbia CNMTL, accessed March 2, 2013, http://socialjustice.ccnmtl.columbia.edu/index.php/ The_Nation_of_Islam; Muhammad, *The Man and the WoMan in Islam*, 42.

43. Pseudonym.

44. W. D. Muhammad, "The Family and the Community," *Bilalian News*, November 12, 1976, 15; W. D. Mohammed, "Sisters Only Meeting," Detroit, July 2, 1994, unpublished transcript, 4–5.

45. Muhammad, *The Man and the WoMan in Islam*, 56, 58, 61.

46. Carolyn Moxley Rouse, *Engaged Surrender: African American Women and Islam* (Berkeley: University of California Press, 2004), 148, 150.

47. Edward Curtis also provides a Sunni woman's narrative in which she makes similar points. Curtis, *Black Muslim Religion in the Nation of Islam*, 179.

48. Women, including former sister captains, had a hard time pinpointing when exactly Imam Mohammed changed the name of MGT to MWDC. However, in an old MGT notebook from a woman in Durham, North Carolina, there are notes from a class dated June 25, 1975, and the women are still referred to as MGT sisters. The notebook also contains a memorandum from Rhonda X, "Captain MWDC," dated March 9, 1976, indicating that the name had been changed by that date.

49. These dates are based on rough estimates from former sister captains in two cities: Safiyyah Shahid in Atlanta, Georgia, and Rhonda Muhammad in Durham, North

Carolina. As stated in the previous note, an old MGT notebook included a memorandum from Rhonda X, "Captain MWDC," dated March 9, 1976, indicating that the captain title continued to exist a year after Elijah Muhammad's death.

50. This date is from Gardell. He states that in "January 1976, the 'temples' were renamed 'mosques' and in March 1977, '*masjids*.'" He further states that "minister" was changed to "imam," though it is not clear if it was in March exactly. In an August 1977 issue of *Bilalian News*, the imam is referred to as *Emam* Wallace D. Muhammad. Gardell, *In the Name of Elijah Muhammad*, 110–11.

51. "The weekly M.G.T. classes were overseen by the local Sister-Captain, but were taught by various female teachers, or in Nation of Islam terminology, instructresses." Rahman, "She Stood by His Side," 88; Marsh, *From Black Muslims to Muslims*, 117.

52. Women also had a hard time establishing exact dates for CERWIS, but the majority were confident that it started in the early parts of the transition.

53. Essien-Udom, *Black Nationalism*, 145.

54. Rasheeda Faquir, "Committees in Action," *Bilalian News*, September 10, 1976, 23; "Proclamation: International League of Muslim Women Community Recognition Day," accessed March 3, 2013, http://www.syracuse.ny.us/mayorDocs/2/International%20League%20of%20Muslim%20Women.pdf.

55. Rhena Muhammad, "Wife Beaters: Incidents and Solutions Explored," *Bilalian News*, January 13, 1978, 4; Mildred M. El-Amin, "Family Life," *Bilalian News*, August 24, 1979, 14.

56. *Bilalian News*, September 10, 1976, 26; Samuel Ayyub Bilal, "Bilalian News Salespeople to Visit Mecca," October 14, 1977, 16.

57. Anonymous speaker.

58. Marsh, *From Black Muslims to Muslims*, 110–11.

59. Pseudonym. We use pseudonyms in this section because it discusses sensitive matters related to real communities.

60. Pseudonym.

61. Pseudonym.

62. Pseudonym.

63. Mikal Saahir, "A Tribute to Imam W. Deen Mohammed," accessed March 3, 2013, http://www.athreedayjourney.com/africans-in-america/a-tribute-to-imam-w-deen-mohammed/.

64. Elijah Muhammad, *How to Eat to Live, Book No. 1* (1967; repr., Phoenix: Secretarium MEMPS Ministries, 1997), 20–22, 45–46.

65. The instructions on the December fast in *How to Eat to Live* do suggest a predawn meal, although ultimately it was not recommended as a best practice. Ibid., 46.

66. W. D. Mohammed, "Sisters' Meeting," Chicago, April 23, 1994, unpublished transcript, 34.

67. Pseudonym.

68. Curtis, *Black Muslim Religion in the Nation of Islam*, 178–79.

NOTES TO CHAPTER 3

1. Pseudonym.
2. Paul Delaney, "Many Muslims Disaffected by Changes in Policies," *New York Times*, December 25, 1978, 1.
3. "Elijah's Legacy," *The Chicago Defender* (Daily Edition), March 3, 1975, 9.
4. Arthur Magida, *Prophet of Rage: A Life of Louis Farrakhan and His Nation* (New York: HarperCollins, 1996), 61.
5. Gardell, *Countdown to Armageddon*.
6. "Emam Wallace D. Muhammad's Appeal to Minister Farrakhan," *Bilalian News*, April 28, 1978, 7.
7. "Howard Lee Interview with Abdul Farrakhan," *Africa Overseas: An International Business, Economic and Political Magazine*, No. 50, 1975, 61.
8. Muhammad, *Closing the Gap*, 328.
9. Gardell, *Countdown to Armageddon*, 265.
10. Don Terry, "Million Man March Is Stirring Passions," *New York Times*, October 8, 1995, 24.
11. Louis Farrakhan, *A Torchlight for America* (Chicago: Final Call Publishing, 1993), 105.
12. Audrey Muhammad, "A Virtuous Conversation: The Nation's Next Top Model, Jamillah Farrakhan," *Virtue Today Magazine*, Winter 2008, 11.
13. Louis Farrakhan, "The Divine Value of the Female," accessed March 19, 2013, http://www.finalcall.com/artman/publish/National_News_2/article_8147.shtml.
14. Farrakhan, *A Torchlight for America*, 109.
15. Ibid., 107.
16. Louis Farrakhan, "Men of This World Do Not Desire a Righteous Woman," accessed February 15, 2012, http://www.finalcall.com/artman/publish/Minister_Louis_Farrakhan_9/article_8491.shtml.
17. Louis Farrakhan, "Let Us Make Man," accessed January 15, 2013, http://www.finalcall.com/artman/publish/Minister_Louis_Farrakhan_9/article_8191.shtml.
18. C. Eric Lincoln and Lawrence Mamiya, *The Black Church in the African American Experience* (Durham, N.C., and London: Duke University Press, 1990), 321.
19. Judy Claude, "Poverty Patterns for Black Men and Women," *The Black Scholar* 17, no. 5 (1986): 22.
20. Minister Farrakhan launched the *Final Call* newspaper in 1979. However, the paper was published irregularly until 1984. E. R. Shipp, "Candidacy of Jackson Highlights Split among Black Muslims," *New York Times*, February 27, 1984, A10.
21. Mandates about the requirement to wear the uniform at all times have historically varied according to region and time.
22. Farrakhan, *A Torchlight for America*, 156.
23. In recent years the NOI has increased its online presence via weekly webcasts from Mosque Maryam and Facebook and Twitter accounts.
24. Muhammad, *Closing the Gap*, 28.

25. Ibid., 29.
26. *The Final Call*, November 4, 2008, 20–21.
27. Author interview with Dr. Sayyid Syeed, May 23, 2011.
28. Author interview with Khaleelah Muhammad, July 21, 2012.
29. Amani Muhammad, "Reflections of a Young Auditor," *Youth Creation Community Outreach*, April 2012, 24.
30. Ibid.
31. Jesse Muhammad, "The Exclusive with Ebony S. Muhammad: How She Turned a Vision into a Reality," *Hurt 2 Healing*, March 2011, 25.
32. Pseudonym.
33. Pseudonym.
34. Charlene Muhammad, "New Ready-to-Wear Collection by Mother Khadijah Farrakhan's Newell Apparel," *The Final Call*, August 28, 2012, 36.
35. Zenzile Muhammad, "Uncovering Why We Cover," *Hurt 2 Healing*, August 2010, 16.
36. "Let Little Girls Be Little Girls: A Look into Kameelah's Closet," *Virtue Today*, Winter 2008, 14.
37. Claudette Marie Muhammad, *Sister Claudette Marie Muhammad's Memories* (Chicago: FCI, 2006), 93.
38. Muhammad, *Closing the Gap*, 58.
39. Ebony Muhammad, "One-on-One with Ava Muhammad: Breaking the Barriers of Sexism," *Hurt 2 Healing*, February 2011, 19–20.
40. Pseudonym.
41. Pseudonym.
42. Akilah Worthy, "Communicating Love," *Youth Creation Community Outreach*, April 2012, 18.
43. Dionne X Mahaffey and Richard Muhammad, "12,000 Black Women Join Min. Farrakhan in Atlanta," *The Final Call*, July 20, 1994, 8.
44. Pseudonym.
45. Author interview with Claudette Marie Muhammad, January 26, 2010.
46. "Black Women Gather to Promote Unity at Million Woman March," *Jet*, November 10, 1997, 9.
47. Muhammad, *Message to the Blackman in America*, 106–7.
48. Gibson, *A History of the Nation of Islam*, 25.
49. David Muhammad, "A Brief History of Latinos in the Nation of Islam," accessed October 20, 2012, http://www.finalcall.com/artman/publish/Perspectives_1/article_9164.shtml.
50. Theresa X Torres, "Who Is the Original Man? Latinos Are a Part of the Original Family," *The Final Call*, April 22, 2008, 25.
51. YoNasDa Lonewolf-Muhammad, "A Testimonial: Embracing the Light Within," *The Final Call*, August 28, 2012, 29.
52. Ibid.
53. Author interview with Askia Muhammad, January 13, 2008.

54. Sadiyah Evangelista, "Why She Thinks She Can't Leave Him," accessed March 25, 2013, http://www.h2hmag.info/why-she-thinks-she-cant-leave-him/.

55. Diamante Vega, "Eliminating Stereotypes of Hispanic/Latinos," *The Universal News Journal*, October 2012, 9.

56. Ashahed M. Muhammad, "He Makes All Things New," *The Final Call*, November 11, 2008, 2.

57. Muhammad, *Closing the Gap*, 261.

58. Author interview with Dr. Larry Muhammad, January 31, 2012.

59. "Bringing the Peace" (DVD: Final Call, 2003).

60. Muhammad, *Closing the Gap*, 144.

61. Farrakhan, *A Torchlight for America*, 97–98.

62. Pseudonym.

63. Muhammad, "A Virtuous Conversation," 10–11.

64. Rasul Muhammad, "Why Should You Get Married?" *Virtue Today*, Fall 2011, 12.

65. Audrey Muhammad, "The Ask Hafeez Column Presents: 'The Art of Mating,'" *Virtue Today*, Spring 2012, 12.

66. Pseudonym.

67. Nojma Muhammad, "Badges of Dishonor," accessed March 26, 2013, http://www.modestyinternationalmag.com/page29.html.

68. Muhammad, "The Exclusive with Ebony S. Muhammad," 54.

69. Ebony Muhammad "Do's and Don'ts: 7 Tips to Find Your 'Mr. Right,'" *Hurt 2 Healing*, October/November 2012, 21–22.

70. "Ask Mrs. Mavis," *Hurt 2 Healing*, February 2011, 49.

71. "Waves of the Prophetic: Prophet Valentine Williams Healing Ministries," *Youth Creation Community Outreach* Magazine, April 2012.

72. Louis Farrakhan, "The Honorable Elijah Muhammad and His Student Malcolm X, 28 Years Later—What Really Happened?" (DVD: Final Call, 2003).

73. Gibson, *A History of the Nation of Islam*, 118–19.

74. Ibid.

75. Louis Farrakhan, "Letter from the Honorable Minister Louis Farrakhan," *The Final Call*, September 11, 2006, 21.

NOTES TO CHAPTER 4

1. "Religious Perspectives—Our Leader Imam W. Deen Mohammed 1," accessed March 6, 2013, http://www.youtube.com/watch?v=8faoEmx48RU.

2. "Religious Perspectives—Our Leader Imam W. Deen Mohammed 2," accessed March 6, 2013, http://www.youtube.com/watch?v=xPZ1of9TKxg.

3. "Religious Perspectives—Our Leader Imam W. Deen Mohammed 3," accessed March 6, 2013, http://www.youtube.com/watch?v=TeJZ9xoHwuE.

4. "Religious Perspectives—Our Leader Imam W. Deen Mohammed 4," accessed March 6, 2013, http://www.youtube.com/watch?v=wG6kjh6yxZk.

5. Pseudonym.

6. Pseudonym.

7. Pseudonym.

8. Brian Muhammad, "Unity Prayer Service Marks Milestone for Islam in America," *The Final Call*, October 16, 2012, accessed March 13, 2013, http://www.finalcall.com/artman/publish/national_news_2/article_9274.shtml.

9. "W. Deen Mohammed and Louis Farrakhan Interview," accessed March 7, 2013, http://www.youtube.com/watch?v=328DMQ7TGrs.

10. Ibid.

11. Edward Curtis argues that Imam Mohammed's use of the term Bilalian is one strong example of his continuing Black consciousness. Curtis, *Black Muslim Religion in the Nation of Islam*, 179–80.

12. W. D. Mohammed, "How Islam Encourages Us to Pursue Excellence," February 16, 1997, Detroit, cassette.

13. "Current Full-Time Sis. Clara Mohammed and WDM High Schools," *Muslim Journal*, February 22, 2013, 16.

14. Curtis, *Islam in Black America*, 121.

15. Jamillah Karim, *American Muslim Women: Negotiating Race, Class, and Gender within the Ummah* (New York and London: New York University Press, 2009), 80.

16. Coweta Teen Mothers and Babe Service Center, Inc., accessed March 6, 2013, http://www.cowetateenmoms.org/home/about_us.

17. Immigrant mosques have increased their level of community activism since the attacks of September 11, 2001. Ihsan Bagby, "The Mosque and the American Public Square," in *Muslims' Place in the American Public Square*, ed. Zahid H. Bukhari et al. (Walnut Creek, Calif.: AltaMira Press, 2004), 336; Ihsan Bagby, "The American Mosque 2011: Activities, Administration and Vitality of the American Mosque, Report Number 2 from the US Mosque Survey 2011," Islamic Society of North America, May 2012, accessed June 19, 2013, http://www.hartfordinstitute.org/The-American-Mosque-Report-2.pdf, 10.

18. Aisha al-Adawiya, Ihsan Bagby, and Sarah Sayeed, "The American Mosque 2011: Women and the American Mosque, Report Number 3 from the US Mosque Study 2011," Islamic Society of North America, March 2013, accessed June 19, 2013, http://www.hartfordinstitute.org/The-American-Mosque-Report-3.pdf, 8.

19. See also Karim, *American Muslim Women*.

20. Mohammed, "Sisters' Meeting."

21. Juliane Hammer, *More Than a Prayer: American Muslim Women, Religious Authority, and Activism* (Austin: University of Texas Press, 2012), 37–38, 81–85.

22. Ibid., 132–33.

23. Bagby, "The American Mosque 2011: Activities, Administration and Vitality of the American Mosque," 15–16; Ihsan Bagby, Paul M. Perl, and Bryan T. Froehle, *The Mosque in America: A National Portrait, a Report from the Mosque Study Project* (Washington: Council on American–Islamic Relations, 2001), 47.

24. Bagby, "The American Mosque 2011: Activities, Administration and Vitality of the American Mosque," 16–17.

25. Ihsan Bagby, "A Profile of African-American Masjids: A Report from the National Masjid Study 2000," *Journal of the Interdenominational Theological Center* 29, no. 1–2 (2001–2): 217.

26. Pseudonym.

27. The views of women in the WDM community on woman-led prayer are representative of those of most American Muslim women. *Azizah* magazine conducted a survey in which 82 percent of participants "felt that women should not lead mixed-gender congregation prayers." Hammer, *More Than a Prayer*, 50–51.

28. Wadud, *Qur'an and Woman*, 88–89.

29. Mohammed, "Sisters' Meeting."

30. See Rouse, *Engaged Surrender*, and Karim, "Through Sunni Women's Eyes."

31. Mohammed, "Sisters' Meeting."

32. Ibid.

33. This observation is based on reports of African American female students at Spelman College upon visiting Black *masjids* in Atlanta.

34. Ebony Muhammad, "Motherhood Beyond Biology: An Exclusive Interview with Ava Muhammad," *Hurt 2 Healing*, May 2010, 33.

NOTES TO THE CONCLUSION

1. Author interview with Lorraine Muhammad, April 13, 2012.

2. Pseudonym.

3. Pseudonym.

4. Melissa Harris-Perry, *Sister Citizen: Shame, Stereotypes, and Black Women in America* (New Haven & London: Yale University Press, 2011), 284.

5. *The Final Call*, November 4, 2008, 20–21.

6. Monica Coleman, ed., *Ain't I a Womanist Too? Third-Wave Womanist Religious Thought* (Minneapolis: Fortress Press, 2013).

7. Debra Mubashshir Majeed, "Womanism Encounters Islam: A Muslim Scholar Considers the Efficacy of a Method Rooted in the Academy and the Church," in *Deeper Shades of Purple: Womanism in Religion and Society*, ed. Stacey M. Floyd-Thomas (New York and London: New York University Press, 2006), 39; and Rouse, *Engaged Surrender*, 148.

8. Curtis, *Black Muslim Religion in the Nation of Islam*, 185–86.

INDEX

Abdul-Aleem, Bayyinah, 46, 203, 215, 236, 240–241
Abdul-Ghafur, Saleemah, 219
Abdullah, Shafeeqah, 86, 207, 217–218
Abdullah, W. Muhsinah, 26, 86, 96, 214
Afro-Descendant Upliftment Society, 80
Ahmadiyya Movement, 5
Akbar, Daiyah, 90, 115–116
Akram, Amidah, 108
Ali, John, 111
Ali, Noble Drew, 4, 46
Ali, Sultana, 106–107
Ali, Terri, 228
anti-Semitism, 18
Atlanta Masjid of Al-Islam, 206, 209, 218
Austin, Alan, 5

Berg, Herbert, 11
Beynon, Erdmann, 3–5
Bilalian: W. D. Mohammed abandons the term, 204; W. D. Mohammed coins the term, 75–76
Bilalian News: 1977 issue on the role of women, 93–95, 108; changed to *Muslim Journal*, 204; originally *Muhammad Speaks*, 75, 111–112; women's influence on, 112–113
Black church: NOI's critique of, 3, 41, 44; women's leadership in church compared to that in the Nation, 23–24
businesses, women, 26–27, 41, 61–68, 147, 166–177, 229

civil rights movement, women's leadership in: compared to that in the NOI, 23–24, 58–61, 229; Ella Baker, 24; Johnnie Carr, 24. *See also* Karim, Ana
Clay, Sonji, 1

Collins, Patricia, 29–30
Commission for the Restructuring and Reorganization of the Nation of Islam, 164
Committee to Enhance the Role of Women in Society (CERWIS), 109–111, 231; imams' resistance to, 117–118
conversion to the NOI: over Sunni Islam, 187–188, 224, 236; women's reasons for, 2, 5, 22, 27–29, 40–46, 139–145, 227
Cordell, Carolyn, 107
Coweta Teen Mothers and Babe Service Center, 208
Curtis, Edward, 129, 241–242

Davis, Deborah, 54, 100, 122
Diab, Jamil, 78
diet, 31–32, 52–53, 164–166, 205, 229, 239
dress. See *hijab*; Muslim Girls Training
Durley, Gerald, 180–181

El-Amin, Mildred, 113
El-Amin, Sandra, 94–96, 107–109, 206–208, 218–220, 237, 240
Essien-Udom, E. U., 17, 65, 69
Evanzz, Karl, 3

Faiz, Khayriyyah, 45, 77, 109, 128
Fanusie, Fatimah, 3
Farrakhan, Donna, 19, 148, 169–170, 177
Farrakhan, Khadijah, 134, 146–147, 157, 169–170
Farrakhan, Louis: early career, 134–135; establishing *jum'ah*, 194; gender ideology, 135–138; on music and dance, 167–170; on polygyny, 221; reconciliation with W. D. Mohammed, 21, 141, 180, 182–183; relationship with Church of Scientology, 144–145; relationship with clergy, 19, 141–145;

ABOUT THE AUTHORS

Dawn-Marie Gibson is Lecturer in Twentieth-Century U.S. History in the Department of History at Royal Holloway, University of London.

Jamillah Karim is an independent scholar who specializes in Islam in America, Islam in Black America, and Women and Islam. Her former academic appointment was as Associate Professor of Religious Studies at Spelman College in 2011.